UKCAT 2016

TEXTBOOK
WITH
2000+ QUESTIONS ONLINE

Katie Wren

Simon Johnstone

James Tomkins

Ordering Information:
Quantity sales. Special discounts are available on quantity purchases by corporations, associations, and others. For details, contact the publisher at the address above.

Orders by UK trade bookstores and wholesalers.

Please contact UKCAThelp;

Or visit www.ukcathelp.com

Printed in the United Kingdom.

All content is owned by the authors and official information regarding the test is taken from the official site www.ukcat.ac.uk and the official 2016 UKCATguide

The information within this resource is intended solely as a revision aid for the UKCAT test . Any information within the verbal reasoning sections are extracts produced by the authors and are only their opinions. The material presented is for individual private-study only; public performance of the material without written permission is specifically forbidden. All the learning resources are copyright. The views expressed are those of the authors and not those of any sponsors or partners.

Publisher's Cataloging-in-Publication data

Copyright © 2016 by UKCAThelp

ISBN:

ISBN-13: 978-0-9908538-4-8

ISBN-10:0-9908538-4-5

CONTENTS

INTRODUCTION

Most students, that have reached the stage of preparation for the UKCAT, know how much work is needed in order to maximise their potential. The vision for this book is to provide the reader with an in-depth breakdown of the exam in order guide you through the most important aspects of the UKCAT. This book uses a different approach to learning aimed to provide you with the required functional skills with minimal effort.

What is in this book and how to use it effectively

This guide contains over 750 practice questions; including the new style of questions that have been introduced to the UKCAT in 2016. The core of the book's contents focuses on understanding the concepts and skills that the UKCAT examines. The aim is to become familiar with the principles and thought-processes behind the test. Thus, it will allow for a flexible and fluid approach to virtually any question offered. By purchasing this book you also receive access to over 2,000 questions online; simply enter the code VBIT1loml at the checkout at ukcathelp.com. If you are having problems with the code please email info@ukcathelp.com with the receipt of purchase.

The UKCAT is a modified IQ test. Its purpose is similar to tests such as the Wechsler Adult Intelligence Scale, Wisconsin Card Sorting Test and many more. These tests provide results that medical and dental schools use as a means of assessing candidates. In order to understand the UCKAT the following breakdown will gently touch on several important theories in neuroscience. This will help to gain an appreciation of how the brain works in each specific section, and therefore disarm some of the sections that candidates find most daunting. More importantly, knowledge of precisely what the sections are testing, will help to guide candidates in the right direction. Thus the key is to learn the system, but not to blindly memorise facts.

CHAPTER 1: THE BREAKDOWN

THE BREAKDOWN

From this point onwards you will practice your ability to learn new things and to know what the sections are testing. By the time of your exam, you will be in a position where you can effectively recall the prior information from this breakdown and know how to tackle the sections in an efficient and effective manner.

INTRODUCTION

Firstly, the concept of working memory can be viewed as similar to a bridge, with one end of the bridge containing sensory information from your eyes, nose and ears. On the other end of the bridge there are learned processes for understanding that information. They both come together to create working memory. Simply take this example:

1+5= ?

The information received from the eyes contains the shapes within the problem "1 + 5 =?" This is processed by those learned ways of understanding information to know that 1, 5 are numbers. Then in context of the other symbols it activates the skills in addition and to solve the example, 1 + 5 = 6. Thus the bridge between the two components of working memory formulates the answer 6. Most of this calculation is executed without much conscious thought or even effort. The entire exam is testing these types of bridges, but different sections connect to different learned processes of understanding information.

More detail is provided in the following sections of the book to ensure that the correct bridges to success are recognised and made more familiar. On the theme of numbers, the next chapter covers the Quantitative Reasoning (QR) section. This will provide the information needed to develop those skills and overcome any challenging problem. QR works in a similar way as the example by just activating skills that are normally covered in GCSE level mathematics.

QUANTITATIVE REASONING

Some of the key skills required for this section will be reviewed. Please note that pen and paper will be available for the test and there is a calculator provided on the screen. Use them, but use them wisely as they may use up important time.

A summary of the essential skills that will be covered is listed below, please be aware that this list is not exhaustive.

- Rounding up and down

- Unit conversions

- Reading graphs

- Calculating means, medians and mode

- Percentages & Ratios

Please note that for students that are studying A-level Maths this section may appear very simplified, but it will serve useful as a section to revise on some of the facts. When practicing these questions, try not to be too dependent on a calculator, in order to improve your mental arithmetic (and to save time in the test).

Tip - Highlight the key information in the data, understand what the question is asking and find the numbers that will give you the answer.

Rounding up and down:

Often calculations give answers to many decimal places. The answer will require rounding to the closed whole number or 1 decimal place. It is very rare to get an answer that is to two decimal places or longer. How do we round up and down efficiently?

The way to do this is if the number is five or greater you round the value up. If less than five you round it down. Imagine that a child who wants pizzas will only eat if they know their appetite will be satisfied. If there is half a pizza or more they will eat it. Anything less than half a pizza and is thrown away. The following is an example.

- If the number is **≥5 you round up**, for example 1.5 rounds up to 2
- If the number is **<5 you round down**, for example 1.4 rounds down to 1

If the answer is like 2.3931, and you want to round it to a whole number or 1 decimal point depending in the question and answers.

For the nearest whole number, you always round the 1st decimal, 2.3931 rounds to 2. **3 is less than 5, it is less than half a pizza so you'll throw it away.** This same rule applies to round the answer to 1 decimal place, you have to round the 2nd decimal place, 2.3931 rounds to 2.4, **9 is greater than 5, is more than half a pizza so you'll take it.**

Have a go at rounding the following numbers to a whole number:

a) 21.4 rounds to ………. b) 17.8 rounds to ……….

Have a go at rounding the following numbers to 1 decimal:

c) 47.35 rounds to ………. d) 19.949 rounds to ……….

Answers

a) 21 (4 < 5) b) 18 (8 > 5) c) 47.4 (5 ≥ 5) d) 19.9 (4 < 5)

Tip – If a question is difficult and it is unclear whether to round up or down, just remember pizza and which slices get eaten or thrown away.

Unit conversions:

Desired Units = Units to be converted x Factor required to convert the Units

In simple terms:

Desired Units = current units x amount needed to convert

For example convert 60kg to pounds (currently in kilogram and require pounds lbs)

1kg = 2.2 lbs. In the UKCAT QR questions the factor needed to convert the units will be provided. Hence:

Desired Units (Pounds) = 60kg x 2.2

Desired Units = 132lb

132lb = 60kg

How will this be presented in the exam?

Information from the past exams shows up to 50% of your questions will be in this format with a table/graphs of data. Most questions ask to compare between different values of the data. Within the table/graph or explicitly in the question, lies the factor that is needed to convert the units. Here follows an example of this, first analyse the data to find what is required to find to the answer:

A factory has been redesigned after recent advances in technology. The old and new factories are compared in the table below. All units are per hour, unless otherwise stated. Daytime refers to the time when the factory is in production.

Category	Old factory	New factory
Daytime energy usage	20 units	23 units
Night-time energy usage	6 units	2 units
Daytime greenhouse emissions	50g	40g
Night-time greenhouse emissions	16g	10g
Power costs	£10/unit	£9/unit

What do you think is the 3 key components in this information?

1) _____

2) _____

3) _____

The 3 key components are: 1) There is an old factory 2) There is new factory present 3) There is data comparing the two factories in terms of energy, emissions and power costs.

The data allows comparison of the two factories in energy, emissions and power costs. Here is an approach to this question, using the data in the table.

In one day, if the new factory was producing for 16 hours, what was the cost of power?

- What does the question want? Cost of power. What information is available? Hours in production.
- To get to the Cost of power, first calculate the power from the hours in production and not in production.
- In the statement above the table, it states that "Daytime refers to the time when the factory is in production". In one day (24hours), 16hours is in production and 8hours not in production, which is night-time energy usage.

---

16 x 23 (Power used in production) =

8 x 2 (Power used not in production) =

Total Power used in one day=

Now convert the units of Power into cost

Your answer for Total energy used x Power costs =	
....	x £9 =

The answer is: £3456. If this same result was not achieved, work back from the answer to look for any errors.

Percentages: Percentage is a proportion of 100.

A percentage is a proportion out of 100. This could to be shown as a decimal. This is important to remember as this provides a shortcut for most percentage based questions. Percentage can be easily converted as a proportion out of 100 or 1 which represents the whole portion. Here is how to change percentage into a decimal and how to calculate the percentage, the proportion of a given sample:

How does 87% = 0.87?

87% = 87 out of 100. This can placed in a fraction as $^{87}/_{100}$ which equals 0.87.

From a decimal you can calculate the percentage by x 100, 0.87 x 100 = 87, which is 87%

Using this principle work out a percentage from the following question.

Here is the previous table from unit conversions:

A factory has been redesigned after recent advances in technology. The old and new factories are compared in the table below. All units are per hour, unless otherwise stated. Daytime refers to the time when the factory is in production.

Category	Old factory	New factory
Daytime energy usage	20 units	23 units
Night-time energy usage	6 units	2 units
Daytime greenhouse emissions	50g	40g
Night-time greenhouse emissions	16g	10g
Power costs	£10/unit	£9/unit

What is the percentage increase in power cost per unit of the old factory compared with the new factory?

a.1% b. 9% c. 12% d. 10% e. 11%

To calculate the percentage of increase in the power cost per unit comparing the old factory to the new factory, first work out the change between the two factories.

10 - 9 = 1

Next calculate what proportion the change of power cost per unit is to the old factory

1 /10 = 0.1

 Change the decimal into a percentage

0.1 x 100 = 10, which is 10%, the answer is d. 10%, the power cost per unit is 10% higher in the old factory.

An easy formula to use whenever the question asks about the percentage of the change or the difference:

The difference between the two values/The value the question want you to come it to x 100

Ratios: Ratios is comparison of proportion compared to each other

Ratios are not very different from percentages however also require the calculation of proportions. The only difference being that instead of using a value out of 100, values are calculated out of other values. Now, here is an example:

If there are six sweets in a pot, John received four sweets while Jack received two what is the proportion of sweets John received compared to Jack?

Firstly, the question highlights that there needs to be comparison of the proportions of John to Jack i.e John : Jack.

Write down the values in a way that compares John : Jack. 4:2. This is the answer.

Whenever a ratio is required, always aim to put it in the most simplified form.

Both values, 4 and 2, can be divided by 2 to give you 2:1

Now here is a UKCAT style question:

Below is a pie chart showing the burgers that 425 people chose at a fast food restaurant.

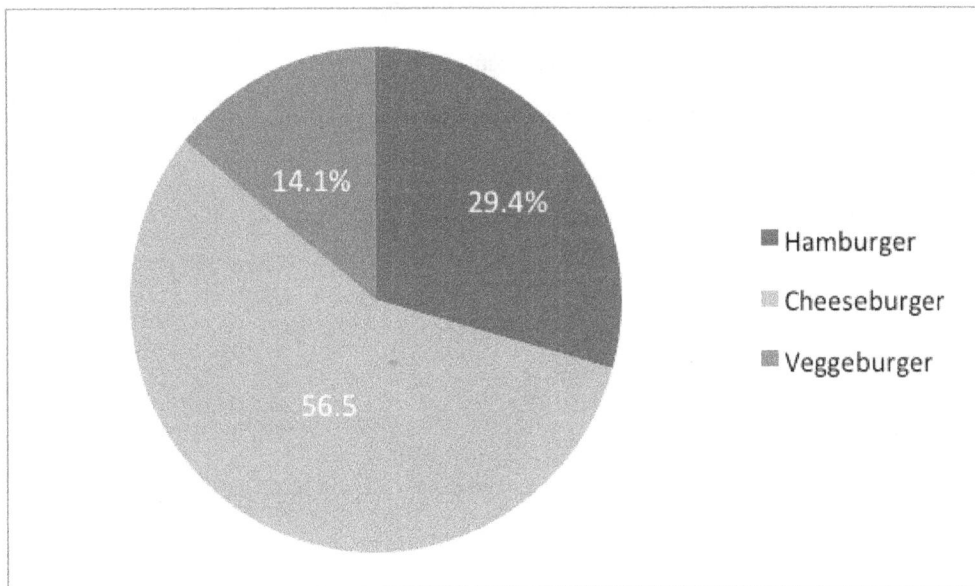

Hamburger = 29.4%, Cheeseburger = 56.5%, Veggeburger = 14.1%

Regardless of the type of question in any of the sections, aim to highlight the key components of the data and the information provided to reach the answer. In order to reinforce this, write down the two key components of the pie chart data.

1) _____

2) _____

The two key components are:

1) There are three different types of burgers.

2) The data is represented in a circle and the proportion out of 100 that each burger represents is also given. Now break-down a question:

What is the ratio of number of Cheeseburgers to Veggeburgers?

a.   240:60 b. 4:1 c. 12:85 d. 425:60 e. 85:12

The question asks to compare Cheeseburgers : Veggeburgers

Is the amount of Cheeseburgers : Veggeburgers known? No, therefore work out this value

What values are known? The total number and the percentage in relation to this.

Using this work out the amount of Cheeseburgers and Veggeburgers

Cheeseburgers:

56.5% proportion of 425 = 425 x 0.565 which equals 240.125. This rounds down to 240.

Veggeburgers:

14.1% proportion of 425 = 425 x 0.141 which equals 59.925. This rounds up to 60.

So now know the ratio is 240:60

Aim to put it to the values in the simplest form. 240 and 60 can be divided by 60 to give you 4:1

The answer is b. 4:1

Alternatively another solution to this question is to find the ratio between the percentages (as the total number is a constant) - 54 ÷ 14 = 4

Reading graphs

There is a wide range of graphs that could be used in the UKCAT. Most graphs only require data extraction to derive a value from it. The way to read from a bar graph will not be covered here (this can be found in GCSE Maths textbooks). Therefore the focus is on the most common example: pie charts.

In the example below, the approach to a pie chart question will be demonstrated.

The previous data from will be used to focus on the question rather than analysing the data. Firstly, a key thing to understand is that a pie chart is the representation of data in a form of a circle, a whole circle = 360°

Below is a pie chart showing which shows types of burgers 425 people chose at a fast food restaurant.

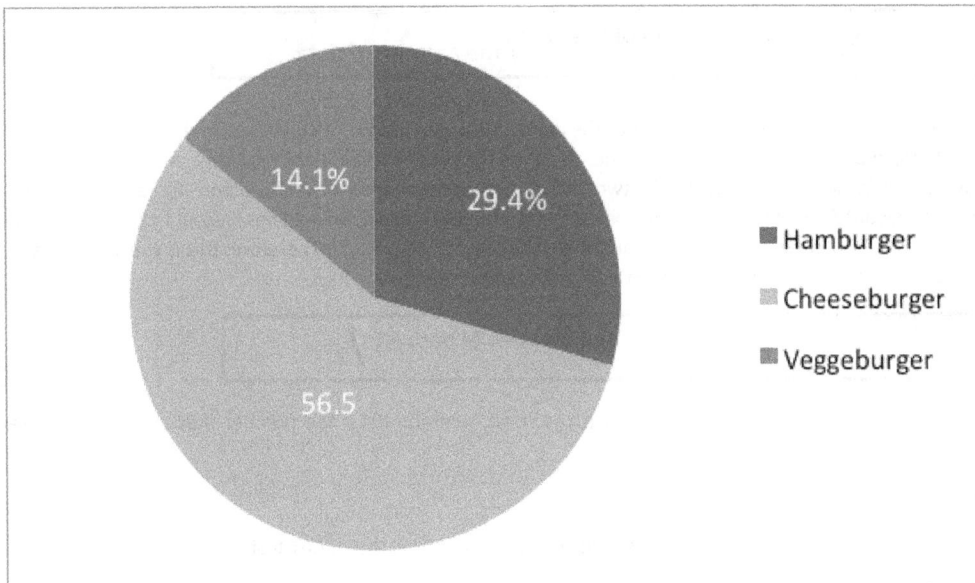

Hamburger = 29.4%, Cheeseburger = 56.5%, Veggeburger = 14.1%

What angle does the Cheeseburger section take up on the pie chart? Give answer to the closest whole angle

a. 57 b. 203 c. 204 d. 202 e. 56

Going back to two key components, what data is known? This is the proportion out of 100% that Cheeseburgers represent. Remember that a full circle, 100%, = 360°.

Here is how to calculate the answer:

Proportion out of 100 that represents Cheeseburgers = 56.5%

Full circle (100%) is 360°, Let's swap 360° for 100.

Angle of the section Cheeseburger takes up is = 56.5% of 360°

0.565 x 360° = 203.4°. Rounded to closest whole angle = 203°

Calculating mean, median and mode

What is the mean? The mean is often used interchangeably with the word average. It is the sum of the values divided by the number of values. The aim is to find out the value represents all of the data.

$$\text{The mean} = \frac{\text{Sum of the data}}{\text{the amount of data}}$$

What is the median? This is the value at the middle of the data. This is most easily calculated by first rearranging all the data in order of size. Then, in order to find the middle value, calculate the total number of values. After this, add one to the total number of values and divide this new number by two. For an even total number of values a non whole number is derived. To make this clear, layout four coins, or any four objects that are easily available in a line. Place a finger on the middle point of the objects. This is in between the second and the third object, (hence 2.5). Therefore, this is the same as adding the two values that the midpoint is in between and then, dividing that number by 2.

$$\text{The median} = \frac{\text{the amount of data} +1}{2}$$

Mode is the more straightforward concept. Simply, it is the most common data: the number that appears most frequently.

Now, here is a UKCAT style question:

Below is a stem and leaf plot showing the average scores of people that took the UKCAT test on a specific day at a test centre. The left column represents hundreds, the right represents tens.

```
4 | 8 9
5 | 0 1 2 3 3 6 8 8 8
6 | 2 3 4 5 5 5 5
7 | 0 1 2 3 3 8
8 | 1 3
```

What do you think are the 2 key components in this plot?

1) _____

2) _____

The two key components in this plot are: 1) The left column represents hundreds and the right column represents tens 2) The data is already ordered in value.

Now work out the following:

What is the modal score?

a. 630 b. 580 c. 650 d. 650 e. 580

What is the median score?

a. 650 b. 645 c. 630 d. 635 e. 640

What is the mean score?

a. 600 b. 619 c. 640 d. 629 e. 630

The data is arranged in ascending order value, which speeds up the process of working out the mean, median and mode.

1) What is the modal score? c. 650 - is the score that occurs the most.

2) What is the median score?

$$\textbf{The median} = \frac{\textbf{the amount of data +1}}{\textbf{2}}$$

The total number of students is 26, so the midpoint would be the 13.5th score, to work this out, add the 13th and the 14th value, 630 + 640 = 1270. Now divide this number by 2. 1270 ÷ 2 = 635, the answer is d. 635.

1) What is the mean score?

$$\textbf{The mean} = \frac{\textbf{Sum of the data}}{\textbf{the amount of data}}$$

480 + 490 + 500 + 510 + 520 + 530 + 530 + 560 + 580 + 580 + 580 + 620 +630 + 640 + 650 + 650 + 650 +650 + 700 + 710 + 720 + 730 + 730 + 780 + 810 + 830 = 16,360. Mean is 16,360/26 = 629.23, so 629

d. 629

The aim is to be able to perform all of these skills without even having to think about it. This will be achieved by understanding the concepts. Practicing UKCAT questions is a valuable resource, but, an even better resource is to master these in real life. Open up a pack of Haribos, and calculate the ratio of, for example, gummy rings to cola bottles to other sweets. Convert the units: If the ratio is 3 : 5 : 2 and the packet costs £1.00, what is the cost of each type of sweet? £1.00 ÷ 10 gives the total number i.e the sum of the ratios. One sweet in the ratio is worth 10p and so five cola bottles is worth 50p of the packet. What is the percentage increase of cola bottles to gummy rings? This will not only help to understand the skills but it will also improve mental arithmetic and reduce dependence on a calculator.

As the precise content of the questions that will come up in the exam is unknown, by practising this it will build the right bridges and help to maintain a relaxed, flexible and adaptable approach to the questions. These are the key skills in achieving the best in this section.

Content the past exams suggest that the other 50% of questions will be in a statement format. The values that needed to answer the question will not be presented obviously in a table or graph. It requires the ability to read the statement and pick out key information from it.

VERBAL REASONING

Now how the brain sees and processes verbal information will be covered.

What is the Verbal Reasoning section testing? – It is testing the ability to analyse and critique verbal information presented in a passage. It combines the verbal processing and the ability to read the passage and highlight key information that will achieve the right answer, like in the QR section.

Here is a practice passage, which is part of an interactive breakdown. Get involved, circle the answers that are correct and write down the answer in the spaces provided. Any mistakes made are the best resource in order to develop and improve.

Below is an extract from an article on the Food Industry:

Traditional restaurants present their diners with a regimented menu; meanwhile diners themselves are becoming more concerned as to the exact contents of their meals, particularly given the high media interest in health and nutrition.

"How many times have we left plates of unfinished food at the end of a meal? Or left having felt hungry? Have you ever really wanted to order a particular dish, but didn't because it came with mushrooms, but you wanted something else? We all have different dietary requirements and desires – the time has come for this to be reflected in restaurant menus. Yes, a printed menu usually has a variety of options, but these menus fail to cater to differences in size of appetite, health-consciousness, allergies and intolerances, all at the same time!"

The problem we have identified is that customers wanting to express themselves in the above ways are required to overcome many obstacles to achieve this goal. From the hassle of embarrassing conversations with waiters, who then communicate this to the kitchen, to the hope that the final plate will account for the requested changes.

We aim to solve this by allowing our customers' exact requirements to be communicated directly to the kitchen using the ingenious interface of an iPad app. Not only does this allow for an engaging, novelty experience, but it also serves an important purpose in cutting out the unnecessary steps in getting what the customer wants.

"From 2013 onwards, restaurants will need to make customisation a cornerstone of their food"

- Technomic Inc., the food industry's leading research analyst.

Questions

1)   The passage was written by Technomic Inc.

True   False   Can't Tell

2)   The passage was probably not written by Technomic Inc.

True   False   Can't Tell

3) The first quote was from Technomic Inc.

True   False   Can't Tell

4) The first quote may be from Technomic Inc.

True   False   Can't Tell

5) The passage states that restaurants generally have strict menus.

True   False   Can't Tell

6) Customers who do not wish to customise their meal tend to have an easier time ordering than those that do.

True   False   Can't Tell

7) Customers will have to bring their iPad to order at this restaurant.

True   False   Can't Tell

8) Customers will require an iPad to order at this restaurant.

True   False   Can't Tell

9) According to the text, waiters embarrass customers.

True   False   Can't Tell

10) The text suggests that-

a)   Customers are often embarrassed when talking to waiters about altering a meal on the menu;

b)   iPads are the best way to offer customisation to customers in restaurants

c)   When customers request changes, the final plate often does not include these

d)   Vegetarians have hard times in restaurants.

How to process the passage

Each paragraph of a passage is written with a certain objective. Skim read the passage, and highlight the objective of that paragraph. This allows the quick and efficient location of the answer to the question. Do not attempt to memorise the passage as visual information decays quickly and the concise meaning of the passage is lost.

Here is an example of how to breakdown the passage into this format:

Below is an extract from an article on the Food Industry:

"Traditional restaurants present their diners with a regimented menu; meanwhile diners themselves are becoming more concerned as to the exact contents of their meals, particularly given the high media interest in health and nutrition."

Current ways of doing things and changes in the demand of restaurants

"How many times have we left plates of unfinished food at the end of a meal? Or left having felt hungry? Have you ever really wanted to order a particular dish, but didn't because it came with mushrooms, but you wanted something else? We all have different dietary requirements and desires – the time has come for this to be reflected in restaurant menus. Yes, a printed menu usually has a variety of options, but these menus fail to cater to differences in size of appetite, health-consciousness, allergies and intolerances, all at the same time!"

A quote highlighting the negative experience customers have when ordering a customised meal

"The problem we have identified is that customers wanting to express themselves in the above ways are required to over-come many obstacles to achieve this goal. From the hassle of embarrassing conversations with waiters, who then communicate this to the kitchen, to the hope that the final plate will account for the requested changes."

Current problems in the process of ordering a customised meal

"We aim to solve this by allowing our customers' exact requirements to be communicated directly to the kitchen using the ingenious interface of an iPad app. Not only does this allow for an engaging, novelty experience, but it also serves an important purpose in cutting out the unnecessary steps in getting what the customer wants."

Solution to the problems of ordering a meal, how to supply the demand of the customer

"From 2013 onwards, restaurants will need to make customisation a cornerstone of their food"

-        Technomic Inc., the food industry's leading research analyst.

Concluding quote

How to process the questions

The questions are notoriously difficult in this section. Here the question is going to be broken down into two key components:

1. **Where to look for the answer**

2. **What is the question asking?**

1) The passage was written by Technomic Inc.

Where to look for the required information: The passage – The whole passage is referred to.

What information is the question specifically interested in: Written by Technomic Inc - identify the author, is it Technomic Inc?

2) The passage was probably not written by Technomic Inc.

Where to look for the required information: The passage – The whole passage is referred to.

What information is the question specifically interested in: Probably not written by – The author is not Technomic Inc

3) The first quote was from Technomic Inc.

Where to look for the required information: The first quote of the passage (A quote highlighting, negative customers experience when ordering a customised meal)

What information is the question specifically interested in: The author is Technomic Inc

4) The first quote may be from Technomic Inc.

Where to look for the required information: The first quote of the passage (A quote highlighting, negative customers experience when ordering a customised meal)

What information is the question specifically interested in: may be from Technomic Inc. – could the author be Technomic Inc.?

5) The passage states that restaurants generally have strict menus.

Where to look for the required information: Although the words "The passage" may lead you to think the location is within the entire passage, the latter "restaurants generally have strict menus" leads to the section - Current ways of doing things and changes in the demand of restaurants.

What information is the question specifically interested in: do restaurants generally have strict menus?

6)   Customers who do not wish to customise their meal tend to have an easier time ordering than those that do.

Where to look for the required information: The comparison of the experience of ordering food - A quote highlighting, negative customers experience when ordering a customised meal

What information is the question specifically interested in: comparison of the experience of customers who want to order food without customising it Vs those who do. Customers who don't customise their meal have an easier time ordering than those who do. The question can also be rephrased as Customers who customise their meal have a harder time ordering than those who don't.

7)   Customers will have to bring their iPad to order at this restaurant.

Where to look for the required information: an iPad app is offered as solution to the problem so any information about the iPads will be in the section - Solution to the problems of ordering a meal, how to supply the demand of the customer

What information is the question specifically interested in: Is there any clear indications that a customer will have to use their own iPad?

8)   Customers will require an iPad to order at this restaurant.

Where to look for the required information: Same as above

What information is the question specifically interested in: Is there any clear indication that a customer will have to use an iPad to order at this restaurant

9)   According to the text, waiters embarrass customers.

Where to look for the required information: "The text" is misleading. The word waiter would be mentioned in either the experience or problems of ordering a customised meal

What information is the question specifically interested in: Do the waiters embarrass the customers?

11)   The text suggests that-

In this format of questions, there is a leading statement and the challenge is to choose one of the four options presented that best suits the statement. The statement holds the key to what information is required. Out of the four options, the statement looks for either, what statement is TRUE or what is FALSE. Be careful reading the statement. It is often asked in an over complicated manor.

What information is this statement interested in? The text suggests that or, in simple terms, which of the following statements is true.

a)   Customers are often embarrassed when talking to waiters about altering a meal on the menu;

Where to look for the required information: as mentioned in the explanation of 9) either the experience or problems of ordering a customised meal

b)   iPads are the best way to offer customisation to customers in restaurants

Where to look for the required information: iPads, indicates the section - Solution to the problems of ordering a meal, how to supply the demand of the customer.

c)   When customers request changes, the final plate often does not include this.

Where to look for the required information: key focus is communication that is looked upon in the section - Current problems in the process of ordering a customised meal.

d)   Vegetarians have hard times in restaurants.

Where to look for the required information: key focus is experience, so the section - A quote highlighting, negative customers experience when ordering a customised meal.

Remember, the leading statement aims to either find the TRUE option among the FALSE/ CAN'T TELL options, or the FALSE/ CAN'T TELL option among the TRUE options. For this example the leading statement aims to find the TRUE option among the FALSE/ CAN'T TELL options.

Answers

1. Can't Tell. The final quote has been attributed to Technomic Inc., but there is no author given for the whole passage.

2. True. If the passage had been written by Technomic Inc., it probably would not have specified where the final quote came from. The word "probably" is aimed to create ambiguity with the answer. A common pitfall students fall into is to focus on this ambiguity and select can't tell

3. Can't Tell. The first quote of passage is the entire second paragraph. The author has not stated the source of the quote, so this may or may not be true. With any doubt the answer is can't tell.

4. True. As there is no one credited to the first quote, this is a possibility. Key word in this question is "may be", stating ambiguity. A simplified form of this question is – Is there any ambiguity about the author of the 1st quote?

5. False. The passage states this is for traditional restaurants, not restaurants in general. "Traditional restaurants present their diners with a regimented menu"

6. True. "Identified is that customers wanting to express themselves in the above ways are required to overcome many obstacles to achieve this goal" so compare the two diners who want the same meal. The text suggests that, customers who wish to change the meal in the menu have to overcome obstacles. And therefore have a harder time ordering the same meal.

7. Can't Tell. "ingenious interface of an iPad app" The passage does not state whether customers would have to bring their own iPad, or whether the restaurant would provide them with one.

8. True. The passage says that an iPad app will be used, so it can assumed an iPad will be needed.

9. False. "From the hassle of embarrassing conversations with waiters" A common pitfall students make, is because visual information decays rapidly over time. The brain remembers the sentence as, customers + embarrassing + waiters. When it comes to processing a sentence, it is faster to recognise words in a sentence that do not make sense but are grammatically correct. Under exam pressure and in a state of anxiety, students recognise the key words, customers + embarrassing + waiters and the fact they are grammatically correct. However, failing to recognise the real meaning of the question. The way to avoid this trap is, to read over the abstract and question concisely and consistently for each question. Do not choose an answer until both the question and the area it focuses on are fully understand.

10. The text suggests that-

a) Customers are often embarrassed when talking to waiters about altering a meal on the menu. The passage states that customers have embarrassing conversations with waiters. "From the hassle of embarrassing conversations with waiters." Therefore this option is TRUE

Why are the others False/Can't tell?

b)   iPads are the best way to offer customisation to customers in restaurants

"The ingenious interface of an iPad app. Not only does this allow for an engaging, novelty experience, but it also serves as an important purpose in cutting out the unnecessary steps in getting what the customer wants" – There is no reference to how effective it is, or whether it is the best way. Therefore this option is CAN'T TELL

c)   When customers request changes, the final plate often does not include these

The quote - "to the hope that the final plate will account for the requested changes" is about the uncertainty of whether the final plate will have the changes included. There is no specific information such as figures to show the final plate does not include the changes. Therefore this option is FALSE

d) Vegetarians have hard times in restaurants.

There is no reference to vegetarians in the passage so, this mean their experiences in restaurants are not known. Therefore this option is CAN'T TELL.

Key takeaway points –

-       Avoid the common pitfall of rushing to an answer.

-       Make sure the breakdown of the passage helps to locate where the required information for the questions can be found.

-       Breakdown each question to create a concise meaning of the question

-       Reread the passage for each question – visual information decays quickly. The interpretation of what has been read has to be refreshed for each question.

-       Do not compensate with existing knowledge. If it is not in the text having looked through the entire passage, it is likely to be either a False/Can't Tell answer.

Again, UKCAT questions is a valuable resource. But try to master theses skills in real life! Next time a passage is available to read, whether it is from a newspaper or online, break it down and highlight the key objective of each paragraph.

Understanding is the key - the content of the questions that come up in the test are unknown, it allows building of the right bridges and connections to virtually handle any question that can come up.

Next, a thorough and in-depth explanation of the Abstract Reasoning section follows. This section is quite tricky. Again, a break is recommended at this point.

ABSTRACT REASONING

So far, a basic understanding of the principals of problem solving in the UKCAT exam has been gained. Abstract reasoning is not all that different from other sections. The focus of this section is the analysis of shapes and being able to recognise patterns within them. The mind processes visual information in two ways simultaneously: what and where. One important pitfall to avoid is changing the shapes into symbols, giving them meaning from prior memory. For example, often, when looking at an arrow shape it is easy to spend too much time trying to look for a connection to do with direction. The way to avoid this is to remember that the shapes are in abstract. They hold no greater meaning than just a shape.

Before the breakdown of this section, have a pen handy. It will be required to draw in a box. This is key because it will help to develop the skills tested in this section. It is recommend that a pen is used because any mistakes will provide vital insight to the thought process involved, and highlight areas that are not understand clearly. It will show how to improve the skills in this section.

Key aspects to look at:

- Symbol

- Size

- Quantities

- Colour

- Symmetry

- Direction

- Positioning

- Angles

- Multiple Rules

This is a long list, however it is unnecessary and to consuming to try to remember this entire list . It would also be ineffective because under exam pressure there is an increased likelihood that it will be difficult to recall all the cold facts like this. Fortunately, many of these aspects like Symbol, Size, Colour, can be observed and processed without having to put much thought into it. A good way to progress is to use mistakes as learning tools. Try to remember sections forgotten and missed out and make sure this is not repeated. As the questions progress, if it is difficult to find a pattern, try starting again in a effort to look at the aspects that can be found naturally.

Information from the past exams, suggest that 90% of your answers will be in the format of: "what set does this box fall into" - A, B or neither. The other 10% of the answers will be in the format of "what box completes the series." Provided is an in-depth breakdown of each format because the way to tackle these formats are different. A good starting point for both formats is to think - what is the pattern in the Set/Steps of the series?

Now, go through this sample question: For the following questions see if the box falls into either: Set A, Set B or Neither. In the designated spaces, write down what the pattern could be.

Set A

Set B

What do you think is the key information and information you can eliminate in order to find the pattern?

_____

_____

_____

_____

_____

_____

_____

_____

_____

_____

_____

As stated previously, a common pitfall that applicants make is focusing solely on trying to recognise patterns that are not there. The purpose of the shapes is to be overwhelming and intimidating. Once a shape is recognised, the mind naturally processes this as a symbol looking for meaning and patterns. In this example the arrow shape often gets processed as a symbol that indicates direction. Most students are drawn to look for directions and changes regarding the direction. This is an attempt to distract from the real, simple pattern. From the Sets direction of the arrow can be discarded because it inconsistently points in different directions. In order to understand this process of eliminating unnecessary shapes, the question above is used but the arrows have been replaced with circles.

What could the pattern be?

_____

_____

_____

_____

_____

_____

_____

_____

_____

_____

_____

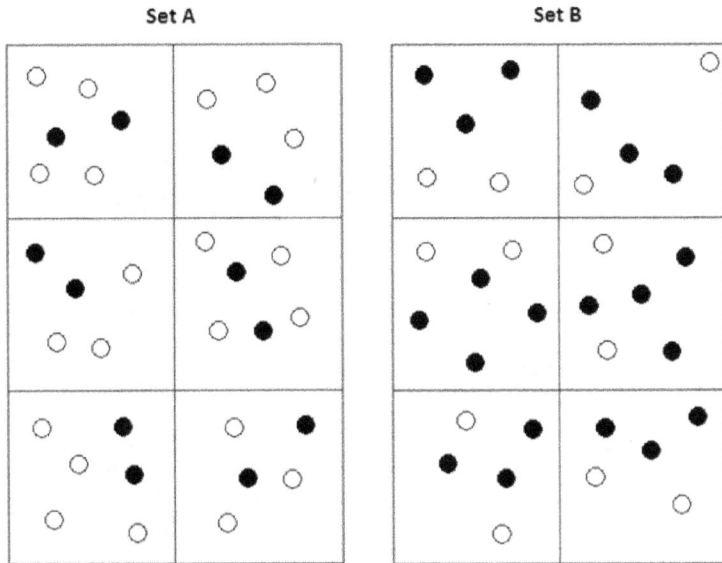

Set A   Set B

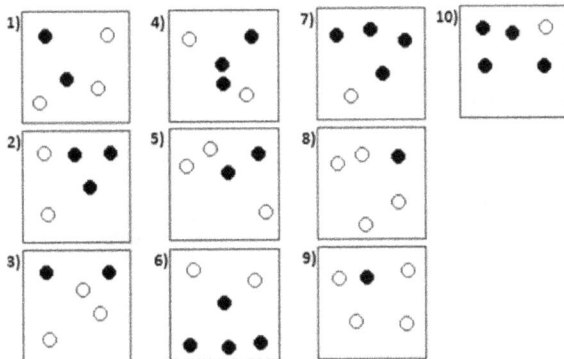

Now, the arrow has been eliminated, the pattern is a lot easier to recognise.

A key point to take away from this is do not become preoccupied with what the shape means in real life and try to look for an overcomplicated pattern. The shapes are in abstract; they do not represent anything else but a shape.

Rule: Set A has two black shapes, Set B has two white shapes.

Answers

1) A

2) B

3) A

4) B

5) A

6) B

7) Neither

8) Neither

9) Neither

10) Neither

Attempt the following example, what can be seen?

Set A   Set B

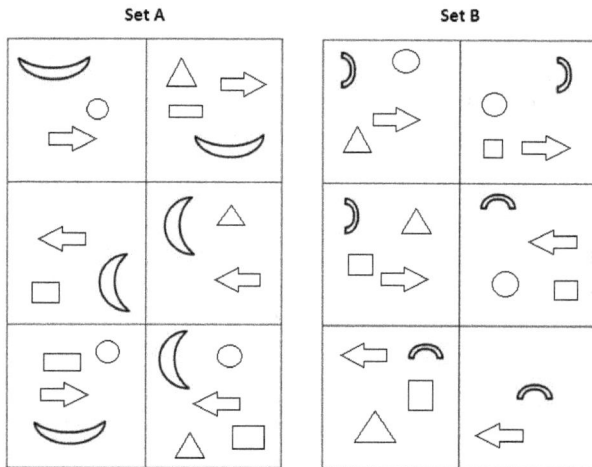

What do you think is the key information and information you can eliminate in order to find the pattern?

_____

_____

_____

_____

_____

_____

_____

_____

_____

_____

_____

Firstly, what is consistent?

Both sets contain triangles, ovals, quadrilaterals and a crescent shape. There is not a clear indication of a change in size, colour or quantities in the sets.

There seems to be no clear pattern in the amount of shapes, type of shapes or even position of the shapes for either A or B as there are some boxes without triangles, ovals etc.

One thing that is noticed is the change in the crescent shape in A and B. Also one shape, which is consistent in the boxes of A and B, is the arrow. So now simplify the example and try to notice the pattern now.

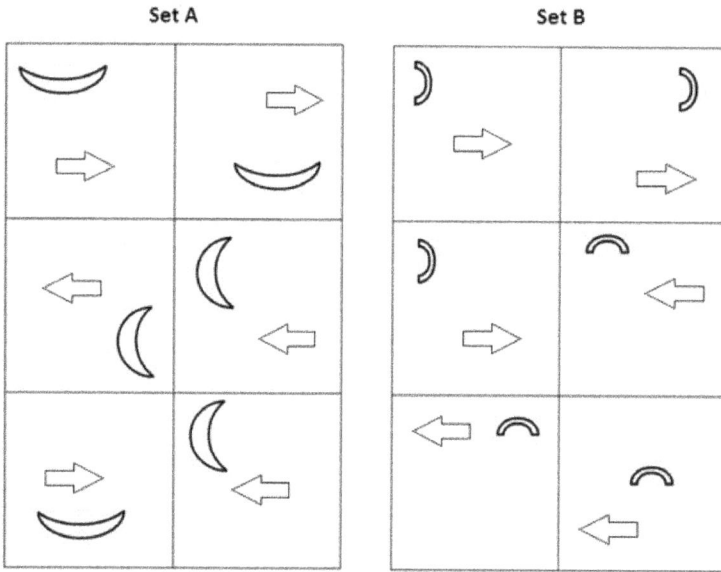

Set A   Set B

What seems to be changing? Firstly specify

 = 0°

The arrows are rotated to either, 90° or 270°.

The plane of the crescent shape also changes, from on a vertical or horizontal axis. Is there a connection between the two shapes? Simplified further:

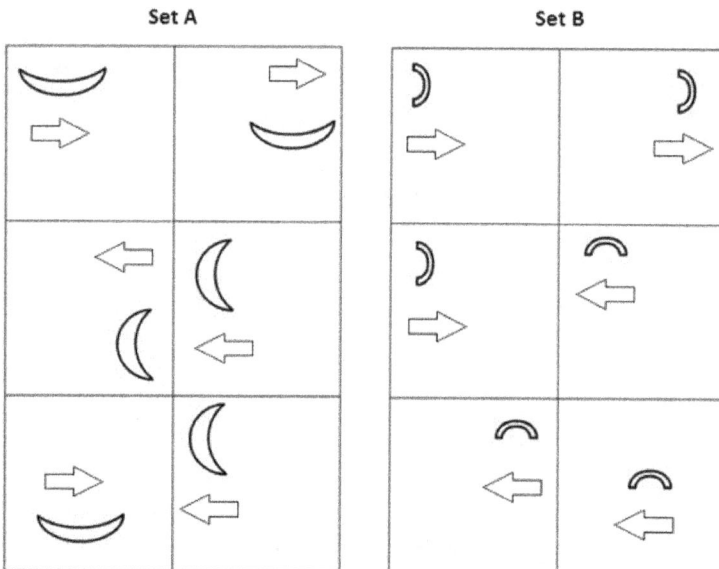

Set A   Set B

In Set A, if arrow is at 90°, the crescent shape is on the Horizontal axis, if at 270°, the crescent shape is on the Vertical axis

In Set B, if arrow is a 90°, the crescent shape is on the Vertical axis, if at 270°, the crescent shape is on the Horizontal axis

Or vice versa if the crescent shape is on the Horizontal axis, the arrow is a 90°

Admittedly, although it would have been easier to state the arrow as left or right, that would change the arrow shape into a symbol. The arrow can be replaced with any symbol that has one line of symmetrical such as:

Which Set does this box fall into, A, B or neither?

Answers

1) A

2) A

3) Neither

4) B

5) A

6) B

7) B

8) B

9) A

10) Neither

Have a go at this example.

Set A   Set B

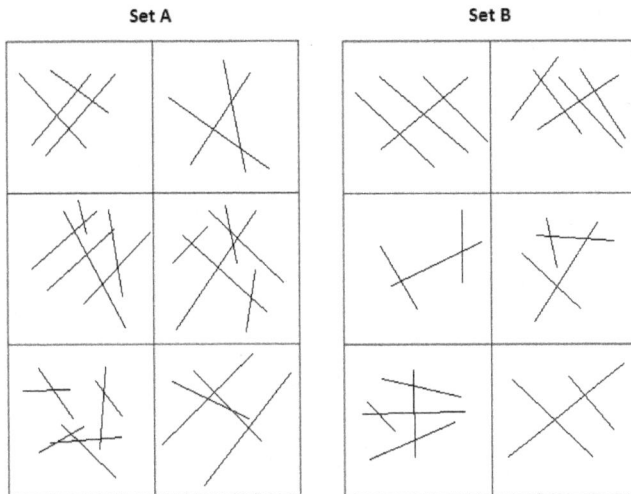

What do you think is the key information and information you can eliminate in order to find the pattern?

The mind processes visual information as what and where. In context of this question, what is simple, there are just Lines. There is not any other shape involved in the question. That eliminates the concerns about colour and shading. The length of the lines vary within both sets of data so that can be eliminated. The quantity of the lines are also varied so this can be eliminated that. What can be eliminated from possible factors that make up the pattern? This could include the positioning, angles and symmetry and so on.

This leaves the key question, where is the pattern in these Sets? To overcome the intimidating lines and make them easier to process, they will be simplified using the information stated above. Here the edges have been trimmed off the lines. Focus on where the pattern lies.

Set A	Set B

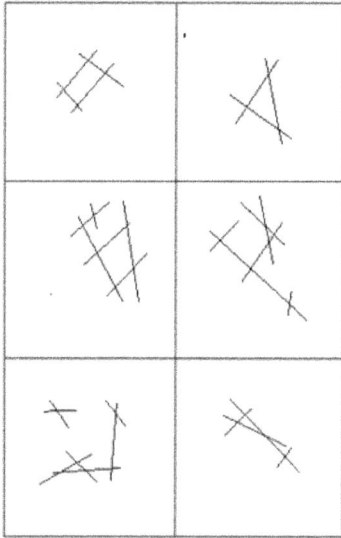 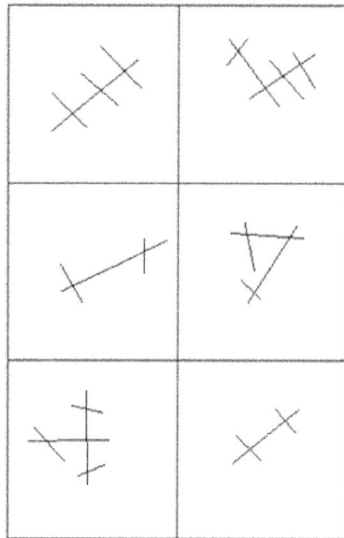

What can the pattern be? Is it the amount of lines that cross one specific line?

Set A has one enclosed space. Set B has no enclosed spaces. This might be harder to see in the box of the second column of the third row in Set A:

Set A

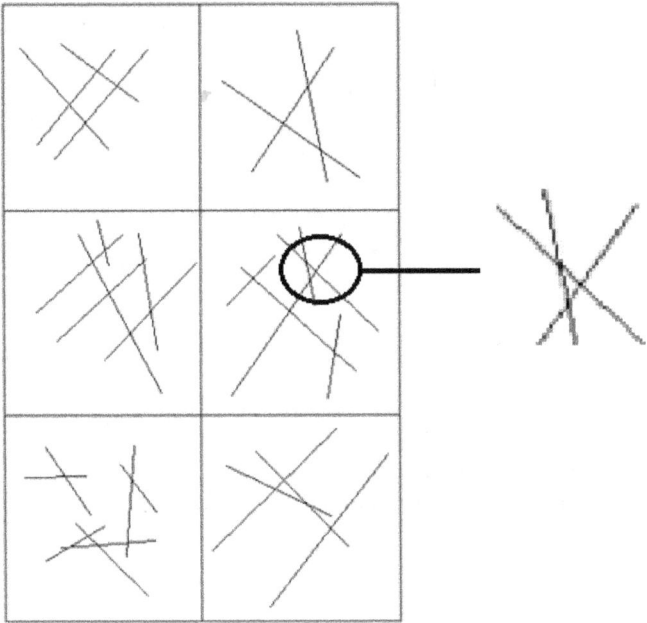

Here are the accompanying questions to gain a familiarity with this format. Where to boxes fall? Choose between: Set A, Set B or Neither

Answers

1) A

2) B

3) B

4) A

5) A

6) B

7) A

8) A

9) B

10) A

Here is the second format of questions. It requires all the skills of decoding and recognising and eliminating information stated above. The question will be laid out like this: four steps will be provided that are changing in sequence, the question will then ask to pick the fifth step in the series.

The breakdown of this example follows and will provide a guide through the process. Please draw in the designated boxes in the following example, grab a pen and pick up on your mistakes.

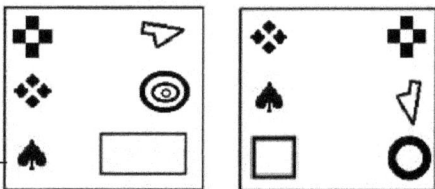

Draw what you think is the next box in this series

What is consistent? There are 6 distinguishable shapes. Three lines on each vertical border of the box.

Going from the 1st step to the 2nd, what stays the same? The shapes:

❖ , ♣ and ♠ do not change. The shape ▽ will undergo some form of rotation.

There are still 6 distinguishable shapes. Three lines are on each vertical border of the box. So presume the three shapes will stay the space in the following step. What has changed? All the shapes seem to have moved one position in a clock wise direction, so presume that:

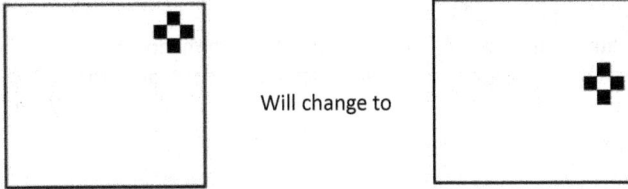

Will change to

The shape ▽ has rotated at 90°, so we can presume:

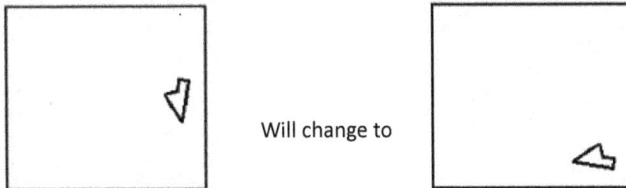

Will change to

Now having gained an understanding of what is happening and what to look for, what will the remaining two shapes will transform into?

Draw what you think the remaining two shapes will transform into and conclude with what you think the next box in series would look time now

39

The answer

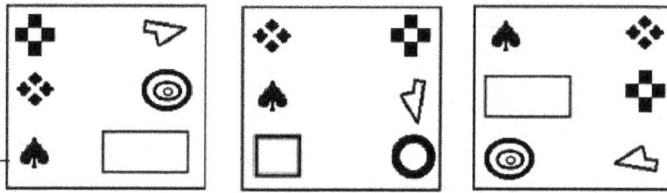

Did the box drawn match up to the answer? If not, try and build up on the pattern assumed from Step 1-2 to Step 2-3. Eliminate any incorrect patterns and analyse the ones that fit.

Hopefully insight has been gained about the information required, and how to process the information in a way that will give an accurate pattern. To reinforce the process of looking at previous step to get your pattern, draw the box for the fourth box in the series, using steps 2-3.

Draw what you think is the next box in this series

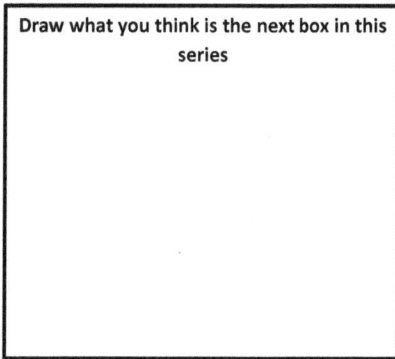

The answer

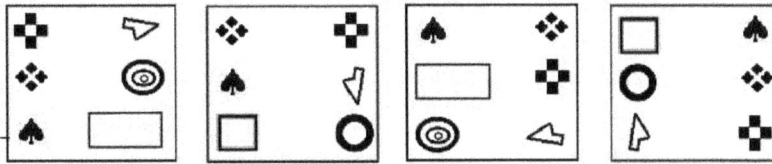

This example was broken down to help provide a guide through the process needed to get to the right pattern. Now, here is how how this type of question will come up in the UKCAT, with a small change to the layout.

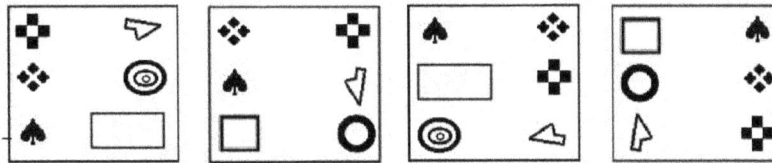

From the following options, which figure completes the series?

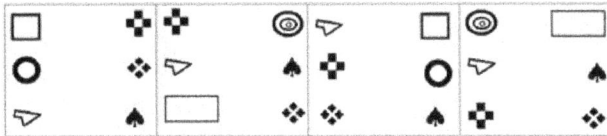

Draw your answer here

The answer is:

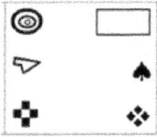

Key takeaway points-

• These are shapes NOT symbols

• What is consistent in the data? Aim to eliminate useless shapes that are placed to overwhelm and distract, focus on the shapes that will help to lead to a correct pattern.

• Breakdown each shape, analyse what it does. Is it useful or useless? Does it change? If so find out a reason why.

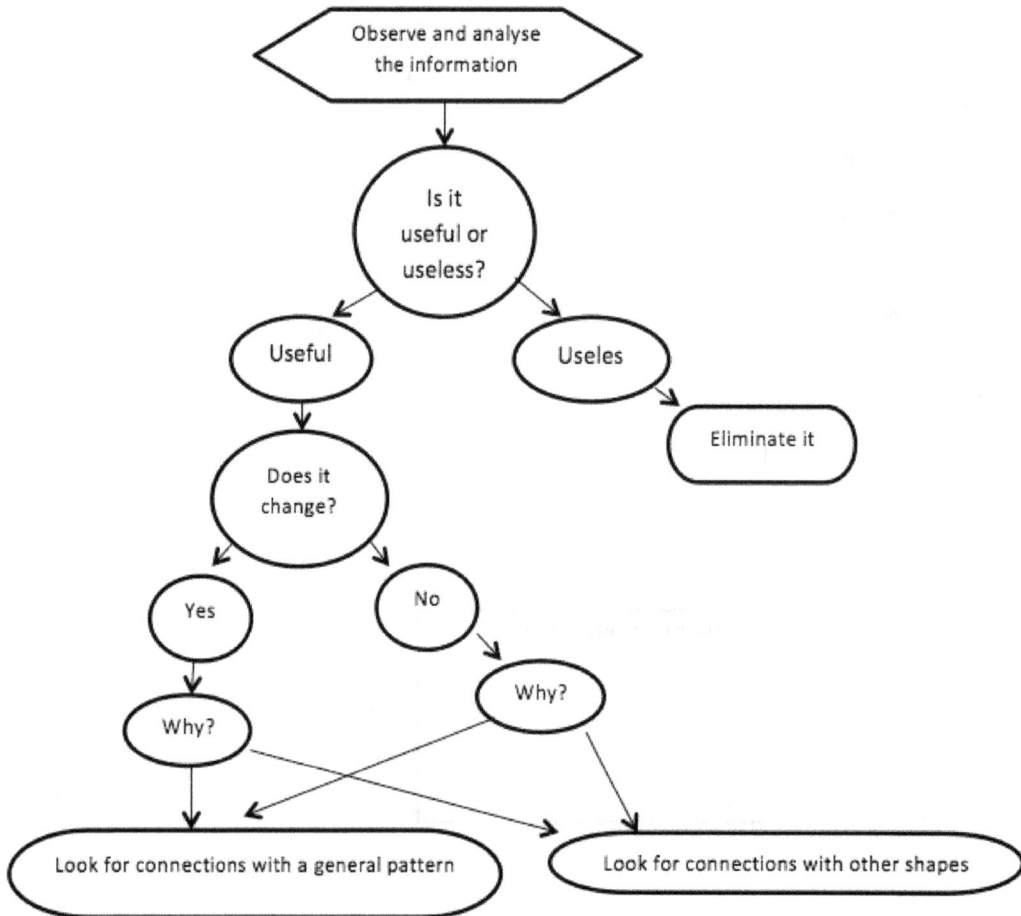

SITUATIONAL JUDGMENT TEST

This section is a more straightforward part of the exam. It is a personality test that is ethically and patient based. Patients place a significant amount of trust in medical professionals to take care of their health. This applies in many different settings such as in a hospital, or a dental surgery or even the opticians. What qualities are expected of the healthcare practitioner who oversees patient care? The aim of the Situational Judgment Test is to assess whether candidates display these qualities. Now the key qualities that are expected from medical professionals will be broken down and will provide a good framework to handle these questions but this is not an exhaustive list:

Main priority is the care of the patient, this means it is important to display:

- Trust.

- Integrity.

This expands to an umbrella of key ethical aspects:

- Being polite and considerate – Respect the patient.

- Be a good listener; understand the patients concerns and preference in general but more importantly in regards to their care and treatment.

- Patient confidentiality.

This is essential because candidates are in a position of responsibility this means:

- Be prepared to explain your actions.

- Prepare to act quickly if the patient is going to be compromised in terms of safety, or any other aspect such as comfort or dignity.

- Be responsible for your knowledge and skills; and understand limitations in that knowledge.

- Co-ordinate with others in ways, which are in best interest of the patient.

- Judgment of capacity and consent.

In summary, the key is to display a respect for human life. These are all of qualities expected from a medical professional overseeing patient care.

Now work through an example of a scenario and choose the most appropriate the action to take in the scenario:

A drug addict visits her GP. She says she is finding her treatment tough, and has relapsed once. She has a young son. Social services previously found her fit to look after him, but this was before the relapse. She says she finds it tough to look after him at the moment. How appropriate are each of the following responses.

Now examine this situation, like the Verbal reasoning analyse the situation, write down key aspects of patient care that are being tested.

Write down the key aspects of patient care that you think the situation wants you to look at
_____
_____
_____
_____
_____
_____
_____
_____
_____
_____
_____
_____

A drug addict visits her GP. – The patient is a drug addict; a key area to start thinking about is the capacity to make decisions. Are the decisions made in the best interest of the patient? Responsibility of the health of the patient both physically and psychologically lies with the GP. She says she is finding her treatment tough, and has relapsed once. – Again the patient's care needs to be addressed by the GP, who will need to listen to the patient's concerns regarding her treatment and management. Why is she finding it difficult? Is there an alternative treatment? She has a young son. Social services previously found her fit to look after him, but this was before the relapse. She says she finds it tough to look after him at the moment. – Here is the moral dilemma, faced with the conflicting situation of patient confidentiality versus the care of her son. Key points to remember, healthcare professionals are meant to be trustworthy and act with integrity. The patient's care is the primary concern not the care of the son. How appropriate are each of the following responses.

Circle the answer that is most correct.

1) Although consent should be sought, if the child's safety is at risk, there is a case to call social services anyway.

a) A very appropriate thing to do

b) Appropriate, but not ideal

c) Inappropriate, but not awful

d) A very inappropriate thing to do

2) The doctor should support the patient at all times.

a) A very appropriate thing to do

b) Appropriate, but not ideal

c) Inappropriate, but not awful

d) A very inappropriate thing to do

3) If the child's safety is at risk, there is a case to call social services without consent.

a) A very appropriate thing to do

b) Appropriate, but not ideal

c) Inappropriate, but not awful

d) A very inappropriate thing to do

4) Help the patient to get back on track.

a) A very appropriate thing to do

b) Appropriate, but not ideal

c) Inappropriate, but not awful

d) A very inappropriate thing to do

5) Determine whether the child is at risk, but this may take a while.

a) A very appropriate thing to do

b) Appropriate, but not ideal

c) Inappropriate, but not awful

d) A very inappropriate thing to do

The model answers

1) Although consent should be sought, if the child's safety is at risk, there is a case to call social services anyway. = Appropriate, but not ideal. Here there is a good reason for doing so and this action can be justified. However, if the patient does not consent, it violates patient confidentiality and trust.

2) The doctor should support the patient at all times. = A very appropriate thing to do. The patient is the key priority and the main focus of care should be with her.

3) If the child's safety is at risk, there is a case to call social services without consent. = Inappropriate, but not awful. Similar reasons as 1) but the key difference is that consent is directly avoided. The focus of best interests is not the patient but the son.

4) Help the patient to get back on track. = A very appropriate thing to do. This is the best choice as the focus is on the patient's care and treatment. It also promotes working in a trustworthy manner and protecting patient confidentiality.

5) Determine whether the child is at risk, but this may take a while. = Appropriate, but not ideal. The key point to take away from this question and these questions in general is that the care of the patient is the main priority, be a good listener and understand the patient's concerns. Aim to maintain trust, integrity and patient confidentiality.

Now, here is another example to help internalise the key qualities that are looked for in the SJT. This will be in the format of the 2nd style of questions:

A newborn baby is suffering from a congenital disease. Treatment is available, but if successful, would result in the baby having a severely reduced quality of life. The medical team has to decide what to do. How important is it to take into account the wishes of the baby itself when deciding how to respond to the situation?

Write down the key aspects of patient care that you think the situation wants you to look at

Now here is the breakdown of the situation:

A newborn baby is suffering from a congenital disease.

– Newborn baby, unable to consent to treatment, decisions must be made by the parents.

Treatment is available, but if successful, would leave result in the baby having a severely reduced quality of life.

– As a medical professional the best treatment must be provided, weighing the benefits and more importantly the harm of the treatments given to the patient. This is important for both operations and also the possible side effects of drugs. It is important that the patient can make decisions with full knowledge of what can go wrong. It is key that clinicians are effective listeners and communicators in order to address the patient's preference and concerns.

The medical team has to decide what to do.

– Whenever working in a team, it is important to be aware of any limitations and know how to work with members of other medical professionals to provide the best treatment for the patient.

How important is it to take into account the wishes of the parents when deciding how to respond to the situation?

Questions: Circle the answer – for this format of questions, answers are given in terms of greatest importance.

1) **This is an important factor. If the quality of life is severely reduced it may be better to not attempt the treatment. However this is more of a factor for the family to decide on.**

a) Very important

b) Important

c) Of minor importance

d) Not important at all

2) **The decision ultimately lies with the parents.**

a) Very important

b) Important

c) Of minor importance

d) Not important at all

3) **The medical team should give their professional views, but ultimately the decision lies with the parents.**

a) Very important

b) Important

c) Of minor importance

d) Not important at all

4) **This is an important factor as it could be a contributing factor to the parents when making the decision.**

a)   Very important

b)   Important

c)   Of minor importance

d)   Not important at all

5) **The cost is not why the decision is being made, so is not an important factor.**

a)   Very important

b)   Important

c)   Of minor importance

d)   Not important at all

The model answers:

1)   If the quality of life is severely reduced it may be better to not attempt the treatment. = This is of minor importance. Although quality of life is an important factor for the medical team to consider this is more of a factor for the family to decide on. The only goal is to provide the best treatment for the patient and the judgment of what effect this will have on the patient is the patient's decision or in this case the parent's choice. In this example, what seems important from clinical perspective might not be important to the patient. It could go against their belief system.

2)   The decision ultimately lies with the parents. = Very important. As mentioned above, the key is the patient. The parents are making the decision for the child because the child does not have the capacity to consent to the treatment. The decision of the parents must be respected as if it was the patient making the decision.

3)   The medical team should give their professional views, but ultimately the decision lies with the parents = Very important. The healthcare professional's role is to provide the best care and treatment for the patient and to voice these choices to the patient/parents from a professional point of view. It is the patient's choice on which treatment to choose.

4)   Quality of life of the baby after the treatment is a contributing factor for the parent's decision. = This is an important factor, as it could be important to the parents when making the decision. The parents are making the decision for the child, the considerations of the parents with regards to the quality of life is their choice to make.

5)   The cost of the treatment. = Not important at all. The cost of treatment is not important when providing the best treatment for the patient's health. The key role is of a medical professional is to maintain and improve life. Cost plays no part in this aspect.

Key take away points:

•   The patient always comes first, respect their concerns and wishes about the treatment, in order to provide the treatment, which is best for them.

•   Be honest and act with integrity.

•   Be trustworthy; only break patient confidentiality if there is no other choice in terms of health of the patient.

- Have a respect for human life.

There are an enormous amount of resources for SJT in terms of scenarios available online. Also there are many different medical ethical guidelines that further expand on key qualities of a medical professional. It is recommended that these resources are used to help achieve a satisfactory band rating.

Hopefully at this stage the sections of UKCAT have become more familiar and approachable. The aim has been to develop candidates' skills to the point where questions are answered without putting much thought into it. Similar to the example of the child who learns to recognise words and what they mean, this stage of skill development is vital to understanding the sections of the UKCAT. The focus is to guide candidates to the point where they can master these skills and execute them naturally. There is a clear need to practice and practice for a minimum of four weeks. If this is not possible, the UKCAT may be more of a challenge. Using the skills highlighted in the breakdown will help candidates achieve a better score. A good source of extra UKCAT style questions to practice on can be found for free online. But, as stated before to really master these skills and prepare for the exam, try to use real life examples. This will help to build the right bridges to success and maintain a relaxed, flexible and adaptable approach that can handle virtually any of the questions that appear. There are also other books that offer extra questions to practice on. Questions in the old format are not the most representative of what UKCAT 2016 is based upon. However, they are still useful to practice these skills and understand the process of how to handle these sections.

Keep coming back to the breakdown sections to master the skills required for the exams.

CHAPTER 2 : EXAM FORMAT

EXAM FORMAT

You are given 120 minutes (2 hours) for the UKCAT and 150 minutes (2 hours and 30 minutes) for the UKCAT special needs test. This is a long time to stay focused; nonetheless, with the right preparation it can be done.

There is a maximum score of 900 for each section. Some universities use aggregate scores and have a cut- off score (generally over 600) , where candidates with a lower score than the cut- off are not considered; whereas, others require a certain minimum score in each of the sections in order to be considered. This varies from university to university and most colleges do not make public what method they use. For the test, remind yourself that each question counts and time wasted = lower scores.

We have kept it simple by homing in on important facts and information in order to give you a full picture of the exam. It's up to you to do the practice tests for each section and work hard up until your test date. We suggest that you focus on one section at a time to start with and really dig deep into why you're making mistakes and aim to improve with each question. There's absolutely no point in doing hundreds of questions without actually understanding the reasoning behind them. Even after you manage to complete this book, use real life situations and free online question in combination with the breakdown to get to where you want to be.

Using the 'one section at a time' strategy will enable you to identify early on where your strengths and weaknesses lie. For instance, if verbal reasoning is your weakest section, you can then start reading long articles in newspapers/online and see how much you can remember or how long it takes you to read it critically; the aim here is to identify your weakness early so that you can transform it into a strength. A low score in any one of the sections will lower your average and hence, it is important to tackle your weaknesses whilst keeping up your strengths. Most universities take into account an aggregate score and therefore, this technique will pay off in the long run.

Please note that for the UKCAT 2016 - the decision analysis has been removed and a 'Decision making' section has been added - this book will not cover this section as it is not marked for the 2016 cohort.

UKCAT 2016 Breakdown Table

Subtest	Duration	Information	Test Items
Verbal Reasoning	22 minutes	11 passages of text need to be evaluated	44 items
Quantitative Reasoning	25 minutes	9 sets of tables, graphs, pie charts etc	36 items
Abstract Reasoning	14 minutes	13 sets of abstract shapes	55 items
Situational Judgement Test	27 minutes	20 scenarios	68 items
Total Time	120* minutes		

*This time includes the Decision making section which will not be marked for your test.

You are not allowed to take anything into the test. You will be provided with one/two laminated sheets to write on.

An on-screen calculator will be provided which can be found on the top left hand corner of your screen

Some Tips before we get started on the practice questions

- You reap what you sow. It is imperative that you maximise your time until the test. We advise that you don't rely on how much you're peers are doing.
  Gauge your own capability and build a working pattern in order to develop accuracy and speed with your skills.

- Depending on how long you have until your test, you need to devise a daily study plan. Some candidates prefer to work a couple of hours every night, whereas others prefer to work five hours, every couple of days and then take a few days off. Do what works for you.

CHAPTER 3 : VERBAL REASONING

VERBAL REASONING

This section is the Verbal Reasoning practice section, we recommend you refresh your memory on how to approach this section on pages 15 - 23.

What should you expect?

This section is designed to test your ability to read and critique the information presented to you.

There will be 11 passages of text, which can be about anything ranging from science topics to current affairs or even a passage from a storybook etc . You are expected to answer 44 questions based on these 11 passages. Remind yourself that they are not testing your pre-existing knowledge, but **rather** your ability to carefully analyse information.

Format 1

The question will be in the form of a statement and you have to choose whether the answers will be one of 'Yes'/'True, 'No'/'False' or 'Can't tell'.

Read the short passage below and determine the correct answer.

The production of smart phones and tablets continues to increase considerably, with demand particularly high in developed nations like Northern America, Tokyo and Britain. The rapid diffusion of technology and fast growing technological benefits are resulting in enhanced consumption, and the market is likely to quadruple over the next decade. With old players like Nokia who have now been left behind, while new contenders like Apple and Samsung take the lead, the future shows no signs of slowing down for this market and we can look forward to new entrants in this multi- billion industry.

Statement: Smart Phones and tablets are the fastest growing field in the Technological industry.
A.True   **B.** False   **C.** Can't Tell

True- If the statement can directly be justified by the passage, or if you were to put the statement in to the passage it wouldn't be out of place.

False- If there is something in the statement that is completely the opposite to what it states in the passage, or if you placed the sentence within the passage, it would outrightly stand out

Can't tell - Choose this option if there exists even **a shred of ambiguity** or uncertainty, particularly when the passage doesn't directly imply this but it could be true if more information was given to you

Solution: According to the passage, "The production of smart phones and tablets continues to increase considerably, with demand ...is likely to quadruple over the next decade". Nonetheless, the passage does not explicitly state that smart phones and tablets are the fastest growing field in the technological industry. Based on current knowledge, we may be tempted to make assumptions and assume that the answer is true. However, **remember Rule #1**, the correct answer here is **'Can't Tell'**

Format 2

The options presented will take the form of an incomplete statement or a question, there will be four response options available. Students are required to choose the best or most suitable response. Candidates can only select a single response. Remember Rule # 1 and base your answer solely on the information provided in the text, so that you can confidently move on to the next, without any lingering doubt in your minds.

Some example questions are given below:

The author most likely agrees with all of the following except:
- Which of following claims is best supported by the passage?
- Which conclusion can be drawn from the passage?
- Which of the following assertions would strengthen/weaken 'some argument' that appeared in the passage?
- Which of the following statements is most/least likely to be true?

Simply understanding what the question requires of you is important in this test as time management is of the essence.

A helping hand before you crack on:

1. This section requires a lot of concentration and being the first section, this works to your advantage.

2. If you are finding any one question extremely difficult, do not panic. Instead, eliminate the obvious incorrect answers, like what we have done in the breakdown, and then try and choose between the remaining two

3. The test is not negatively marked, so don't leave anything blank. Flag questions and come back to them. It's always better to make a wise guess rather than lose a mark.

4. You have 22 minutes (one minute for instruction) to complete 44 questions. So once you have read the instruction keep in mind that you have around 30 seconds to do each question. This sounds like no time, but the more you practice the easier it will become.

For this practice section we have

Format 1 - 15 passages

Format 2 - 15 passages

Format 1 and 2 - 8 passages

Verbal Reasoning questions - Format 1

1.   It has been known for years that there is a very strong relationship between smoking and increased risk of lung cancer. Doctors recognised in the 1940's and 50s that cigarettes seemed to be causing an epidemic in lung cancer. Scholars started noticing the parallel rise in cigarette consumption and lung cancer. The first studies were mainly case-control epidemiology, where they looked at groups of lung cancer patient compared to cancer-free controls. They were able to show that people with lung cancer were far more likely to have smoked. It wasn't until a study done in 1954 that showed that a smoker of 35 or more cigarettes a day increased their chances of dying of lung cancer by a factor of 40, that people started to believe that the link had been proven beyond reasonable doubt.

There have been many studies looking into why even after all this evidence about the carcinogenicity of cigarettes it still took decades for people to start to change their behaviour. When asking members of the US public in 1954 if cigarette smoking was a cause of lung cancer only 41% answered yes. A poll was done in 1960 amongst American doctors, which showed that only 1/3 considered smoking a 'major cause of lung cancer'. It also showed that nearly 50% of doctors in the USA were still smoking regularly.

a.   The relationship between smoking and lung cancer was first noticed in the 1940's

A. True   B. False   C. Can't Tell

b.   It was shown that smoking 35 or more cigarettes a day increases risk of dying from lung cancer by 40 times

A. True   B. False   C. Can't Tell

c.   By 1960s smoking was considered a major cause of lung cancer by the majority of doctors.

A. True   B. False   C. Can't Tell

d.   Even with all the evidence against cigarettes, it took decades for people's behaviour to change

A. True   B. False   C. Can't Tell

2.   There has been a lot of research into the positive effects of single sex education. One of the commonest points of discussion relating to the positive effects of single sex classrooms relates to the dominant presence of boys in classrooms and that they tend to be more disruptive. This is speculated to have a negative effect on engagement and therefore achievement of girls. On of the biggest points of discussion recently is that some research has shown all round positive effects of single sex schooling for girls. It states that girls are more confident and assertive and shows that they feel free to pursue academic excellence in the more gender atypical areas of science, technology and maths. All-girls schools consistently report highly competitive GCSEs and low drop out rates. They also indicate that the students are less likely to study gender-stereotyped subjects in school if at a single-sex school.

Some researchers suggest that it may actually be very difficult to make these sorts of comparisons between single sex and coeducational schools, as is it very hard to only control the one variable in these studies. Some researchers feel that the results may be due, in part, to the broader factors that are often characteristic of single-sex schools rather than purely from the separation of girls from boys.

a.   Boys are thought to be more disruptive in class which may affect education of girls

A. True   B. False   C. Can't Tell

b.   Students only study gender-stereotyped subjects at single-sex schools

A. True   B. False   C. Can't Tell

c.   Researchers feel that some of the benefits seen in single-sex schools are due to more than just separating girls from boys

A. True   B. False   C. Can't Tell

d.   Co-educational schools have high drop out rates

A. True   B. False   C. Can't Tell

3.   Cambridge University was founded in the 13th century. For many centuries it was only open to male students, however this all changed in 1869 with the establishment of Girton College and then Newnham in 1872, which were both set up for women students. The first women were examined in 1882. Although women were permitted to study at the University, attend lectures and sit the exams, they were not given degrees until 1947 when they were given full membership to the university. The number of undergraduate students increased after the war, partly due to the full admission of female students and also the foundation of 3 more colleges, New Hall, Churchill and Robinson. By now there were 3 female only colleges, with all the other colleges still only admitting male students. In the 1970's, Churchill, Clare and Kings's allowed admission of women for the first time. Magdalene was the last all male college in both Cambridge and Oxford to admit women in 1988, despite protest of some of the students. Now there are no all-male colleges in Cambridge, however there are still 3 female-only colleges in Cambridge, making Cambridge the only university in the UK that has admission policies that discriminate against gender.

a.   The first female students took exams at Cambridge university in 1869

A. True   B. False   C. Can't Tell

b.   The first degrees given to female students were in 1947

A. True   B. False   C. Can't Tell

c.   In 1985 not all colleges accepted women

A. True   B. False   C. Can't Tell

d.   Newnham, Girton and New Hall are the 3 female-only colleges

A. True   B. False   C. Can't Tell

4.   Hawk-eye is a complex computer system that is used in numerous sports, such as cricket, tennis and association football, as a near real-time technological adjudicator. There are multiple high-speed cameras placed at different locations around the stadium from which the ball can be tracked from different angles. This data is triangulated and used to statistically work out the most likely path of the ball as a moving image. This 'prediction' of the path of the ball can then be used by judges to help them make decisions about infringements of the rules. It is only accurate to within 5mm but it has been accepted by governing bodies in tennis, cricket and association football as a technological means of adjudication. It was developed in the UK and was originally implemented in 2001 in cricket. Now it has become an integral part of over 20 sports and every year covers events across more than 400 stadiums in over 50 countries. In 2011, the company was sold to Sony and now has offices around the world.

a.   Hawk-eye Is used in badminton

A. True   B. False   C. Can't Tell

b.   Was used first as a technological adjudicator in tennis

A. True   B. False   C. Can't Tell

c.   The technology is used to predict the likely path of a ball, from multiple cameras within the sports stadium

A. True   B. False   C. Can't Tell

d.   Hawk eye has been accepted because of its complete accuracy

A. True   B. False   C. Can't Tell

5.   In 2005 London was selected to host the 2012 Olympics. After winning the bid, work began on a 246 hectare Olympic Park in the east end of London.   By opening in 2012, 30,000 people worked on the project that included 5 new permanent venues. The biggest venue that was built was the Olympic stadium.   It was designed by architects to be flexible. It was built to hold 80,000 during the Games but this could be reduced after the games finished by removing 55,000 seats in the upper tier. Sustainability and legacy were 2 important factors when designing and building the Olympic park and this is seen in the ability of the stadium to be reduced in capacity so that it would become a permanent venue for professional sports. West Ham eventually won the bid to take over the Stadium and they will start to use it in the 2016/17 season.

70,000 volunteers helped to "make London 2012 happen". Games Makers and Young Games Makers were selected to be on the frontline to assist the millions of visitors and all the athletes. More than 240,000 people applied and 86,000 were interviewed for these posts. With 8.8 million tickets for sale, the roles for the Games Makers varied from ticket checkers to drivers and event stewards to welcome desk officials.

a.   The capacity of the Olympic stadium was built to be flexible

A. True   B. False   C. Can't Tell

b.   West Ham football club started to play at the stadium after the Olympics ended

A. True   B. False   C. Can't Tell

c.   One of the roles of the Games Makers was to help direct the visitors

A. True   B. False   C. Can't Tell

d.   Over half the people who applied to be a Games Maker were interviewed for the role

A. True   B. False   C. Can't Tell

6.   Jersey is one of the Channel Islands, lying 19 miles from France and 85 miles from the UK. Although Jersey is the biggest of the Channel Islands, the island is only 9 miles from end to end and 5 miles wide. It has a population of 100,800. The maximum speed limit on the island is only 40mph and is often restricted to 15mph in many places. Jersey is part of the British Isles, not the United Kingdom, which includes England, Wales, Scotland and Northern Ireland. Although the main language spoken in Jersey is English, all their road signs are also in French and there is a lot of French influence on the Island. The climate is very temperate due to its location and it is often warmer, with more sunshine hours than in the UK. This means that there is often good weather to enjoy the quality and variety of beaches on offer.

a.   Jersey is part of the British Isles even though it lies closer to France than the UK

A. True   B. False   C. Can't Tell

b.   All road signs are in 2 languages

A. True   B. False   C. Can't Tell

c.   The average speed that cars can drive is less than 20mph

A. True   B. False   C. Can't Tell

d.   The weather is often better in Jersey than in England

A. True   B. False   C. Can't Tell

7.   The National Minimum Wage is the minimum pay per hour most workers are entitled to by law. In 2015, the National Minimum Wage was £6.70 for people aged 21 and over. The living wage is the minimum income necessary for a worker to meet their basic needs. This differs from the minimum wage and in the UK has been more than the National Minimum Wage, meaning that many families fail to have the salary to meet requirements for basic quality of life and rely on government help for additional income. However, from 1st April 2016, the National Living Wage of £7.20 per hour will be mandatory for anyone aged 25 and over. The government believe that insisting on this increase in minimum salary will reduce the reliance of the public on top ups from the state. The response from employees has been positive, however 54% of employers surveyed said that this increased will have a significant impact on their wage bill. 30% of employers are planning on responding to this by improving efficiency and increasing productivity. Surveys showed that the National Living Wade will have the biggest impact in retail and hospitality as well as in the healthcare sector. There are fears that this change could lead to a loss of 60,000 jobs with 1/5 of employers cutting staff numbers to compensate for the higher wage threshold.

a.   The National Minimum Wage in March 2016 was £6.70

A. True   B. False   C. Can't Tell

b.   The National Minimum Wage ensures that all families have enough money to support themselves

A. True   B. False   C. Can't Tell

c.   Over half of all employers will be impacted significantly by the increase in Minimum Wage

A. True   B. False   C. Can't Tell

d.   Thousands of people may lose their jobs as a result of the increase in wage threshold

A. True   B. False   C. Can't Tell

8.   Thalidomide was created in 1953 by a German company called Grunenthal Group. After realising it was an effective antiemetic it was licensed to be used in pregnancy to prevent morning sickness. In the 1950's the use of medications in pregnancy was not controlled and drugs were not thoroughly tested for harmful effects to the fetus. At the time scientists did not believe that drugs taken by a pregnant woman could cross the placental barrier to reach the fetus. Thousands of pregnant women were prescribed thalidomide to relieve their nausea. The first babies with severe limb deformities as a result of this drug were born in 1959. However ,it wasn't until 1961 that the drug was withdrawn from the market after an Australian doctor wrote to the Lancet about the correlation he had noticed between the increase in babies born with severe limb deformities and mothers taking thalidomide. By the time the drug was taken off the market due to massive pressure from the public it had caused about 10,000 cases worldwide, of which only 50% survived. In 1968, a compensation settlement of £20 million was agreed with Distillers, the company who distributed the drug in the UK. This was administered by the Thalidomide Trust to all affected individuals and families.

a.   Drugs have always been tested for their safety to growing fetuses

A. True   B. False   C. Can't Tell

b.   Thalidomide was removed from the market due to doctors complaining

A. True   B. False   C. Can't Tell

c.   The first babies born with affects from the thalidomide was in 1953

A. True   B. False   C. Can't Tell

d.   Thalidomide resulted in about 5,000 people living with limb deformities

A. True   B. False   C. Can't Tell

9.   Antarctica is the Earth's southernmost continent containing the South Pole. It is the 5th largest continent in area, measuring 14,000,000 square km, of which 98% is covered in ice. It is the coldest, driest and windiest continent and is considered a desert due to only 200mm of precipitation falling per year. There are no permanent human residents but there are up to 5,000 people living there throughout the year at research stations. During the coldest part of the year, temperatures fall to -63OC. Ernest Shackleton was chosen to go on the Antarctica expedition in 1901 on the ship "Discovery". Shackleton with 2 others trekked towards the South Pole, they didn't reach it, as Shackleton became very ill and had to return home. In 1911, the South Pole was reached by Roald Amundsen for the first time. 1914 saw Shackleton returning to Antarctica with the ship "Endurance" with a plan to cross the continent via the South Pole. The ship became trapped in ice and later sank, after which Shackleton's journey became a survival mission to find help. Shackleton published an account of the "Endurance" expedition in 1919 called 'South'. 100 years later, Henry Worsley arrived in Antarctica to complete the first ever solo unsupported crossing of Antarctica. He wished to walk 943 miles across the continent unassisted in the spirit of his idol Shackleton 100 years after the failed Endurance expedition. He battled the extreme weather conditions but only 30 miles short of his destination he made the decision to not continue further as this trek had finally took its toll on him. He not only wanted to be the first person to make this solo crossing but also raise support and money for The Endeavour Fund to assist wounded soldiers. In the 71 days he managed alone Henry Worsley raised over £100,000 for this cause.

a.   No humans live on Antarctica

A. True   B. False   C. Can't Tell

b.   Shackleton died on the failed "Endurance"' mission

A. True   B. False   C. Can't Tell

c.   Worsley had walked over 900 miles before having to pull out of his mission

A. True   B. False   C. Can't Tell

d.   No females have ever reached the South Pole

A. True   B. False   C. Can't Tell

10.   Agricultural products and foodstuffs such as Gorgonzola, Melton Mowbray pork pies, Camembert, Herefordshire Cider and Champagne are protected by 3 European Union schemes. These are responsible for protecting the reputation of these foods and therefore allow producers to obtain a premium price for the authentic products. The protected designation of origin (PDO), protected geographical indication (PGI) and traditional specialities guaranteed (TSG) all work to ensure that certain products protected by them can only be labelled as such if they come from the designated region and are produced in the specified manner.   For example, Champagne is a sparkling wine that is produced from grapes grown in the Champagne region of France and that is pressed and fermented using unique regimes. Even though there are many sparkling wines produced worldwide, only wine that meets the requirements may be legally labelled as Champagne within the EU and many other countries. It has been protected within Europe since 1891 under the Madrid system treaty and more recently other countries worldwide have passed laws or signed agreements not to use the term "Champagne" for other products from outside the EU.

One of the newest additions to the scheme was Herdwick sheep. In 2013, they were given protected states by the PDO. This means that meat can only be described as Lakeland Herdwick if It comes from the Herdwick breed and was born, raised and slaughtered in Cumbria. Farmers are very happy as this will help them to protect a traditional farming system and help give them a sustainable future.

a.   To be called 'Champagne', the sparkling wine needs to be produced using specific grapes and methods

A. True   B. False   C. Can't Tell

b.   Champagne is protected worldwide

A. True   B. False   C. Can't Tell

c.   Protecting Herdwick Lamb will help farmers in Cumbria maintain their livelihoods.

A. True   B. False   C. Can't Tell

d.   The only requirement is that the product has to have come from a specific area.

A. True   B. False   C. Can't Tell

11.   Valentine's Day is an annual holiday celebrated on February 14. It's origins come from a Western Christian feast day honouring a saint named Valentinus. One of the popular martydom stories associated with the Valentines is an account of Saint Valentine of Rome which stated that he was imprisoned for performing weddings for soldiers who were forbidden to marry. According to legend, he healed the daughter of his jailer and wrote her a letter signed "your valentine". It was in the 18th century that it turned into a day when lovers presented flowers, confectionary and sent cards known as valentines to their loved ones.

Today, mass produced greeting cards have taken over from handwritten ones and there is a huge industry for valentine's gifts and paraphernalia. In the UK just under half the population spend money on valentines. Approximately £1.3 billion is spent every year on cards, flowers, chocolates and other gifts. It is estimated that in the US 190 million valentines are sent each year, with half of those sent to family members other than spouse.   For some companies it is the second biggest day for sales of products after Christmas Day, these include the card company Hallmark, Hersheys (chocolate store) and jewellery stores such as Tiffany. Some people now see it as a Hallmark holiday due to the commercialisation of the day.

a.   Over £1,000,000 are spent every year on Valentine's day

A. True   B. False   C. Can't Tell

b.   A popular story associated with the day is about Saint Valentine who signed a love letter signed "your valentine"

A. True   B. False   C. Can't Tell

c.   Cards sent on 14th February were called 'Valentines' from the 1700's

A. True   B. False   C. Can't Tell

d.   The majority of cards sent in the US on Valentines are to people's siblings or children

A. True   B. False   C. Can't Tell

12. In the UK, women are entitled to 52 weeks of Statutory Maternity Leave. Half of that is Ordinary Maternity Leave and the other half Additional. Taking this much time off after you've had your baby is not compulsory but all women must take 2 weeks off after the baby is born. Fathers are entitled to 2 weeks Paternity leave that must be taken after the child is born, but before they are 56 days old. As of April 2015 a new system has been introduced called Shared Parental Leave. This was designed to give parents more flexibility. Parents are able to share a period of leave, therefore they can decide to have time off together or take it in turns. The mother must be entitled to maternity leave and must share the responsibility for the child. The other partner must also be an employee and they must have worked for their employer for 26 weeks at the end of the 15th week before the child is due. If they satisfy these tests they are both entitled to share the leave. The parents are entitled to 50 weeks of leave, with 37 paid weeks. The leave may be taken at any time before the child's first birthday and each parent can book up to 3 blocks of leave in this year. During the 37 weeks of paid leave the rate of pay is £139.58 or 90% of average weekly earnings (whichever is lower).

a. Women do not have to take any maternity leave

A. True   B. False   C. Can't Tell

b. To be entitled to Shared Parental Leave the mother's partner must have been working for his or her employer for the whole of gestation

A. True   B. False   C. Can't Tell

c. Both parents are paid for 37 weeks leave

A. True   B. False   C. Can't Tell

d. If the parents earn £800 a month then they will be paid £139.58 a week

A. True   B. False   C. Can't Tell

13.   UNESCO World Heritage Sites are places of importance to cultural or natural heritage that are believed to be of interest to the international community to preserve. These sites of natural, scenic and historic significance are protected and preserved so that present and future generations can enjoy them. There are currently 936 World Heritage Sites located in 153 countries. The majority of these are cultural sites (725) with 183 being natural sites. For a site to be inscribed onto the list it must meet the criteria set out by the organisation. These include things such as it bears a unique testimony to a cultural tradition or civilisation which is living or has disappeared, or it is an area of exceptional natural beauty and aesthetic importance. The first world heritage site was the Galapagos Islands in Ecuador.

As of July 2014, Italy has 51 sites inscribed on the list. This makes it the country with the most World Heritage Sites in the world. 4 of the sites in Italy are shared with other countries. 4 sites are of the natural type, whilst all the others are cultural, meaning that Italy also has the largest number of "cultural" heritage sites in the world. The World Heritage Sites in Italy range from an active volcano to entire cities, from individual towers to coastlines and include the Dolomites, The City of Verona, Historic Centres of Florence and Rome, the archaeological area of Pompeii and the Amalfi Coast. The sites are all travel destinations for those seeking history and culture and range from

a.   One criteria for being inscribed onto the list of World Heritage Sites, is that it the site is a unique area that highlights cultural traditions of past generations

A. True   B. False   C. Can't Tell

b.   There are now over 900 cultural World Heritage Sites in the World

A. True   B. False   C. Can't Tell

c.   Italy has both the most World Heritage Sites in the world and the most cultural sites.

A. True   B. False   C. Can't Tell

d.   The Leaning Tower of Pisa is one of the 51 sites in Italy

A. True   B. False   C. Can't Tell

14.   On the 26th December 2004 an earthquake measuring more than 9 on the Richter scale started a tsunami that ended up killing a quarter of a million people. The earthquake was as a result of the Indo-Australian Plate subducting below the Eurasian plate. This caused the seafloor to lift up, displacing the seawater above and creating the waves. This was the 4th largest earthquake of recent times. The tsunami hit 13 countries with Indonesia being the worst affected. By the time the Tsunami reached the shores the waves were up to 15 metres high and swept in quickly and with little warning. The only warning in some places was a rapidly receding ocean, people who knew what that meant gave a warning to those around them to get to high ground as quickly as possible. Some experts say that this would have given people up to 5 minutes to get to high ground. Therefore, there may have been plenty of time for more people to save themselves if only they knew what to do. The tsunami destroyed thousands of miles of coastline, destroyed homes and shattered lives. Very soon after the disaster, people all over the world were aware of the magnitude of the disaster. The scale of the generous public response was unprecedented, about $14 billion dollars was raised internationally in a very short time frame as humanitarian aid to help all those affected at a time of great suffering.

a.   The tsunami was triggered by the biggest earthquake of recent times

A. True   B. False   C. Can't Tell

b.   The waves created reached heights of 15m

A. True   B. False   C. Can't Tell

c.   If people knew the warning signs thousands of lives could have been saved

A. True   B. False   C. Can't Tell

d.   The humanitarian response was worldwide, very quick and on a massive scale

A. True   B. False   C. Can't Tell

15.   Alzheimer's disease is the most common form of dementia, accounting for 60-70% cases. It is a chronic neuro-generative disease that starts slowly but progresses over time.   The symptoms include short-term memory loss, problems with language, disorientation, mood swings and behavioural issues. Gradually, all body functions are lost and the disease leads to death. The average life expectancy is 3-9 years after diagnosis. Alzheimer's has been identified as a protein mis-folding disease. The accumulation of abnormally folded beta-amyloid protein being the hallmark of Alzheimer's disease. There is a hypothesis that these proteins when deposited within the brain are toxic to neuronal cells, resulting in their death. This leads to degeneration and atrophy of the affected regions of the brain. Currently, there is no cure for Alz-heimer's. There are some medications that can improve the symptoms, however they cannot prevent the eventual degen-eration of this progressive disease.

There has been new excitement in the field with the discovery by a laboratory in Cambridge that a stain-like drug may be able to prevent the onset of Alzheimer's. The drug Bexarotene has been shown to prevent onset of amyloid plaque deposi-tion in worms that were genetically programmed to suffer the same progression as people with the disease. Scientist be-lieve that it stops the "primary nucleation" of the amyloid protein seen in early Alzheimer's, which prevents its aggregating into the classic plaques. The hope is that if this works in humans that it would stop the process before aggregation starts. Therefore, it may work as a prophylactic drug to halt the early biological events of Alzheimer's. The scientists feel that this may then be able to be marketed as a neurostatin to decrease risk of Alzheimer's disease if taken in your 30s or 40s.

a.   Alzheimer's is an incurable disease

A. True   B. False   C. Can't Tell

b.   Bexarotene has been shown to be effective at stopping progression of Alzheimer's in humans

A. True   B. False   C. Can't Tell

c.   Neurostatins will become the next prophylactic drug to prevent progression of this neurodegenerative disease

A. True   B. False   C. Can't Tell

d.   Bexarotene is thought to prevent aggregation of the amyloid protein into the toxic plaques that are characteristic of Alzheimer's

A. True   B. False   C. Can't Tell

Verbal reasoning format 1

answers

1.a. C - The passage states that doctors first noticed the relationship between increased rates of lung cancer and smoking in the 1940s and 50s, however it doesn't state whether this was the first time that this relationship was noticed. Therefore you can't tell.

1b. A - The passage states that in a study done in 1954 showed that a 'smoker of 35 or more cigarettes a day increased' their risk of dying from lung cancer by a 'factor of 40'. Therefore, it is true that it has been shown.

1c. B – This is false as the passage states that only 1/3 of doctors considered smoking a 'major cause of lung cancer'.

1d. A – This is a paraphrase of the first sentence in the 2nd paragraph and is therefore true.

2a. A – The passage states that boys tend to be 'disruptive' in classrooms and this is thought to have a negative effect on engagement and therefore achievement of girls, which implies that their education may be affected by this behaviour.

2b. B – The passage states that they are less likely to study 'gender-stereotyped subjects' at a single-sex school; therefore this statement that they only study these subjects is false.

2c. A – the passage states that some of the positive results may be due to the broader factors characteristic to single-sex schools rather than purely separation. Therefore this is true.

2d. C – The passage states that all-girls schools have low drop out rates, it does not mention what the drop out rates are at co-educational schools therefore you can't tell.

3a. B – The passage states that women were first admitted in 1869 when Girton was established, however they weren't examined until 1882.

3b. A – The passage states that women were not given degrees until 1947, therefore this statement is true.

3c. A – Magdelene remained all-male until 1988, when it was the last all-male college to admit women, therefore it is true that there were all-male colleges in 1985

3d. C – The passage states that there are still 3 al-female colleges in Cambridge, however you can't tell from the passage, which these 3 are.

4a. C – From the passage you cant tell whether it is used in badminton. The passage states that it is used in numerous sports at the beginning and then at the end that it is a part of over 20 sports but is doesn't mention whether one of them is badminton.

4b. B – The first sport that it was' originally implemented in' was cricket in 2001

4c. A – The passage states that there are 'multiple high-speed cameras' around 'the stadium' from which the ball is tracked to work out a prediction of its most likely path.

4d. B – The technology has been accepted despite that fact that it is only accurate to 5mm. Therefore this is false as Hawk eye is not completely accurate.

5a. A – This is true as the passage states that the stadium aws 'designed to be flexible' and the capacity was built to seat 80,000 during the games but could be reduced by removing 55,000 after the Games ended.

5b. B – West Ham won the bid to make the stadium into their permanent venue after the Olympics but that passage states that they will start to use it in 2016 not straight after Games ended in 2012.

5c. C – You can't tell this from the passage. The passage only states that there was a variety of roles for the Games Makers, which included ticket checking, driving, event stewarding and being officials on the welcome desk, it doesn't specifically say whether they helped direct visitors.

5d. B – this is false, as the passage states that 240,000 people applied to become a Games Maker and only 86,000 were interviewed. 86,000 is less than half of 240,000, therefore this is false.

6a. A – The passage states that Jersey is only 19 miles form France whereas it is 85 miles from the UK, therefore it is true that it lies closer to France than UK. It also states that 'Jersey is part of the British Isles', therefore this statement is true

6b. A – The passage states that the main spoken language

is English and that 'all their road signs are also in French', which impies that they are in 2 languages.

6c. C – Although the passage states that cars are 'often restricted to 15mph in many places' you cant tell from the passage whether the average speed they can drive around Jersey is this low.

6d. A – The passage states that 'it is often warmer' in Jersey than in the UK and that there is 'often good weather' on the Island. From which you can say that it is true that the weather is often better than in England, which is part of the UK.

7a. A – The passage states that the National Minimum Wage in 2015 was £6.70 and that this wasn't going to change until 1st April 2016, therefore it would still stand as correct in March 2016.

7b. B – This contradicts the sentence in the passage that says that National Minimum wage is less than the National Living wage and therefore may families fail to have the salary to meet their basic requirements and rely on the government to top this up.

7c. C – Although the passage states that 54% of employers said that this will have a significant impact on their wage bill, this is only a majority of those surveyed, therefore you can't tell whether this is representative.

7d. A – The passage states that there are fears that 60,000 could lose their jobs, therefore it is a possibility that thousands may lose their jobs, so this statement is true.

8a. B – This is false as the passage states that in the 1950's "drugs were not thoroughly tested for harmful effects to the fetus" therefore they have not always been tested for these negative side effects.

8b. C – the passage states that the drug was removed from the market after a letter from a doctor in Australia who had noticed a correlation between thalidomide use and limb deformities. However it also states that the drug was also taken off the market due to "massive pressure from the public". Therefore, you can't tell whether this was just due to complaints from doctors or from public pressure as well.

8c. B – The drug was created in 1953, however the first babies born with severe deformities, as a result of thalidomide, wasn't until 1959.

8d. A – This is true as the passage states that there were about 10,000 cases of thalidomide deformities, of which only 50% survived. This works out as about 5,000 who then lived with limb deformities as a result of thalidomide.

9a. B – There are no permanent residents on Antarctica, however there are people who live on Antarctica in research stations, so this is false.

9b. B– Shackleton published an account of the failed "Endurance" expedition in 1919, 5 years after he left for the expedition, therefore he could not have died on the expedition.

9c. A – This is true as the passage states that Worsley "wished to walk 943 miles" in total, however he pulled out 30 miles short, which means that he walked over 900 miles.

9d. C – From this passage you can't tell whether any women have ever reached the South Pole. It only mentions the names of men who have reached the South Pole, however it doesn't specifically state that this is true nor does it give a full list of all those who have reached the South Pole, so you can not tell.

10.a A – This is true, as the passage states that to be called Champagne the sparkling wine needs to be "produced from grapes grown in Champagne region of France" and "pressed and fermented using unique regimes".

10b. C – You can't tell this from the passage. The passage states that it is protected legally within EU and that other countries worldwide have passed laws or signed agreements not use the label Champagne. However it is not clear whether this is a worldwide agreement or just in a select few countries.

10c. A – The passage states that the protection of Herdwick lamb will help farmers in Cumbria protect a traditional framings system and help them have a sustainable future, therefore this is true.

10d. B – This is false, as the passage states that the requirements are that the products not only need to come from a specific region, but also need to gave been "produced in a specific manner"

11a. A – The passage states, "approximately £1.3 billion is spent on cards, flowers…" Therefore this is true

11b. C – You can't tell if this is true of false from the passage. The passage does state that one account is of a Saint Valentine who sent a letter to his guard's daughter whom he healed whilst imprisoned and signed it "your valentine". However it does not mention what the nature of the letter was, therefore you cannot tell whether it was a love letter or not.

11c. A – This is true, the passage states that from the 18th century (1700's), lovers "sent cards known as valentines".

11d. B – The passage states that half of card sent in the US are to family members other than the spouse, therefore it is false that the majority of cards sent in the US are to siblings or children.

12a. B – Although taking Maternity Leave is not compulsory, all women must take 2 weeks off work after their baby is born, therefore this is false

12b. B – The partner must have worked for their employer for "26 weeks at the end of the 15th week before the child is due", therefore this is false.

12c. B – The parents are entitled to 50weeks of leave, with 37 paid, but this is shared between the 2 of them, not each. Therefore this is false.

12d. A – This is true, as if the parents earn £800 per month then they would have an average of £200 per week. £139.58 is lower than 90% of £200 (£180), so this is what would be paid.

13a. A – The paragraph states that to be inscribed they must meet the criteria set out by the organisation. These include bearing a unique testimony to cultural tradition, which has disappeared.

13b. B – This is false as the paragraph states that there are currently 936 sites worldwide, with 725 being cultural.

13c. A – This is true. Italy has the 'most World Heritage Sites in the world' and also the 'largest number of "cultural" heritage sites in the world'.

13d. C – You can't tell this from the paragraph. Although it states that there are individual towers on the list on sites in Italy, you can't tell whether the Leaning Tower of Pisa is one of these.

14a. B – This is false. The earthquake that triggered the tsunami was the '4th largest earthquake of recent times'.

14b. A – This is true as the paragraph states that the waves were up to 15m high by the time they reached the shores.

14c. C – Can't tell this. Although the paragraph states that if people knew what to do there would have been time for more people to save themselves, you cannot tell how many people would have been saved, if any, if people knew the warning signs.

14d. A – The scale of the generous public response was unprecedented, with billions of dollars being raised internationally in a very short time frame.

15a. A – Alzheimer's is a chronic disease that progresses over time and 'there is currently no cure'.

15b. B – this is false as the paragraph states that Bexarotene has been shown to work in worms with a genetically similar disease to Alzheimer's in humans, not in human studies.

15c. C – Although this is seen as the aim of the drug from the paragraph, you can't tell whether it actually will or if this is just hope.

15d. A – Through stopping the "primary nucleation" of the amyloid protein, scientist believe that Bexarotene prevents aggregation of this into the classic plaques in Alzheimer's.

Verbal Reasoning questions - Format 2

1.   Data from the 2011 census and Office for National Statistics showed that Cambridge has 59,865 working residents and approximately 94,776 people who work in Cambridge. Over 50% of the Cambridge workforce consists of in-commuters from other local authorities; 73% of them commute by car or van, 9% by bus, 8% by bicycle and 8% by train into Cambridge. 2,457 residents commute into London for work. 43% of residents who commute from within the local authority of Cambridge to their workplace within Cambridge do so by bicycle, this is the highest proportion in the UK, and another 23% walk. This data showed that the age profile of in commuters was older than the age profile of out-commuters.

This is compared to London, where they have the highest proportion of workers who commute using public transport (49.9%). Only 31.4 % of Londoners commute to work by car, taxi or motorcycle. There has been a 144% increase in the number of Londoners who commute to work by bicycle, from 77,000 to 155,000.

a.   **The proportion of workers who live in Cambridge and commute to work by bicycle is nearest to:**

a.   Three-fifths

b.   Four-tenths

c.   One-quarter

d.   One-third

b.   **Which of these conclusions must be true?**

a.   Most people commute into Cambridge by public transport

b.   Most people commute into Cambridge by car

c.   Most people commute within Cambridge by bicycle

d.   Most people commute within Cambridge on foot

c.   **The author would least likely agree with the assertion that:**

a.   Commutes in London are not representative of commutes in Cambridge

b.   There is data about the means by which people commute to work

c.   The highest proportion of workers who commute by bicycle is in Cambridge

d.   There is negligible difference between the proportions of workers who commute by car in Cambridge and London

d.   **The majority of the workforce in Cambridge**

a.   Commute from inside Cambridge centre

b.   Commute from local authorities around Cambridge

c.   That commute from within the local authority commute by bicycle

d.   That commute from another local authority commute by public transport

2.   Obesity in children is becoming a huge issue in the UK. The statistics for 2014/15 showed that 1/3 of children aged 10-11 were overweight, 19.8% of these are classified as obese. Even at aged 4-5 over 20% of children are overweight or obese. This has a huge impact on risk of numerous diseases in children. Jamie Oliver, the chef, has started a campaign to install a "sugar tax" to try and combat sugar intake in children and therefore childhood obesity. This issue has stemmed from the argument that increased sugar intake in children's diets has a damaging impact on their health, not only related to obesity and obesity related diseases, such as type 2 diabetes, but also on the state of children's teeth. There is evidence to say that 26,000 primary school aged children were admitted to hospital last year due to tooth decay caused by sugar, this amounts to £30 million a year spent on pulling children's teeth out. He has urged ministers to be "big and bold" when tackling this issue. Experts believe introducing a tax of 20p per litre of sugary drink could generate £1 billion per year, which could be reinvested into the NHS and schools to tackle obesity and diet-related disease. Not only does he want to introduce this tax to generate funds but also to send a strong message to the food industry. Also, he wants to increase education of the public about the issue and increase information given to people about healthy alternatives.

a.   The statistics for levels of obesity in UK in 2014/15 showed:

a.   2/3 children 10-11 were underweight

b.   Less than 20% of children 10-11 were overweight

c.   Less than 20% of children aged 4-5 were overweight or obese

d.   More than 20% of children between 4-5 were overweight or obese

b.   Jamie Oliver is trying to:

a.   Introduce a tax to combat obesity in adults

b.   Introduce a tax of 20p per sugary food item

c.   Increase education about the problems associated with high sugar diets

d.   Combat fat intake in children

c.   All of these statements are true, except:

a.   Increased sugar intake is linked to obesity and type 2 diabetes in children

b.   The "sugar tax" could generate £1 billion

c.   Up to 25,000 children were admitted to hospital with tooth decay last year

d.   Jamie Oliver wants to reinvest the money generated into the NHS and schools

d.   According to the passage the 'sugar tax" would:

a.   Combat all child health issues

b.   Raise funds to reinvest into the food industry

c.   Help tackle the problem of childhood obesity in UK through combating sugar intake

d.   Be a "big and bold" move to educate the public about eating healthily

3.   The UK passed the first law on drink driving in 1872. This was applicable to driving carriages, horses and steam engines as automobiles did not exist then. It wasn't until 1925 that the law changed to include "mechanically propelled vehicles". However, this failed to define the offence and didn't have guidelines on how to prove the guilt of the party. Therefore, only drivers who were readily perceived to be drunk whilst driving were arrested. 1962 saw the introduction of the Road Traffic Act, which provided analytical tests to detect the presence of alcohol in bodily fluids, however it still failed to stipulate a specific alcohol concentration that was the upper limit. As the number of drivers increased in the 60s so did the number of accidents. Deaths and injuries associated with drink driving became hot topics in the news and soon drink driving was socially unacceptable. The Road Safety Act, 1967, made it illegal to drive after consuming so much alcohol that the concentration in your breath exceeded 35μg in 100ml of breath or 80mg of alcohol in 100ml of blood. In 2012, drink driving was the cause of 280 deaths and 1,200 serious injuries. In 2014, the alcohol limit in Scotland was reduced to 50mg of alcohol per 100ml of blood, or 22μg per 100ml breath to bring this in line with most other European countries. Since doing this police figures show that offences related to drink driving have fallen by 17%. There are now campaign groups within the England who think that the drink drive limit should also be reduced there.

a.   The reduction in alcohol limit in Scotland:

a.   Was to 50μg per 100ml of breath

b.   Brought the specific concentration made illegal down to similar levels to the rest of Europe

c.   Has reduced offences related to drink driving by 1/4

d.   Was reduced in 2014 by 30mg of alcohol per 100ml blood

b.   Which are these statements is true:

a.   The first law on drink driving included all vehicles on the road today

b.   Before 1962 only people who were obviously seen to be drunk were arrested

c.   The specific concentration of alcohol that was the limit was set by the 1st Road Traffic Act

d.   The Road Safety Act set the limits that are still in use in the UK today

c.   Which of these does the passage agree with most:

a.   By the 1960s most accidents were due to drink driving

b.   Death by drink driving became big news headlines which drove the campaign to make it socially unacceptable

c.   The majority want England to follow Scotland in reducing the drink drive limit

d.   It took more than a century to define the offence of drink driving

d.   The drink drive limit is set as:

a.   35μg per 100ml breath in Scotland

b.   80mg per 100ml blood in England

c.   22μg per 100ml blood in Scotland

d.   50mg per 100ml blood in England

4.   Since April 2015, an outbreak of Zika virus has spread from Brazil to the majority of South and Central America and the Caribbean. By October 2015, it had reached epidemic levels and by early 2016 cases had been confirmed in every country in the Americas, except Chile and Canada. The Zika virus is transmitted by Aedes mosquitoes, which are the same mosquito that transmit dengue and yellow fever. About 1 in 5 people infected with Zika virus become ill, the most common symptoms are fever, rash, joint pain or conjunctivitis, muscle aches and headaches, it has been described as a bit "flu-like". Since the beginning of the epidemic, Zika virus infection has been associated with increases in babies born with microcephaly and an increase in Guillain-Barré syndrome. As of the beginning of 2016, Brazil had reported 3,530 cases of microcephaly, a dramatic increase from less than 150 in 2014, which has coincided with the epidemic of Zika virus infection. A strong link has been suspected between Zika virus and microcephaly in babies, however this has still not been proven as a definite causation relationship. There have been no controlled scientific studies, however from a few cases where the infant did not survive, fragments of the Zika virus have been found in the placentas and tissues of the babies, which has led people to believe that a causation will be proven very soon. Until then, many experts believe that until proven otherwise people should take the necessary precautions to protect themselves and their unborn children from the believed devastating effects of Zika virus

a.   **The Zika virus is spread by:**

a.   The same mosquitoes that spread malaria

b.   The Aedes mosquitoes that also transmit West Nile virus

c.   The same mosquitoes that transmit yellow fever

d.   The Anopheles mosquitoes

b.   **Which of these statements is Zika virus infection not associated with:**

a.   Babies born with microcephaly

b.   Guillain-Barre syndrome

c.   Flu-like symptoms

d.   Cough

c.   **Which of these statements is true:**

a.   Zika virus is endemic to Brazil

b.   So far in 2016, there have been more than 3000 cases of microcephaly reported in Brazil

c.   There is a definitive causal relationship between the Zika virus and microcephaly

d.   There were no cases of microcephaly before the Zika epidemic

d.   **Which of these statements does the passage agree with most:**

a.   By 2016 there had been cases across all the Americas

b.   People should still protect themselves and unborn children even if no causation found yet

c.   There is a strong link between Zika virus and Guillain-Barré syndrome

d.   Controlled scientific studies have found Zika virus in placental tissues

5.   The "Oscars" or Academy Awards is an annual awards ceremony to recognise excellence in the film industry. It is hosted by the Academy of Motion Picture Arts and Sciences and the nominees and winners are decided by the Academy's voting membership.   The release of the nominees for the 88th Academy Awards has sparked a big debate about the lack of diversity in the nominees and the membership of the Academy membership. In the four Oscars acting categories all the nominees were white for the second year running, sparking a discussion on diversity in Hollywood. Jada Pinkett-Smith called for a boycott over the all-white list of nominees to try and incite changes within this industry. The president of the Academy, Cheryl Boone Isaacs, the first African-American president, said that she was disappointed with the lack of diversity within the nominations. The Academy membership is about 6,000, however this is made up of largely white males. Some people believe that the lack of diversity in this membership has a knock on effect on the lack of diversity in the nominees and winners. Therefore to be able to diversify the winners, the members of the Academy who decide the nominations needs to be made more diverse and inclusive. Isaacs agrees that "big changes" are required and hopes to alter the makeup of the membership to drive a change before next year.

a.   The Oscars:

a.   Are for film and television

b.   Are also called the Academy Awards

c.   Have 3 acting categories

d.   Are hosted by the British Academy of Film and Television Arts

b.   Which statement is not true about the Academy membership

a.   It is made up of mostly white males

b.   The makeup of the membership may have a knock on effect on diversity of nominees

c.   The current president feels that its makeup is diverse

d.   It has over 5,000 members

c.   Which of these statements would the passage agree with most:

a.   The lack of diversity in the membership probably doesn't affect the nominations

b.   Changes are needed within Hollywood and the membership

c.   There should always be some black people nominated for awards

d.   There are no people of ethnic minority within the Academy membership

d.   Why was there a boycott called after the announcement of the 88th nominations:

a.   There were only a few black nominees

b.   There were no black nominees for the first time

c.   The 4 main acting categories had only white nominees

d.   Because Jada's husband, Will Smith, was not nominated for an award

6.   The European Union is a politico-economic union of 28 member states that are located primarily in Europe. Each of the countries within the Union are independent but they all agree to trade under agreements made between the nations. It was created after the Second World War to try and avoid conflict through making the countries economically interdependent. The EU operates a single market allowing free movement of goods, capital and people between all member states through the development of standardised laws. The union maintains common policies on trade, agriculture and regional development. It has delivered peace, stability and helped raised living standards. With the introduction of the Euro in 2002, monetary union was established in 19 member states. By the end of 2016, there will be a referendum in the UK to on whether to stay in the EU or not. The people pro-leaving the EU feel that the UK is being held back by the EU through its charges and rules on business and trade. They want to gain back full control of the borders to reduce the number of EU nationals that are coming to work here through the "free movement" policy of the EU. The other side of the argument is that Britain's economy is fuelled by EU membership and that Britain is more secure as part of the Union. Big businesses are often in favour due to the ease of moving money, people and products around the world thanks to the Union.

a.   All of these statements are true, except:

a.   The 28 member states are independent but agree to common policies

b.   The EU has helped provide stability in Europe since WWII

c.   The Euro was rolled out across more than three-quarters of the states

d.   There are standardised laws and rules between the countries

b.   The idea behind the EU was to avoid conflict by making the countries:

a.   Politically interdependent

b.   Economically independent

c.   All dependent territories

d.   More reliant on each other economically

c.   Which of these are true:

a.   The UK will leave the EU in 2016

b.   The EU has altered living standards

c.   The EU consists of multiple markets that trade together

d.   People are only able to move freely between selected member states

d.   Which of these agree with the passage most strongly about the arguments for and against leaving the EU posed by the referendum in the UK

a.   Those wishing the UK to leave feel that the free market makes trade difficult

b.   Those wishing the UK to stay feel that the UK would be more secure as part of the Union than apart.

c.   Those wishing the UK to leave feel that the UK's economy is boosted by being a member

d. Those wishing the UK to stay feel that the border control is essential.

7.   Lance Armstrong was an American road-racing cyclist. He won the Tour de France in 7 consecutive years, from 1999 to 2005. At 16 he began competing as a tri-athlete but began is career as a professional cyclist in 1992. He had a run of success between then and 1996, including the World Championship in 1993 and multiple European victories. In 1996, he was diagnosed with stage 3 testicular cancer that had spread to his brain, lungs and abdomen. Initially, he was told that he had a 20-50% chance of survival, but after having his final chemotherapy in December 1996, he was declared cancer-free in February 1997. It was in 1998 that he made his cycling comeback with the team US postal. It was with this team that he won his Tour de France titles between 1999 and 2005 and a bronze medal at the 2000 Olympics in Sydney. The win in 2005 meant he had won a record breaking 7 consecutive Tours. He also achieved the record for completing the Tour with the fastest pace, an average of 26mph. He retired from cycling in 2005, but returned to compete in the 2009 Tour, in which he failed to win the yellow jersey. Ever since winning the 1999 Tour de France Armstrong has been the subject of doping allegations. In 2012, he was found to have used performance-enhancing drugs and been the ringleader for the most successful doping program that cycling had ever seen by the US Anti-Doping Agency. He did not deny the charges at the time and even confessed that some of the allegations were true in an interview in 2013. As a result of this he was banned from competing in all sports for the rest of his life and was stripped of all his achievements after 1998, including the 7 yellow jerseys from the Tour de France wins.

a.   Lance Armstrong was a professional cyclist from:

a.   1992-2012

b.   1996-2005

c.   1992-2005

d.   1992- 2009

b.   In 1996, Lance Armstrong was diagnosed with:

a.   Testicular cancer with spread to his bones

b.   Lung cancer

c.   Metastases in his brain from a primary testicular tumour

d.   Stage 2 testicular cancer

c.   Which of these did Lance Armstrong not win:

a.   2000 Olympics

b.   2001 Tour de France

c.   1993 World Championship

d.   2005 Tour de France

d.   Which of these least likely agree with the paragraph:

a.   Lance Armstrong came out of retirement to cycle the Tour in 2009

b.   Lance always denied the charges of doping

c.   The 7 yellow jerseys were not the only achievements stripped from Lance

d.   He was the ringleader of a massive doping programme from 1998

8.   The total prison population in England and Wales is 85,163, which amounts to 148 people per 100,000 in the population. This leaves England and Wales with the highest per capita prison population in Western Europe. On a global scale, England and Wales is at the midpoint of imprisonment rates worldwide. The world's highest imprisonment rates are in the United States, where it is 724 people per 100,000. Prisons within England and Wales are crowded, running at above 100% occupancy levels. Of the 80,000 people in jail in England and Wales, only 5.5% of them are female, therefore men are 22 times more likely to be imprisoned than women. Out of the prison population within Britain, 10% are black and 6% are Asian. This represents a 7% increase from the proportion of the population that they represent. There is now a greater disproportionality in the number of black people in prisons in England and Wales than in the United States.

The number of prisoners in England and Wales has significantly increased by over 40,000 since 1993 and the latest figures estimate that the prison population will increase to 86,700 by June 2016. It is believed to be due to the greater use of longer custodial sentences within the Justice system and the rise of indeterminate sentences. There are now fears that the prison system is going to face an unaffordable population and with increasing budget cuts this will become unsustainable. Therefore some people feel that more effort needs to go into trying to divert people from prison in the first place and if that fails trying to prevent them from reoffending so they do not return.

a.   All of these statements are true, except:

a.   There are problems with crowding at prisons within England and Wales

b.   Nearly 95% of the prison population are male

c.   The prison population is increasing significantly over time

d.   10% of the prison population are from ethnic minorities

b.   Which of the statements are true about prison populations:

a.   The prison population in the UK is 85,000

b.   England and Wales have one of the highest per capita prison populations in the world

c.   The United States have more than 700 people imprisoned per 100,000 population

d.   England and Wales have similar per capita prison populations to the rest of Western Europe

c.   Black populations in prisons in England and Wales:

a.   Generally have longer sentences

b.   Represent the same proportion of black people in the population

c.   Are less disproportional than in the USA

d.   Total about 8,000 people

d.   Which of these statements would the passage most agree with to prevent unsustainable prison populations

a.   Cutting down of the use of longer custodial sentences

b.   Ensuring that all sentences have a determinate length

c.   Trying to use avenues other than custodial sentences to keep people out of prison

d.   Imprison all re-offenders

9.   The Giant Panda is the rarest member of the bear family. They mainly live in bamboo forests in the mountains of central China, where they eat almost entirely bamboo. The bears have black fur on their ears, eye patches, muzzle, legs and shoulders with the rest of their coat being white. Some people speculate that this is to help them camouflage into their snowy and rocky surroundings. The giant panda is listed as endangered in the World Conservation Union's Red List of Threatened Species. There are only 1,864 left in the wild with more than 300 living in zoos and breeding centres. The biggest threats to giant panda's in the wild are hunting, mainly accidental killing and habitat loss through deforestation. Although, the Panda's diet consists almost entirely of bamboo, their digestive systems are more similar to carnivores than herbivores. Therefore most of what they eat is passed as waste. Consequently, they have to eat up to 80 pounds of bamboo a day get enough nutrients, which results in them spending 10-16 hours a day foraging and eating. They spend the other 8-14 hours of the day sleeping or resting. In the wild a female panda can only produce offspring at most every other year. This is due to her ovulating only once a year and the baby cub staying with her for up to 3 years. Most Pandas will only successfully raise 5 to 8 cubs in her lifetime. This slow breeding rate prevents the population from recovering quickly from hunting and habitat loss.

a.   **Giant Panda's have black fur on their:**

a.   Ears, nose, back

b.   Eye patches, legs, feet

c.   Tummy

d.   Ears and shoulders

b.   **Approximately how many Giant Pandas are left living?**

a.   1,800

b.   1,900

c.   2,000

d.   2,200

c.   **Which of these is not a threat to the Giant Panda?**

a.   Accidental killing

b.   Poaching

c.   Loss of bamboo forests

d.   Change in climate

d.   **All of these statements are true except?**

a.   Giant Panda's spend most of their day eating

b.   Giant Panda's population increases in size quickly

c.   Giant Panda's are more suited to eat meat

d.   Giant Panda's can only get pregnant once a year

10.   The ozone layer protects life on Earth by absorbing UV light, which can damage DNA in plants and animals. During the early 1980s scientists began to realise the ozone layer was beginning to thin over the South Pole each spring. This area of thinning ozone came to be known as the ozone hole. The discovery of the ozone hole opened the world's eye to the effects of human activity on the atmosphere. It was found that CFCs upon reaching the stratosphere were broken down by UV light to release chlorine. The chlorine catalysed the destruction of the ozone. In 1989 CFC's were banned from being produced along with other ozone-depleting chemicals. Due to the close proximity of Australia to the Antarctic ozone hole the UV radiation levels in Australia are much higher than in the rest of the world. Australians are exposed to up to 15 % more UV than Europeans, due to proximity to the ozone hole and that due to the Earth's orbit, Australia is closer to the sun during summer.

Therefore, Australians have one of the highest rates of skin cancer in the world. 2 in 3 will be diagnosed with skin cancer by the age of 70, with skin cancer accounting for 80% of cancers diagnosed each year.   During the 1980's rates of skin cancer in Australia started to spiral and there was a dramatic increase in mortality rates from melanoma. SunSmart was developed to try and reach Australians with the message to reduce risk through changing attitudes towards tanning and sun protection. The first launch of the campaign involved a cartoon seagull singing 'Slip! Slop! Slap!'. The idea was to encourage people to slip on a shirt, slop on suncream and slap on a hat to protect them from the sun and to try and prevent people getting sunburned which is a marker increased risk of skin cancer. This campaign has been running for more than 25 years and has been shown to be a worthwhile investment. Since then behaviour has changed dramatically and deaths from skin cancers has started to slow.

a.   **The ozone hole:**

a.   Was discovered in 1980

b.   Is an area of thinning in the Southern Hemisphere

c.   Is the same thickness all year around

d.   Was created by natural reactions

b.   **Which of these would the passage least agree with as to why UV levels are higher in Australia compared to the rest of the world?**

a.   Proximity to Antarctica

b.   Earth's orbit

c.   More sunshine hours

d.   The sun gets closer to Australia than Europe

c.   **Which of these are true about skin cancer in Australia?**

a.   Skin cancer is the one of the least diagnosed cancer in Australia

b.   Three quarters of the population will develop skin cancer

c.   There was a dramatic increase in diagnosis of skin cancer in 1980s

d.   Rates of death from skin cancer has reached a plateau since 1980s

d. **Which one of these agrees most strongly with the SunSmart message?**

a.   It was first delivered by a video of a live seagull

b.   It encourages people to prevent getting tanned in the sun

c.   It was aimed at changing attitudes towards tanning and sun cream use

d.   It encouraged people to wear hats and shirts to stop the need for suncream

11.   J K Rowling was born on 31 July 1965 in Yate, Gloucestershire. As a child she wrote fantasy stories, which she used to read to her sister. She studied English at A-level and went on to study French and Classics at Exeter University. After graduating she began working for Amnesty International when she conceived the idea for Harry Potter in 1990 whilst delayed on a train to London. However, it took 7 years for her to get the first book, Harry Potter and the Philosopher's Stone, published. Rowling was training to be a teacher when Harry Potter was accepted for publication by Bloomsbury. It quickly became a best seller and was translated into many different languages. Before she had even written the first book, J K Rowling had planned all 7 books in the series. So following the success of the first Harry Potter book, the others were all subsequently published. The final book in the series, Harry Potter and the Deathly Hallows became the fastest selling book ever when it was released in 2007. The series is now published in 78 languages and over 450 million copies have been sold worldwide. She is the UK's best-selling living author and her fortune was estimated to be about £560 million in the 2008 Sunday Times Rich List. She has received many awards since then including an OBE for services to children's literature in 2000. In October 1998, Warner Bros purchased the rights to the first 2 films, with Harry Potter and the Philosopher's Stone being released in the cinemas in November 2001. On signing a contract with Warner Bros, Rowling insisted that the films were to be shot in Britain with an all-British cast. It was announced in 2015 that J K Rowling was adding to the Harry Potter franchise through an eighth instalment that will be presented on stage. The play, Harry Potter and The Cursed Child, will follow the lives of the main characters now they are grown up.

a.   J K Rowling's jobs have included all but one of these:

a.   Teacher trainee

b.   Author

c.   Movie star

d.   Employee of Amnesty International

b.   Which of these is true:

a.   The idea of Harry Potter came to her on a plane

b.   After the success of the first book she planned the other 6 books

c.   Harry Potter was published by Bloomsbury

d.   The first book was published in 1996

c.   All of these are true except:

a.   The series are published in nearly 80 languages

b.   J K Rowling is the UK's best ever selling author

c.   J K Rowling won an order from the Queen in 2000

d.   The seventh book was the fastest selling book of all time

d.   Which one of these is most true about the Harry Potter franchise after the books:

a.   The film rights were bought by Warner Bros for all films in 1998

b.   J K Rowling insisted that the films were shot in Britain

c.   There will be an eight instalment in the form of another book

d.   Harry Potter and the Cursed Child will follow the lives of the characters from where the 7th book finished

12.   Les Miserables is a French novel written by Victor Hugo, which is considered one of the greatest novels of the 19th century. The novel explores the history of France from 1815 to the June Rebellion in Paris in 1832. It follows the lives and interactions of several characters, examining politics, moral philosophy, justice and love. Les Miserables is one of the longest novels ever written, with 1,900 pages in the French edition. Hugo explained that he wanted the book to be for everyone. The release of the book was highly anticipated and was an immediate commercial success, being highly popular since it was published. Les Miserables was adapted into a musical which premiered in Paris in 1980. The music was written by Schonberg who made it into a sung-through musical based on the novel by Hugo. This production closed after 3 months when the booking contract expired. In 1983, the producer Cameron Mackintosh was asked to produce an English-language version of the show. This version premiered in London 1985. At the opening, critical reviews were negative, however public opinion differed with record orders at the box office and sold out shows. The London production has been running ever since, making it the second-longest running musical in the world and the longest-running musical in London. Attempts to adapt the stage musical into a film had been tried since the late 1980s, but it wasn't until 2011 that a screenplay was written. In 2012, a British musical film based on the book was released with a very famous and well-known cast. The film won multiple Golden Globe Awards, 4 BAFTAs and was nominated for 8 Academy Awards.

a.   The book Les Miserables:

a.   Was written in 1900s in French

b.   Explores the history of France until the June Rebellion in 1830

c.   It is the longest novel ever written

d.   Is written as interwoven stories of many characters covering multiple topics

b.   How many pages does the book have:

a.   One thousand nine hundred in English

b.   Less than two thousand when written in French

c.   Two thousand in the French Edition

d.   One thousand eight hundred

c.   Which of these is not true about the stage musical:

a.   Premiered in 1980 in Paris

b.   English-language version was produced by Schonberg

c.   Critical reviews opposed public opinion

d.   It is the longest-running musical in London

d.   Which of these are most true:

a.   The stage musical was adapted into a film in 1990

b.   The British musical film was released in 2011

c.   The film was very successful, winning 8 Academy Awards

d.   Many of cast were well-known faces in the film industry

13.   Mount St Helens is located in the state of Washington, USA and is part of the Cascade Volcanic Arc. This is a segment of the Pacific Ring of Fire that includes over 160 active volcanoes. This volcano is famous for its eruption in 1980 which killed 57 people. The eruption of the volcano was sparked by an earthquake that measured 5.1 on the Richter scale and caused a massive rock debris avalanche as the north face of the mountain collapsed. This avalanche caused the release of pressurised gases within the volcano, which then lead to a massive explosion, sending hot gas, ash and rock away from the volcano. Anyone near to the volcano died instantly as a result of the avalanche. The massive explosion resulted in nearly 150 square miles of forest being blown over or left dead. The plume of ash rose thousands of metres and then drifted downwind to cover eastern Washington and beyond. For more than 9 hours a plume of ash erupted, eventually reaching more than 12 miles above sea level. Ash was found on top of cars and roofs as far as Alberta, Canada the next morning. The magna from within St Helens burst out to form a large-scale apyroclastic flow that flattened everything in its path for more than 600 square km. The volcano continued to erupt until 1986, building a lava dome in the process. This lava dome is now 920 feet high. The area around Mount St Helens was left a vast and gray landscape, replacing the forested slopes that once grew there. In 1982, the area was converted into a National Volcanic Monument that is now left alone to respond naturally to the disaster. Slowly plants began to grow again and birds and animals have found their niches once more within the new forest. There are now thousands of visitors to Mount St Helens to explore the crater and the surrounding park.

a.   Mount St Helens is not:

a.   Part of the Pacific Ring of Fire

b.   In Washington DC, USA

c.   Famous due to its deadly eruption in 1980

d.   In a volcanic Arc that includes more than 150 active volcanoes

b.   The eruption in 1980:

a.   Was triggered by an earthquake that was less than 5 on the Richter scale

b.   Caused the south face of the mountain to collapse

c.   Killed 57 people

d.   Triggered a massive explosion wiping out over 150 square miles of forest

c.   Which of these would the paragraph agree with least about the plume of ash that rose from the volcano?

a.   It erupted for nearly 10 hours

b.   It rose to above 12 miles higher than sea level

c.   Ash travelled as far as Canada that same day

d.   The immediate plume of ash was created by an explosion that also sent gas and rock from the volcano

d.   Which of these is true about the aftermath?

a.   The volcano settled down in less than 5 years after the first eruption

b.   A lava dome was created on the volcano, measuring 920 metres high

c.   The area around the volcano was converted into a National Monument to allow it to respond naturally

d.   The landscape is still vast and grey due to the death of the surrounding forest

14.   The Berlin Wall was erected in August 1961 to completely cut West Berlin from Eastern Germany. The Communist government of East Germany began building this wall of barbed wire and concrete to keep the Western "fascists" from entering Eastern Germany. The official purpose was one of stopping Westerns from undermining the socialist state, but the real effect was to slow the mass defections from East to West. There had been nearly 3 million people who had fled from East to West, many of them teachers, doctors and engineers. On August 12th 1961, 2,400 refugees left East Germany for the West in one day. It was the very next day that the officials from the East started erecting the wall. The order to build the wall was given by the Soviet Union President, Krushchev, to stop the flow of emigrants by closing the border. It only took 2 weeks to build a temporary wall that divided the city. After the wall was built, citizens from East Berlin could only enter West Berlin through 3 checkpoints. Very soon people could only get across the border under special circumstances. Over time the wall was replaced with a sturdier wall that was more difficult to climb over. It was 12 foot tall by 4 feet wide and had an enormous pipe on top to make climbing over almost impossible. The wall came to symbolise the Iron Curtain that separated Western Europe from the Eastern Bloc during the Cold War. By 1989, the Cold War was coming to an end, there were a series of political changes in the Eastern Bloc that liberalised the authorities and eroded the power of pro-Soviet governments in Poland and Hungary. On 9th November 1991, after weeks of unrest, the government of East Berlin announced a change in relations with the West and that from midnight citizens of the GDR were free to cross the wall. At midnight people flooded through the checkpoints and there was the greatest street party as a celebration of unity of Berlin for the 1st time since the Second World War ended.

a.   The Berlin Wall was erected to:

a.   Cut off East Berlin from Western Germany

b.   Keep Westerners out of Communist East Germany

c.   Prevent defections from West to East

d.   Stop flow of immigrants

b.   Which of these are true about the Wall?

a.   It was built in less than 2 weeks

b.   It was made of concrete and barbed wire with an enormous pipe on top

c.   It has 3 checkpoints in that allowed people to move freely between the 2 sides

d.   It measured 12 foot by 4 metres

c.   Which of these is not true about the fall of the Wall?

a.   Citizens from the East were free to cross the wall from 10th November 1991

b.   The fall of the wall marked unity of Berlin for the first time since 1945

c.   The wall started to fall as soon as the Cold War started to come to end

d.   The fall of the wall symbolised the end of the Iron Curtain separating East and West Europe

d.   Defections from East to West:

a.   Consisted of mainly doctors and teachers

b.   Reached nearly 3 million before the wall was erected

c.   Were the official reason for erecting the Wall

d.   Reached a peak of over 2,500 in one day on the 12th August 1961

15.   The Equal Pay Act 1970 was introduced to prohibit discrepancies between men and women in terms of pay and conditions of employment. This Act allows an employee to claim that they are entitled to 'equal pay' if they are employed on 'equal work'. Definitions of equal work include, doing the same work as another employee, using the same level of skill as the other employee, that the work they do is of equal value to that of the other employee or that the work done is rated the same as the other employee. This Act has now been repealed but has been replicated in the Equality Act 2010. This Act brings together many Acts, which are all related to anti-discrimination. It requires equal treatment in access to employment, regardless of age, disability, race, sex, religion.

However, 45 years after the first Act brought in to end gender pay inequality, research shows that there is still a large gender pay gap within the UK. It has been shown that female graduates earn up to £8,000 less than male counterpart, with the biggest gap being amongst lawyers. The Office for National Statistics said that the gap between men and women's pay for full-time workers was 9.4% in April 2015. However, other research has stated that the gender pay gap stands at 19.1%. This equates to women earning 80p for every £1 a man earns. The Prime Minister said that he wants to close the gender pay gap within the next generation. One of the strategies that has been announced to facilitate this is a policy that requires large companies with more than 250 employees to publish their gender pay gap online and reveal the numbers of men and women at each pay range. This will then be used to create a gender pay gap league table that will highlight discrepancies between the salaries of men and women. People hope that this will create the pressure on large companies to drive women's wages up to close this pay gap, as was seen with MPs salaries after they were forced to be open and known. Many people hope that this new transparency of wages will be one step towards helping women across Britain and extending opportunities to all.

a.   Definitions of 'equal work' include all but:

a.   Doing the same work as another employee

b.   The work done by you and another colleague has the same value economically

c.   That the work done is rated the same as another colleague

d.   Equal work is not dependent on skill set

b.   Which of these are true:

a.   Women earn up to £8000 more than men

b.   Lawyers are the most equal profession in terms of pay gap

c.   On average women earn 80p for every £1 earned by a man

d.   The gender pay gap is nearly 20% in full-time workers

c.   The new policy will:

a.   Make it a legal requirement for all companies to publish their pay gap online

b.   Hopefully create pressure to drive men's wages down in line with women's

c.   Only be applicable to companies with 250 employees

d.   Be used to create a gender pay gap league table to highlight companies with discrepancies

d.   Which of these does the passage agree with most?

a.   The Equal Pay Act is still in force now

b.   The Gender Pay Gap will be closed within the next generation

c.   The gender pay gap was closed in politics after salaries were forced to be transparent

d.   The Gender Pay Gap has reduced to only a few percent between male and female salaries

Verbal reasoning format 2

answers

1a. B – 43% of residents who live in Cambridge and commute within the local authority cycle to work, therefore this is closest to four-tenths (40%)

2b. B – 73% of the people who commute into Cambridge from other authorities 'commute by car or van', therefore B must be true. Only 17% commute in on the bus and train (public transport). Within Cambridge only 43% cycle (which is less than half so not a majority, whilst 23% walk.

3c. D – anything that contradicts the passage the author is not likely to agree with. Therefore D is the correct answer as there is quite a big difference between the proportions of workers who commute by car in Cambridge (73%) and London (31.4%). The other answers are supported by the passage.

4d. B – Over 50% of the Cambridge workforce consists of people who commute in from other authorities, therefore B is correct, as the majority of the workforce commute from other local authorities around Cambridge.

2a. D – The passage states that over 20% of children are overweigh or obese between the ages of 4-5

2b. C - The last sentence states that Jamie Oliver also wants to increase education about the public issue surrounding high sugar diets. He is trying to combat obesity mainly in children, not adults. The 20p tax would be on a litre of sugary drinks according to the passage. He is trying to combat sugar intake in children.

2c. C - The passage states that 26,00 children were admit-

ted to hospital with tooth decay last year, which is more than 25, 000.

2d. C – The sugar tax would 'try and combat sugar intake in children, therefore childhood obesity'. The passage states that it would combat obesity and therefore obesity and diet-related disease in children. The money raised would be reinvested into NHS and schools, not the food industry and Jamie Oliver urges ministers to be "big and bold" when tackling the issue of childhood obesity.

3a. D – The passage states that the drink drive limit in Scotland was reduced from 80mg to 30mg of alcohol per 100ml of blood, which is a reduction of 30mg making D the correct answer. The limit was reduced to 22µg per 100ml of breath not 50µg, so A is wrong. B is also wrong as the passage states that it brought the limit down to similar levels to the rest of Europe, however the passage states that it was now in line with most other European countries, the statement implies all, whereas most is not the same as all. The figures show that the reduction in offences was 17% which is not the same as ¼ or 25%.

3b. B – Before the introduction of the 1st Road Traffic Act that 'provided analytical tests to detect presence of alcohol' only drivers 'readily perceived as drunk' were arrested. Therefore B is correct. This 1st Act didn't 'stipulate specific alcohol concentration', so C is wrong. The Road Safety Act set the limits that are still in use in England and Wales but not Scotland any more, so D is wrong. A is wrong because the first law passed was not applicable to automobiles as they did not exist in 1872.

3c. B - Any statements that are contradictory to what is in the passage will be wrong. It needs to be a statement that supports the passage. This is B because this is a rephrase of a sentence within the passage.

3d. B – The drink limit in England is 80mg per 100ml of blood or 35µg per 100ml of breath. In Scotland it is 50mg in blood and 22µg in breath.

4a. C – The passage states that Zika virus is transmitted by the Aedes mosquitoes that also transmit Yellow Fever

4b. D – This is the only symptom or disease that is not mentioned in the passage

4c. B – The passage states that by the time it was written there had been 3,530 cases of microcephaly reported in Brazil. The rest of the statements contradict the passage or cannot be implied from the passage

4d. B – This is a rephrase of the final sentence in the passage, therefore it must be the one that it agrees with most as it supports the passage. The other statements contradict the passage, therefore cannot be correct.

5a. B – The first sentence of the passage states that the Oscars are also called the Academy Awards. The passage states that they are to recognise 'excellence in the film industry' and that they are hosted by the 'Academy of Motion Picture Arts and Sciences' with 'four Oscars acting categories'. A, C and D all contradict these statements from the passage.

5b. C – The current president, Isaacs, agrees that '"big changes" are required and hopes to alter the makeup' before next year of the membership which is largely white males so not very diverse.

5c. B - This is the statement that supports the passage the most. The overall message of the passage is that change is required within Hollywood and membership to diversify members and therefore nominees. The other statements either contradict the passage or cannot be inferred as supporting the passage.

5d. C – A boycott was called over the all-white list of nominees. It also states that there were only white nominees in the 4 acting categories for the 2nd year running.

6a. C – You are looking for the statement that contradicts the passage. This is C as it is false. There are 28 member states and only 19 of them joined the Euro, ¾ of 28 would be 21.

6b. D – The passage states specifically that the EU was created to "avoid conflict through making the countries economically interdependent".

6c. B – B is true as is states that living standards were altered, which agrees with the sentence in the passage that says that the EU has "helped raise living standards". A, B and D are all false as they contradict the passage.

6d. B – B is the statement that agrees most closely to the passage, the other statements contradict what the passage states. The passage states that those against leaving the EU believe that "Britain is more secure as part of the Union".

7a. D – The passage states that Lance Armstrong started professional cycling in 1992. It states that he retired from professional cycling in 2005, however he returned again to cycle professionally in 2009.

7b. C – Lance was diagnosed with "stage 3 testicular cancer that had spread to his brain, lungs and abdomen"

7c. A – Lance only came third in the 2000 Sydney Olympics ("bronze medal"). He won all the other titles listed.

7d. B – The answer is the statement that contradicts the passage. This is B as the passage states that Lance "did not deny the charges" against him for doping. Therefore it is false that he always denied the charges so this would be the statement that does not agree with the paragraph.

8a. D – D is false as the passage states that 10% of the prison population in England and Wales are black, with 6% Asian, therefore it cannot be true that only 10% are from ethnic minorities.

8b. C – C is the true answer. The passage states that there are 724 people in prison in the USA per 100,000 population. The other answers are wrong. A because there are 85,000 in England and Wales, therefore there must be more than that imprisoned in the while of the UK. B is wrong because England and Wales are said to be at the "midpoint of imprisonment rates worldwide". D is also wrong because the passage states that England and Wales have the "highest per capita prison population in Western Europe".

8c. D – D is true about the black populations in prison in England and Wales as the passage states that they make up 10% of the prison population. 10% of 85,163 would be about 8,000.

8d. C – The passage would agree most with C, because it states that "more effort needs to go into trying to divert people from prison in the first place", therefore the author thinks that keeping people out of prison by using other avenues would be a good idea. The other statements contradict the passage.

9a. D – The passage states that the Panda's have black fur on their ears, eye patches, muzzle, legs and shoulders, therefore D is true.

9b. D – There are 1,864 left in the wild and over 300 in zoos and breeding centres, therefore there are approximately 2,200 still living.

9c. D – In the passage, hunting (poaching), accidental killing and loss of habitat (bamboo forests) are stated as threats to the Giant Panda. Therefore D is false as it doesn't state that climate change is a threat.

9d. B – The statement that disagrees with the passage is B as the passage states that the Giant Panda's have a slow breeding rate, so cannot recover quickly / increase their population quickly.

10a. B – The passage agrees with B as it states that the ozone hole was an area of thinning ozone over the South Pole that would thin each spring that scientists began to realise in the early 1980s, not discovered in 1980. It states that human activity has an effect on the atmosphere and that CFCs released by humans, not natural reaction, was responsible for the ozone hole.

10b. C – The passage states that Australians are exposed to more UV than Europeans due to factors including, proximity to the ozone hole and Earth's orbit means Australia is closer to sun during summer.

10c. C – C is true. "During the 1980's rates of skin cancer in Australia started to spiral". It also states that 2 in 3 will develop skin cancer and 80% of all cancers diagnosed are skin cancers. It also states that "deaths from skin cancers has started to slow", so hasn't yet reached a plateau.

10d. C – SunSmart was developed to try and change "attitudes towards tanning and sun protection", which makes C agree most likely with the passage. The other statements disagree with the passage therefore are not true.

11a. C – The paragraph states that J K Rowling has worked as an author, a teacher trainee and for Amnesty International. It does not state that she has stared in a movie, therefore C is not true.

11b. C – C is the only statement that agrees with the paragraph, all the others contradict was is written in the paragraph.

11c. B – B is not true, as the paragraph states that JK Rowling is the 'UK's best-selling living author', therefore this

implies that there are some authors who sold more books than her that are now dead. C

11d. B – The paragraph states that JK Rowling 'insisted that the films were to be shot in Britain'. The film rights were bought for the first 2 books originally. The eighth installment is going to be a play and it will follow the lives of the characters when they are grown up.

12a. D – D is the only statement that doesn't contradict the contents of the paragraph. The paragraph states that the story follows the 'lives and interactions of several characters, examining politics, moral philosophy, justice and love.' Therefore D is true. A, B and C are all false.

12b. B – The book has 1,900 pages in the French edition, which makes B true as it states that it has less than 2,000 in the French edition. The paragraph does not state how many pages are in the English edition.

12c. B – B is false as the English-language version was produced by Cameron Mackintosh. Schonberg wrote the music for the original musical.

12d. D – D is the only statement that is true. The paragraph states that the cast were well-known in the British musical film. The screenplay of the musical was written in 2011, and released in 2012. The paragraph states that it was nominated for 8 Academy Awards, it does not mention whether they won any or all of these.

13a. B – The question is asking which of these statements is false. This is B as Mount St Helens is in the state of Washington, not Washington DC.

13b. C – The paragraph states that 57 people were killed. It states that the earthquake measured 5.1, therefore A is false. That the north side of the mountain collapsed with the explosion and that nearly 150 square miles of forest was blown over of left dead, making both B and D false.

13c. C – The ash from the explosion was found in Canada the next day, therefore the paragraph would probably disagree with C the most, as you can't really tell whether any ash reached Canada before this. The ash covered Eastern Washington and beyond immediately.

13d. C – This is true as the paragraph states that the 'area was converted into a National Volcanic Monument that is now left to respond naturally to the disaster'. A, B and D are all false as they contradict statements in the paragraph.

Act 'has now been repealed'. B and D are also false, as the paragraph states that the prime minister 'wants to close the gender pay gap within the next generation' not that it will be closed and it states that some research shows that the gap is still 19.1%, which is not just a few percent.

14a. B – The wall was built to 'keep Western "fascists" from entering Eastern Germany.

14b. B – The paragraph states that the wall was made from 'barbed wire and concrete' and had 'an enormous pipe on top', therefore making B true. The temporary wall was made in less than 2 weeks, but the permanent one took longer to build. The 3 checkpoints allowed only movement under special circumstances and the wall measured 12 feet by 4 feet.

14c. A – C is the only statement that does not agree with the passage. The passage states that the Cold War started to come to an end in 1989, however the wall did not fall until November 1991. Therefore it is not true that it fell as soon as the Cold War started to come to an end.

14d. B – B is the true statement relating to the defections. The passage states that there had been nearly 3 million people who had fled, encouraging the building of the wall. The paragraph states that many of the people who defected were teachers and doctors, but this is not the same as mainly, which implies a majority that many does not. The official reason for erecting the wall was 'to keep the Western "fascists" from entering Eastern Germany' and there were 2,400 refugees who left in one day, which is less than 2,500.

15a. D – The paragraph states that a definition of equal pay includes 'using the same level of skill as the other employee', therefore D is incorrect as it states that equal work is not dependent on skill set.

15b. C – This statement completely agrees with a sentence in the paragraph. All the other statements contradict the paragraph.

15c. D – D is true as the paragraph states that the gender pay gaps published online will be used to 'create a gender pay gap league table that will highlight any discrepancies' between male and female salaries of their employees. The policy will only apply to companies with more than 250 employees, making A and C false. The paragraph states that they hope it will drive women's wages up not men's wages down to equalise them, therefore B is false.

15d. C – The paragraph states that that female MP's wages were driven up to be in line with male MP's wages once they were forced to be open and known, making C true. A is false as the paragraph states that the Equal Pay

Verbal Reasoning questions - format 1 and 2

Stem 1

Below is an extract from an article about a new and upcoming restaurant:

Flaming Jack's is a modern and fun 40-cover American Diner, located in the heart of London's Soho. Themed specifically to appeal to our fashion-conscious, metropolitan clientele, Jack's is elegantly rustic, yet bright and inviting. Serving-up retro American favourites, our menu is appetizing and caters for all tastes. Quality, ethically sourced ingredients and a focus on food 'cooked to order' are a priority at Jack's.

Flaming Jack's is committed to providing the food that diners truly want- customisation is a key ingredient, made possible through our iPad-ordering system. With iPads mounted in a protective shell on each table, diners peruse the menu at their own convenience. Our custom-made app makes it simple and intuitive to modify your meal, with diners being able to select the main ingredients, sauces, toppings and sides as well as adding comments or special instructions for the chef such as allergies.

Orders are sent electronically to the kitchen and customers are notified of how long it will take before they can pick up their food themselves, halving the number of waiting staff needed. Our app will cater for the health-conscious, giving recommendations on the healthiest choices and displaying nutritional information for all items. Diners can pay immediately through each iPad, opting to pay the whole bill or splitting the bill between table members.

We will protect our brand name and logo, whilst our app and its associated intellectual property can be patented and we aim to do this as a matter of urgency.

Questions

1) The article is written by the prospective owners of Flaming Jack's.

    True   **False**   **Can't Tell**

2) According to the text, customers primarily want to be able to customise their food.

    True   **False**   **Can't Tell**

3) The text implies that customers wish to customise their food.

    True   **False**   **Can't Tell**

4) The iPad app will allow customers to change ingredients, sauces and portion sizes as well as other things.

    True   **False**   **Can't Tell**

5) The iPad system makes it cheaper for the restaurant to operate.

    True   **False**   **Can't Tell**

6) Flaming Jack's logo is of an American style.

    True   **False**   **Can't Tell**

7) One thing that is special about Flaming Jack's, is that customers are able to read the menu at their own convenience.

      True   **False**   **Can't Tell**

8) Flaming Jack's provides healthy food.

      True   **False**   **Can't Tell**

9) Customers will be able to communicate directly with the restaurant chef

      True   **False**   **Can't Tell**

10) Which of the following is most likely to be true –

    a. The company's name and logo is in the process of being patented
    b. The restaurant will only require staff to collect payments
    c. People who eat in Soho tend to be fashion conscious.
    d. The restaurant will hire students.

Stem 2

Below is an extract from a restaurant business plan:

'Rodriguez to go' is forecast to generate sales of £258,703 in Year 5 (2018). Net income before interest and tax for the full 2018 financial year is forecast at £46,719.

This assumes:
•The sales forecast is based on sales from the start up restaurant only and does not include the revenue from the intended sister restaurants to be opened in year 3-4.
•Sales volume growth is based on industry standard of 5% growth, for Birmingham restaurants in a similar sector of the industry.

The projected profit indicates a breakeven point of just under 3000 meals a month, which we aim to do by providing an estimated 150 meals per day, giving a profit of £3600 per month.
We aim to gain positive cash balance by year 2. The cash flow forecast includes the assumption of sister restaurants having been opened in year 3 and 4. We hope to expand these restaurants to be larger than the start-up and in similar busy areas of Birmingham. We have therefore forecasted a cash balance of £700,000 by Year 5. This also includes the assumption that further Venture Capitalist funding will be sourced for the expansion of the restaurant to create a chain for franchising.
We require £200,000 to open our start up restaurant 'Rodriguez to go'. This covers, according to affordable loss principles, the rent for one year (£50,000), the rent premium which allows for a lower rental rate throughout the year of (£100,000) and the fixtures and fittings cost (£50,000), including the fixed assets of technology and accessories.

Questions

1) 'Rodriguez to go' will open in 2012.

     True   **False**   **Can't Tell**

2) 'Rodriguez to go' will close in 2018.

     True   **False**   **Can't Tell**

3) 'Rodriguez to go' will make a profit of £258,703 before tax in 2018.

     True   **False**   **Can't Tell**

4) Sister restaurants will be open in year 3-4.

     True   **False**   **Can't Tell**

5) If around 160 meals a day are sold, the restaurant will make a profit.

     True   **False**   **Can't Tell**

6) The majority of the money required for start-up will be spent on rent.

     True   **False**   **Can't Tell**

7) Similar restaurants all have a 5% growth.

     True   **False**   **Can't Tell**

8) It is likely that the company will require further funding to create a restaurant chain.

     True   **False**   **Can't Tell**

9) The company wish to open more than one sister restaurant in the future.

     True   **False**   **Can't Tell**

10) Which is most likely false –

    a. 'Rodriguez to go' will open in 2013
    b. If sales volume growth is below 5%, the restaurant will lose money
    c. The company does not yet have venture capitalist funding
    d. The breakeven point is not 3000 meals per month.

A study summary is given below:

Research overview

This paper explores the patient experience in a satellite dialysis unit, by evaluating service quality through the two proxies of waiting times and patient satisfaction.

Aims and objectives

The aim of this study was to evaluate the service at Northwick Park satellite dialysis unit (NPSDU), and to propose areas of potential improvements. The four objectives of this study were:

(1) To **explore** which factors could affect patient experience in satellite dialysis units through the components of waiting times and patient satisfaction by conducting a narrative literature review

(2) To process map the patient pathway within NPSDU and **identify** factors which affect waiting times

(3) To **identify** factors which affect patient satisfaction at NPSDU

(4) To **propose** recommendations to improve service quality at NPSDU

Methods

To meet our objectives, we carried out two studies adopting a mixed methods approach. Study 1 involved process mapping the patient journey and carrying out structured observations. Study 2 analysed data from predetermined patient satisfaction questionnaires. Quantitative data analysis was conducted on data obtained from both studies, while comments obtained from study 2 were analysed qualitatively using thematic analysis.

Findings

Results showed significant associations between waiting times and type of transport, area of the unit, shift of the day, type of vascular access and mobility. Nurse seniority, however, was found to have no effect on waiting times. Patient satisfaction questionnaires indicated a high level of satisfaction within the unit; the only significant association found was between area of the unit and overall satisfaction with care.

Conclusions

Overall, our study found multiple factors to affect waiting times, but only one factor was found to affect satisfaction. The rationale underlying why these relationships may exist were limited by their somewhat speculative nature, but some were supported by our thematic analysis of patient questionnaires. All in all, this study helped calibrate future research into these important aspects of care.

Questions

1) There are four objectives, each with a different primary goal.

    True   **False**   **Can't Tell**

2) Each study contained different analysis.

    True   **False**   **Can't Tell**

3) Different areas had different waiting times.

    True   **False**   **Can't Tell**

4) The only association found in terms of satisfaction was to do with the area of the unit.

True   **False**   **Can't Tell**

5) All the objectives were clearly met.

True   **False**   **Can't Tell**

6) Senior nurses are just as capable as junior nurses.

True   **False**   **Can't Tell**

7) The recommendations will improve service quality.

True   **False**   **Can't Tell**

8) The recommendations may not improve service quality.

True   **False**   **Can't Tell**

9) The NPSDU operates in different areas.

True   **False**   **Can't Tell**

10) Which out of the following is true:

  a. Each study was analysed in the same way
  b. Study two could not have been analysed in a quantitative way
  c. Study two could have been analysed quantitatively
  d. Study one was solely based on waiting times.

Stem 4

Below is an extract from a research paper:

The NHS National Quality Board (NQB) recently established a working definition of patient experience, guiding its measurement across the NHS (NQB, 2011). A framework consisting of the eight constituent elements of patients' experience of NHS services was formed:

- Respect for patient-centred values, preferences, and expressed needs
- Coordination and integration of care
- Information, communication, and education
- Physical comfort
- Emotional support
- Welcoming the involvement of family and friends
- Access to care

These recent developments in patient experience have guided our study, which focuses primarily on the domain of access to care, concerned with the waiting times of a patient journey.

Waiting times in this study encompasses any time between two steps in the patient journey, consecutive or otherwise. An important disambiguation here is that waiting times do not solely consist of time spent in the waiting room, it includes time spent receiving treatment for example.

Waiting times influence patient experience to the extent that aggression and anxiety are commonly resulting phenomena (Burns and Smyth, 2011). Burns and Smyth (2011) found that waiting times were a key trigger for aggression, accounting for 52% of aggression within the renal unit of St George's hospital.

The opportunity implicated in evaluating this aspect of patient experience is that through better understanding of waiting times we are able to implement strategies focusing on reducing the perceived or actual waiting times to improve patient experience. The NHS earnestly informs patients of the variation in waiting times in an attempt to manage patient expectations. Other means such as: greeting patients as they arrive; live updates about the number and types of cases that staff are presently dealing with; and clear signs explaining the different stages of treatment, are being implemented in certain hospitals to achieve the same end. Such methods to modify patients' perceptions are a powerful management tool to reduce perceived waiting times, and the resulting phenomena of anxiety and aggression discussed above.

Questions

1) The 8 constituent elements of patient experience have been written.

       True   **False**   **Can't Tell**

2) Access to care is the least important of all the elements of patient experience.

       True   **False**   **Can't Tell**

3) The paper was written in 2011.

       True   **False**   **Can't Tell**

4) The article primarily focuses on patient behaviour (aggression and anxiety).

       True   **False**   **Can't Tell**

5) Waiting times are the most important influence in patient experience.

       True   **False**   **Can't Tell**

6) Patient experience and waiting times are the focus of this passage.

       True   **False**   **Can't Tell**

7) Changing patient expectations is thought to help patients have a better experience.

       True   **False**   **Can't Tell**

8) We can assume that hospitals generally inform patients about varying waiting times.

       True   **False**   **Can't Tell**

9) St. George's hospital has a bad record of patient experience.

       True   **False**   **Can't Tell**

10) Which of the following is the most important for patient experience –

a. Respect for patient-centred values, preferences, and expressed needs
b. Access to care
c. Waiting times
d. It is not clear from the text

Below is an extract from a research study:

North West London runs the largest Haemodialysis (HD) programme in the UK with 1,400 patients being treated in eight satellite dialysis units based around one hub, the Imperial College Renal and Transplant Centre (ICRTC), situated in Hammersmith Hospital (Transplant Centre at the Hammersmith Hospital, 2013). Although the number of kidney donations is on the rise, 97.3% of ESRF patients in North-West London are on HD, 72.9% of which attend a satellite dialysis centre to receive treatment (Gilg et al., 2011).

Our study is based in NPSDU, located in West London, with an extremely diverse ethnic population. Compared to London and Great Britain as a whole, West London has a greater population of Asian and Afro-Caribbean ethnicities. Evidence suggests higher incidence of chronic kidney disease (CKD), a precursor to ESRF, among these ethnic minorities (Agarwal et al., 2005; Shulman and Hall, 1991).

At NPSDU, dialysis treatment is carried out from Monday to Saturday, with morning and afternoon shifts daily and an additional evening shift on Mondays, Wednesdays and Fridays.

The unit treats a population of 280 HD patients and has a total of 61 dialysis stations split up into six functionally separate areas. The seemingly bizarre layout of the unit is due to the fact that it was not built for purpose, and expanded incrementally to match growing demand over the years.

NPSDU, like most other satellite units, is nurse-led. While the resource savings enabled through increasing nurse roles has been well documented (RCN 2010), the potential trade-offs with quality in the domain of patient experience in a satellite dialysis unit has not. Therefore, scientific rigor should be applied before conclusions can be drawn on the quality implications in each of its applications, in this case satellite dialysis.

NPSDU provides insight into the drivers of quality at the largest satellite dialysis unit in the UK, which operates in the dominant hub and spoke model (Apira 2010). In studying a unit that lies within London, the area with the highest density of satellite dialysis spokes, we have access to a potentially rich source of data. Thus, we can gain insights into how effectively satellite units, with their unique characteristics, are in line with the NHS' future vision of high quality care for all.

Questions

1) North West London has the highest numbers of CKD in the UK.

True   **False**   **Can't Tell**

2) The article states that West London has the highest incidence of CKD.

True   **False**   **Can't Tell**

3)NPSDU has only morning and afternoon shifts from Monday to Saturday.

True   **False**   **Can't Tell**

4)There are approximately ten dialysis stations in each area of the unit.

True   **False**   **Can't Tell**

5)Quality of patient experience has not yet been looked into, with regards to the satellite unit.

True   **False**   **Can't Tell**

6)The article was written later than 2010 (inclusive).

True   **False**   **Can't Tell**

7)The author believes West London may not be the best place for a study.

True   **False**   **Can't Tell**

8)72.9% of ESRF patients go to a satellite dialysis centre.

True   **False**   **Can't Tell**

9)NPSDU has been generally well received by patients.

True   **False**   **Can't Tell**

10)Which of the following is true:

  e. 72.9% of ESRF patients go to a satellite dialysis centre
  f. 97.3% of patients on HD attend a satellite dialysis centre
  g. Not all patients on HD attend a satellite dialysis centre
  h.   72.9% of patients on HD in London go to a satellite dialysis centre

Stem 6

Below is an extract from a recent News article:

There exists much confusion and controversy amongst healthcare professionals as to the definition of tele-health; even the Department of Health (DOH) definition is subject to varied interpretation. The Royal Society of Medicine, quoting the DOH, defines telehealth as: "patient to clinician: vital signs and general condition monitoring such as blood pressure, weight, mental & physical state." Another recent paper (Hendy et al.) defines it as "the remote exchange of data between a patient, at home, and health care professionals, to assist in the management of an existing long-term condition i.e. COPD, diabetes, heart failure." The first notable inconsistency concerns location. The RSM definition does not specify a home environment, whilst the other does. Similarly, Hendy specifies long-term conditions only, whilst the RSM definition does not specify. The definition chosen in this review is the RSM DOH one, primarily due to its broad nature. By not stipulating the environment in which telehealth is delivered nor restricting to long-term conditions, a far broader range of telehealth services can be analysed and the scope of the review is much increased, whilst still being correct and relevant.

This review considers many forms of telehealth delivery such as telestroke and teleICU. Telecare is **not** considered in this systematic review and is defined as: "the remote, automatic monitoring of an individual's personal health and safety, i.e. mobility, and home environment." The term "telemedicine" is not currently used by the DOH and various definitions exist. Indeed, a 2007 study found 104 peer-reviewed definitions. It is similarly **not** considered in this review, although was included in the search strategy. "Remote care" is an umbrella term describing both telehealth and telecare (Hendy et al.), and was thus appropriately considered.

Questions

1) The paper has given two definitions for telehealth.

    True   **False**   **Can't Tell**

2) The paper uses two definitions for telehealth.

    True   **False**   **Can't Tell**

3) The Royal Society of Medicine definition for telehealth is the one used by most professionals.

    True   **False**   **Can't Tell**

4) We can assume telecare is not part of telehealth.

    True   **False**   **Can't Tell**

5) The author writes that telecare is not a form of telehealth.

    True   **False**   **Can't Tell**

6) The paper does not define telemedicine.

    True   **False**   **Can't Tell**

7) Remote care is a type of telehealth delivery.

    True   **False**   **Can't Tell**

8) The author believes that the RSM definition for telehealth is the correct one.

    True   **False**   **Can't Tell**

9) The author is studying how effective telehealth delivery is.

    True   **False**   **Can't Tell**

10) Which of the following statements is false –

    a. Remote care relates to telehealth and telecare
    b. Telecare is a part of telehealth, but has not been considered
    c. Telecare is not part of telehealth
    d. Telemedicine has many different definitions.

Stem 7

Below is an extract from a recent online article:

Issues regarding implementation of telehealth programs such as training and installation have long been cited as potential pitfalls hindering large scale adoption. It is important to note that even those HCPs who are meant to deliver the service are no exception and hold similar thoughts.

A 2011 cross-sectional, qualitative study conducted in Scotland by Hanna et al. asked GPs their opinions regarding potential non face-to-face consultation methods. Most GPs felt that in order to use the new technologies, adequate frameworks would first have to be implemented including "support and training", along with clear legal advice. The sample size, whilst small at only 20, did cover the whole of Scotland. The study also stated that the results may be generalisable to the UK given the nationally negotiated General Practice contract is similar to Scotland. A key failing was that when discussing results, no specific figures were given, limiting the conclusions that can be drawn.

In a study of telemonitoring by heart failure nurses by Johnston et al., one nurse experienced significant difficulties during installation. She was concerned by her "lack of ability to undertake the installation." She also remarked that there was a lack of time to complete the installation. It must be noted that this was only one nurse, but, given the sample of four, is still significant. Apart from this small sample, a failing was that the nurses were not recruited explicitly for the purpose of this study, and they were interviewed as part of a larger research trial. This raises issues of selection bias, as no details have been given about the initial selection criteria for the larger trial. The nurses may have been selected initially due to their opinions on telehealth, for example. Another failing in the methodology is that the nurses were given the equipment and then left to their own devices. This caused problems such as nurses "cherry-picking" participants known to them and also performing the weight monitoring in a non-standardised fashion. These would potentially alter their opinions, limiting internal validity.

Questions

1) Large scale implementation of telehealth has not worked.
True   **False**   **Can't Tell**

2) The study conducted in Scotland cannot be used as no specific figures were given when discussing results.
True   **False**   **Can't Tell**

3) There was selection bias in the study by Johnson et al.
True   **False**   **Can't Tell**

4) According to the author, it seems there were quite a few drawbacks to the Johnson et al. study.
True   **False**   **Can't Tell**

5) Internal validity can be defined as how warranted a conclusion is.
True   **False**   **Can't Tell**

6) 20 is a small sample size.
True   **False**   **Can't Tell**

7) 4 is a small sample size.
True   **False**   **Can't Tell**

8) The nurse in the Johnson et al. study was not able to perform the installation.
True   **False**   **Can't Tell**

9) We can assume that telemonitoring is a part of telehealth.

10) We can assume the author believes what:

     a.   The nurses should have been allocated participants randomly
     b. Then nurses were biased against telehealth
     c.   Telehealth cannot be rolled out in a large scale
     d. The conclusions drawn from the Scotland study cannot be used.

Stem 8

Below is an extract from a study paper:

Face to face contact is often proclaimed as an invaluable tool in the practice of medicine. It is acknowledged to be the primary means of gathering information from a patient and an essential component of the doctor-patient relationship. With its ever increasing uptake, telehealth has the potential to irrevocably damage this age-old tradition, and thus it is again no surprise to find strong opinions in the literature.

In the Scotland paper Hanna et al., face-to-face consultation was considered central to practice by the GPs, and some did express some reservations about the potential detrimental effect of telehealth on face-to-face interaction. The main complaint was that telehealth would decrease the amount of time spent with the patient and would therefore lead to an inability to build and contribute to the breakdown of existing relationships with patients. Some GPs were more positive. They embraced the evolving doctor-patient relationship and "saw new technologies as providing an opportunity to build a new kind of relationship".

A strength of this paper is the authors' explicit attempts to recruit GPs with varying willingness to use technology, not just those enthusiastic about telehealth (minimising selection bias). They also noted that the study was focussed on the "microlevel communication" between doctor and patient, and recognised therefore that the results would be applicable regardless of the overall healthcare system of a country.

Questions

1) Face to face contact is an example of micro level communication.

     True   **False**   **Can't Tell**

2) The use of telehealth has had a mixed response from GPs.

     True   **False**   **Can't Tell**

3) Telehealth is becoming used more and more.

     True   **False**   **Can't Tell**

4) Face to face contact is the most important way to gain evidence from a patient.

     True   **False**   **Can't Tell**

5) The author believes it is important to use participants who have differing views on the subject.

     True   **False**   **Can't Tell**

6)An example of selection bias would be using just GPs who were positive about telehealth.

     True   **False**   **Can't Tell**

7)Microlevel communication occurs across the healthcare system.

     True   **False**   **Can't Tell**

8)Overall, more GPs were against telehealth than for it.

     True   **False**   **Can't Tell**

9)Overall, more GPs were for telehealth than against it.

     True   **False**   **Can't Tell**

10)Which of the following is most likely to be false :

    a. The paper did not contain much selection bias
    b. The doctor-patient relationship is changing
    c. The paper did not contain any selection bias
    d. The doctor-patient relationship may be changed with this new technology.

Verbal Reasoning questions format 1 and 2 answers

Stem 1

1) **True**. This is a tricky question, even though there is not a specific author, there is a reference to 'our menu'. "We will protect our brand name and logo" this line suggests ownership of the brand.
2) **False**. There is word play in the questions, although the text says 'Flaming Jack's is committed to providing to providing the food that diners truly want- customisation is a key ingredient' The questions states 'primarily want to be able to customise their food' Indicating that the customer want to customise the food, but there is no information that this is what the customer 'primarily wants'.
3) **True.** Here the question states the ' customers want to be able to customise their food' which matches the vision of the restaurant in 'providing the food that diners truly want- customisation is a key ingredient'.
4) **False**. 'app makes it simple and intuitive to modify your meal, with diners being able to select the main ingredients, sauces, toppings and sides as well as adding comments or special instructions for the chef such as allergies' The app will not allow customers to change portion sizes.
5) **True**. 'halving the number of waiting staff needed'. The restaurant requires less staff, so this makes it cheaper.
6) **Can't Tell**. There is no information on what the logo looks like.
7) **False**. This a feature of the restaurant and a benefit to the restaurant as stated : 'iPads mounted in a protective shell on each table, diners peruse the menu at their own convenience'. It does not say that this is unique or special to Flaming Jack's.
8) **Can't Tell**. The text states: 'Our app will cater for the health-conscious' Flaming Jack's allows customers to see the healthiest options, but there is no information on how healthy food is.
9) **False**. 'special instructions for the chef' Customers will be able to communicate with the chef by writing on the iPad app. But not directly with the chef as the question specifies.
10) **C. People who eat in Soho tend to be fashion conscious**. This is the true statement because as the text says 'Themed specifically to appeal to our fashion-conscious, metropolitan clientele'. We can assume that this is linked.

Why are the other options most likely false?

 a. The company's name and logo is in the process of being patented -This is false because 'We will protect our brand name and logo, whilst our app and its associated intellectual property can be patented' It is the app that they're looking to patent.

 b. & d. The restaurant will only require staff to collect payments & The restaurant will hire students - There is no information in the passage to specify this.

Stem 2

1) **False**. ' 'Rodriguez to go' is forecast to generate sales of £258,703 in Year 5 (2018)' It will open in 2013, This is a 5 year forecast ending at 2018, 2018 - 5 = 2013.
 2) **False.** There is nothing to suggest that the restaurant will close in 2018.
3) **False.** 'generate sales of £258,703' , not profit.
4) **Can't Tell**. 'the intended sister restaurants to be opened in year 3-4', but this is a future prediction.
5) **True**. 'estimated 150 meals per day, giving a profit of £3600 per month.', so 160 meals will yield profit.
6) **True**. 'the rent for one year (£50,000), the rent premium which allows for a lower rental rate throughout the year of (£100,000)' which in total is £150,000 of the £200,000 will be spent on rent or the rent premium.
7) **Can't Tell**. 'Sales volume growth is based on industry standard of 5% growth', but we do not know if every restaurant achieves this exact figure (or not).
8) **True.** 'This also includes the assumption that further Venture Capitalist funding will be sourced for the expansion of the restaurant to create a chain for franchising.'.
9) **True**. The text states' We hope to expand these restaurants to be larger than the start-up' restaurants rather than restaurant, indicating more than one.
10) **b. If sales volume growth is below 5%, the restaurant will lose money** We cannot say this is true, as we have not been given exact figures for profit margins.

Why are the other options true?

 a. 'Rodriguez to go' will open in 2013 – Same rationale to the answer as 1)
 c. The company does not yet have venture capitalist funding
         'This also includes the assumption that further Venture Capitalist funding'
 d. The breakeven point is not 3000 meals per month. – 'a breakeven point of just under 3000 meals a month'

Stem 3

1) **False**. There are four objectives but three primary goals, explore, identify, and propose.
2) **False**. 'Quantitative data analysis was conducted on data obtained from both studies, while comments obtained from study 2 were analysed qualitatively using thematic analysis.'   Both studies were quantitatively analysed.
3) **True**. 'significant associations between waiting times and type of transport, area of the unit' The fact that there was an association between different areas and waiting times means that this must be true.
4) **Can't Tell**. There was an association between waiting time and area. We do not know the association in terms of satisfaction.
5) **False**. We cannot see evidence of any recommendations.
6) **Can't Tell**. '. Nurse seniority, however, was found to have no effect on waiting times' There is no information on the capability of the nurses.

7) **Can't Tell**. We do not know if the recommendations will be implemented and if so whether they will be effective or not.
8) **True.** This is a possibility, as we cannot know what will happen in the future.
9) **True.** 'Results showed significant associations between waiting times and type of transport, area of the unit' We know there is a correlation between waiting time and area of unit. So the NPSDU must operate in different areas.
10) ; **Study two could have been analysed quantitatively;** 'Quantitative data analysis was conducted on data obtained from both studies'. The answers could have been therefore analysed in this way.

Why are the other options false?

    a. Each study was analysed in the same way – Same rationale to the answer as 1)
    b. Study two could not have been analysed in a quantitative way - rationale to answer 10)
    d. Study one was solely based on waiting times. – 'Study 1 involved process mapping the patient journey and carrying out structured observations. Study 2 analysed data from predetermined patient satisfaction questionnaires.' Neither of the studies focused solely on waiting time

Stem 4

1) **False.** The box only states 7 of the 8.
2) **Can't Tell**. Although there are 7 of the 8 elements in the box, it isn't ranked, there is no information on which is the most important.
3) **Can't Tell**. Although the references are from 2011, this does not necessarily mean the paper was written then.
4) **False.** 'Burns and Smyth (2011) found that waiting times were a key trigger for aggression, accounting for 52% of aggression within the renal unit of St George's hospital ' this is a quote used to establish the link between waiting times and aggression. This is only a small constituent of the article.
5) **Can't Tell**. Combining with the rationale from 2) that the influences aren't ranked in importance highlights there is no information on whether this is the most important influence..
6) **True**. The bulk of the text is dedicated to one of these two points, also 'which focuses primarily on the domain of access to care, concerned with the waiting times of a patient journey' highlights the aims of the study including waiting times, so we can take this to be true.
7) **True.** 'Other means such as: greeting patients as they arrive; live updates about the number and types of cases that staff are presently dealing with;....Such methods to modify patients' perceptions are a powerful management tool to reduce perceived waiting times' This quote highlights that importance of patient perception and expectation in the patient experience. Therefore we can deduce that this is true.
8) **True.** 'The NHS earnestly informs patients of the variation in waiting times' The article says the NHS does this, so it is safe to assume this is the case.
9) **Can't Tell**. 'within the renal unit of St George's hospital' There is no information given on patient experience as a whole at St. George's.

10) **It is not clear from the text.** The text does not contain any information on which is the most important.

Why are the other options not the most important for patient experience?

The other three options are elements of patient care and as stated previously we do not know what is most important

Stem 5

1) **Can't Tell**. 'North West London runs the largest Haemodialysis (HD) programme in the UK' this doesn't necessarily mean that CKD is the highest in North West London. Although 'Evidence suggests higher incidence of chronic kidney disease (CKD), a precursor to ESRF, among these ethnic minorities' and 'Compared to London and Great Britain as a whole, West London has a greater population of Asian and Afro-Caribbean ethnicities' this does not necessarily mean it has the highest numbers.
2) **False.** The article states that the types of population found in West London have a higher incidence, but does not say that West London itself has the highest incidence.
3) **False**. 'an additional evening shift on Mondays, Wednesdays and Fridays'
4) **Can't Tell**. Although there is 'a total of 61 dialysis stations split up into six functionally separate areas', we do not know if they are evenly spread or not.
5) **True.** 'While the resource savings enabled through increasing nurse roles has been well documented (RCN 2010), the potential trade-offs with quality in the domain of patient experience in a satellite dialysis unit has not.' - that the trade off with quality in the domain of patient experience is not well documented.
6) **True.** The most recent reference is from 2011, so the article must have been written in 2011 or later.
7) **False.** 'Our study is based in NPSDU, located in West London, with an extremely diverse ethnic population. Compared to London and Great Britain as a whole' The author writes that West London has a potentially rich source of data.
8) **False.** '97.3% of ESRF patients in North-West London are on HD, 72.9% of which attend a satellite dialysis centre to receive treatment' 72.9% of patients on HD go to a satellite dialysis centre.
9) **Can't Tell**. There is no information on patient satisfaction.
10) **Not all patients on HD attend a satellite dialysis centre** 72.9% of patients on HD do, so not all of them.

Why are the other options false?

a. 72.9% of ESRF patients go to a satellite dialysis centre – Same rationale as 8)
b. 97.3% of patients on HD attend a satellite dialysis centre – '97.3% of ESRF patients in North-West London are on HD, 72.9% of which attend a satellite dialysis centre to receive treatment'
d. 72.9% of patients on HD in London go to a satellite dialysis centre – 'patients in North-West London'. We do not know the information for the whole of London.

Stem 6

1) **True**. The RSM definition '"patient to clinician: vital signs and general condition monitoring such as blood pressure, weight,

mental & physical state." ' and the definition by Hendy et al "the remote exchange of data between a patient, at home, and health care professionals, to assist in the management of an existing long-term condition' .

2) **False**. 'The definition chosen in this review is the RSM DOH one' The paper chooses the RSM definition.

3) **Can't Tell**. There is no information on whether the RSM definition is the most widely used.

4) **True**. ' "Remote care" is an umbrella term describing both telehealth and telecare' we can assume they are separate.

5) **False**. 'Telecare is **not** considered in this systematic review' The author does not specifically write that Telecare is not a form of telehealth.

6) **True**. The paper says there are '104 peer-reviewed definitions', but does not give a specific one to define telemedicine.

7) **False**. This is just a play with words, '"Remote care" is an umbrella term describing both telehealth and telecare' Telehealth is a type of remote care.

8) **Can't Tell**. The author does not state which is correct, just that he/she will use the RSM 'primarily due to its broad nature'.

9) **Can't Tell**. There is no information on what aspect of telehealth is being studied.

10) **b. Telecare is a part of telehealth, but has not been considered**. As stated in the rationale of 4) Telecare is not a part of telehealth.

Why are the other statements true?

e. Remote care relates to telehealth and telecare - '"Remote care" is an umbrella term describing both telehealth and telecare'

c. Telecare is not part of telehealth - '"Remote care" is an umbrella term describing both telehealth and telecare'

d. Telemedicine has many different definitions. – '"telemedicine" is not currently used by the DOH and various definitions exist. Indeed, a 2007 study found 104 peer-reviewed definitions'

Stem 7

1) **False**. The text merely states 'potential pitfalls hindering large scale adoption.' – implementation has not yet happened.

2) **False**. 'A key failing was that when discussing results, no specific figures were given, limiting the conclusions that can be drawn.' The study's conclusions are limited but still can be used.

3) **Can't Tell**. 'This raises issues of selection bias, as no details have been given about the initial selection criteria for the larger trial.' There may have been selection bias, but we do not know this for sure.

4) **True**. The author lists several problems in paragraph about the Johnston et al study.

5) **Can't Tell**. We do not know what the definition is based on the text only. There is a reference to internal validity 'This caused problems such as nurses "cherry-picking" participants known to them and also performing the weight monitoring in a non-standardised fashion. These would potentially alter their opinions, limiting internal validity' but no clear definition is given.

6) **True**. The author states this. – ' The sample size, whilst small at only 20'

7) **True**. The author states this. – 'given the sample of four, is still significant. Apart from this small sample'

8) **Can't Tell**. 'She was concerned by her "lack of ability to undertake the installation." She also remarked that there was a lack of time to complete the installation.' – there's no specific information stating if the installation was completed or not.

9) **True**. In the beginning of the 3rd paragraph it was started 'In a study of telemonitoring by heart failure nurses'. Later in the paragraph, The author then goes on to write that 'The nurses may have been selected initially due to their opinions on telehealth' so it's safe to presume telemonitoring is a part of telehealth.

10) **a. The nurses should have been allocated participants randomly**. The author says 'problems such as nurses "cherry-picking" participants known to them and also performing the weight monitoring in a non-standardised fashion. These would potentially alter their opinions' It's safe to say the author believes the nurses should have been allocated participants.

Why are the other options NOT what the author believes?

b. Then nurses were biased against telehealth –' The nurses may have been selected initially due to their opinions on telehealth' The author is not sure.

c. Telehealth cannot be rolled out in a large scale – 'potential pitfalls hindering large scale adoption this doesn't mean it can't happen

d. The conclusions drawn from the Scotland study cannot be used. – 'the results may be generalisable to the UK'

Stem 8

Face to face contact is often proclaimed as an invaluable tool in the practice of medicine. It is acknowledged to be the primary means of gathering information from a patient and an essential component of the doctor-patient relationship. With its ever increasing uptake, telehealth has the potential to irrevocably damage this age-old tradition, and thus it is again no surprise to find strong opinions in the literature.

In the Scotland paper Hanna et al., face-to-face consultation was considered central to practice by the GPs, and some did express some reservations about the potential detrimental effect of telehealth on face-to-face interaction. The main complaint was that telehealth would decrease the amount of time spent with the patient and would therefore lead to an inability to build and contribute to the breakdown of existing relationships with patients. Some GPs were more positive. They embraced the evolving doctor-patient relationship and "saw new technologies as providing an opportunity to build a new kind of relationship".

A strength of this paper is the authors' explicit attempts to recruit GPs with varying willingness to use technology, not just those enthusiastic about telehealth (minimising selection bias). They also noted that the study was focused on the "microlevel communication" between doctor and patient, and recognised therefore that the results would be applicable regardless of the overall healthcare system of a country.

1) **Can't Tell**. 'an invaluable tool in the practice of medicine' Although we can probably assume this, there is no link between these two in stated in the text.

2) **True**. 'some did express some reservations about the potential detrimental effect of telehealth on face-to-face interaction.' and 'Some GPs were more positive'

3) **True**. The texts states 'With its ever increasing uptake, telehealth has the potential to irrevocably damage this age-old tradition' implying it is getting used more and more.

4) **True.** It is described as 'primary means of gathering information from a patient', the key word is primary which then relates to most important.

5) **True**. The author states this in the text: 'A strength of this paper is the authors' explicit attempts to recruit GPs with varying willingness to use technology'.

6) **True.** Although we may know the answer from prior knowledge, it is key not to use it and check within the text 'A strength of this paper is the authors' explicit attempts to recruit GPs with varying willingness to use technology, not just those enthusiastic about telehealth (minimising selection bias).' Implies just using GPs who were pro telehealth would be bias.

7) **True.** The author states, 'the study was focused on the "micro-level communication" between doctor and patient, and recognised therefore that the results would be applicable regardless of the overall healthcare system of a country' – we can therefore assume this to be true.

8) **Can't Tell**. There is no information on figures.

9) **Can't Tell.** There is no information on figures.

10) **c. The paper did not contain any selection bias**. – Is most likely to be false because we cannot say for sure if the paper contained absolutely no selection bias, 'A strength of this paper is the authors' explicit attempts to recruit GPs with varying willingness to use technology' the authors went out recruiting GPs on willingness to use technology so this is most likely to be false.

Why were the other options most likely true?

a. The paper did not contain much selection bias – 'A strength of this paper is the authors' explicit attempts to recruit GPs with varying willingness to use technology, not just those enthusiastic about telehealth (minimising selection bias).'

b. The doctor-patient relationship is changing - 'They embraced the evolving doctor-patient relationship and "saw new technologies as providing an opportunity to build a new kind of relationship".'

d. The doctor-patient relationship may be changed with this new technology. – ' "saw new technologies as providing an opportunity to build a new kind of relationship".'

QUANTITATIVE REASONING

This section is the Quantitative Reasoning practice question, we recommend you refresh your memory on how to approach this section on pages 4-14.

This subtest assesses your ability to use mathematical skills to solve problems. You will be given 23 minutes to solve 36 items which may involve interpreting graphs, tables, charts or statements. It is assumed that all candidates are of a reasonable level from GCSE Maths, and therefore, we advise that if students struggle in this area, they should prioritise practising this subtest over the others. Otherwise, a low score here will bring down your average result. Because of all the analysis and data interpretation required for this section, it is important to keep an eye on the clock and move swiftly from one question to the next.

Top tips!!

1. Only use a calculator if you really need to. Most students spend unnecessary time on the calculator to double check answers; this time could be preciously spent on other questions. So get enough practice to feel confident with your answer choices.
2. Practice using the on screen calculator on the mock tests provided by www.ukcat.ac.uk
3. If nerves and the pressure get to you, don't panic! Make a wise guess by ruling out answers that are in the wrong units or too far from what could be correct (remember there is no negative marking)
4. Make sure your answers are in the correct units and to the right decimal place as specified by the question; this is often an easy error that can be avoided.
5. Regularly practice your numerical skills and mental arithmetic using websites and other resources, so that nothing surprises you on the data.

Quantitative reasoning questions

QUESTION 1

A man wants to take his wife and three young children on holiday to somewhere hot and sunny. He is comparing flight and hotel prices to several destinations.

Flights (return)								
	Sun Tours		Easyfly		British Airlines		London Travel	
	Adult	Child	Adult	Child	Adult	Child	Adult	Child
Algarve	£200	£120	£190	£120	£200	£100	£160	£120
Barcelona	£160	£100	£160	£90	£170	£85	£150	£100
Rome	£225	£100	£230	£105	£250	£125	£200	£150
Crete	£280	£140	£260	£150	£280	£140	£230	£175
Hotels (5 nights for whole family)								
	Sun Tours		QuickFind		Sun and Sand		London Travel	
Algarve	£550		£520		£600		£525	
Barcelona	£600		£590		£630		£600	
Rome	£575		£575		£600		£595	
Crete	£550		£500		£490		£500	

Sun Tours offers a 10% discount on the total price if flights and hotels are both booked through their company, whilst London Travel offers £50 cash-back if flights and hotels are both booked through their company.

1) **How much a holiday, with his family, to the Algarve cost through Sun Tours?**

   a. £1310 b. £760 c. £550 d.£1179 e. £1200

2) **What is the cheapest price he can take his family to Rome for?**

   a. £1192.50 b. £1325 c. £1395 d. £1200 c. £1300

3) **What is the cheapest price he can get return flights to Rome if he takes only his wife?**

   a. £450b. £400 c. £405 d. £350 e. £460

4) **What is the difference in price if to go to Barcelona with his family, if he booked through Easyfly and Sun and Sand, compared with British Airlines and QuickFind?**

   a. £1185 b. £1220 c. £15 d. £20 e. £35

5) **Easyfly are having a 15% sale on flights. What is the new price of flights to take his family to Crete?**

   a. £824.50 b. £970 c. £1141 d. £900 e. £950

6) **What is the difference in price if he were to use London Travel for flights and hotels to Barcelona, compared with using London Travel for flights and QuickFind for hotels to book a holiday with his family?**

   a. £50 b. £1200 c. £40 d. £10 e. £1190

7) **What is the cheapest price he can take his family on holiday to Crete for?**

   a.£1460 b.£1377 c. £1530 d. £1435 e. £1480

8) **If Sun Tours reduced their discount to 5%,what would the difference between the old and new price of taking a holiday, with his family, to the Algarve be?**

   a. £50 b. £1244.50 c. £1179 d. £65.50 e. £25

9) **What is the difference in price between Algarve and Barcelona if he books completely through London Travel?**

   a.£50 b. £100 c. £5 d. £57.50 e. £60

10) **What is the cheapest place he can go to with Sun Tours?**

   a. None b. Algarve. c. Barcelona d. Rome e. Crete

QUESTION 2

Below are the prices of various items in a wholesale T-Shirt warehouse.It is recommended that all Jumpers are sold at 3x wholesale price. If the same item is ordered but with different graphics, then the discounts are eligible on the total order.

Plain white Jumpers
£3.00 per item up to 50 items ordered.
£2.75 per item if between 51 and 100 items are ordered.
£2.50 per item if between 101 and 200 items are ordered.
£2.25 per item for 201+ items ordered.

Plain coloured Jumpers
£3.50 per item up to 50 items ordered.
£3.30 per item if between 51 and 100 items are ordered.
£3.10 per item if between 101 and 200 items are ordered.
£2.90 per item for 201+ items ordered.

To add black Graphics
£1 per item for white jumpers.
£1.50 per item for coloured jumpers.

To add coloured Graphics
£2 per item for white jumpers.
£2.50 per item for coloured jumpers.

1) **Someone wishes to buy 55 plain white jumpers. How much will this cost?**

   a .£163.75 b. £151.25 c. £161.25 d. £153.75 e. £152.15

2) **A retailer wishes to buy 50 plain white jumpers and 100 plain coloured jumpers. How much will this cost?**

   a. £480 b. £447.50 c. £460 d. £467.50 e.£470

3) **Someone wishes to buy 100 plain white jumpers with black graphics, and 100 plain white jumpers with coloured graphics. How much will this cost?**

   a. £850 b. £910 c.£950 d, £710 e. £810

4) How much profit can a retailer make on 125 plain coloured jumpers, if sold at the recommended price?

a.£387.50 b. £1162.50 c. £775 d. £825 e. £725

5) A retailer buys 60 plain white jumpers, and 75 plain coloured jumpers with black graphics. He sells most of the items, but has 10 white and 15 coloured jumpers left over. What was the profit/loss?

a. £1050 b. -£1050 c. £1276.50 d. £751.50 e. -£751.50

6) How much will it cost to buy 300 plain coloured jumpers, half with black graphics and half with coloured graphics?

a.£1530 b. £930 c. £1230 d. £1470 e. £870

7) A shop buys 200 plain white jumpers, and 100 plain coloured jumpers. However the shop goes bankrupt, and can only sell them at 1.5x the value they were bought for. What is the difference in profit made compared with if they were sold at 3x the wholesale price.

a.£415 b. £1,140 c. £380 d. £400 e. £1245

8) A retailer sells 200 white jumpers with coloured graphics for a total of £1500 profit. How much must the retailer have been selling each jumper for?

a. £12 b. £7.50 c. £5 d. £9.75 e. £7.25

9) What is the cost of buying 60 plain white jumpers with coloured graphics, and 80 coloured Jumpers with black graphics?

a.£653 b. £669 c. £709 d. £769 e. £753

10) The wholesaler places a 10% discount on all orders. What is the difference between buying 75 plain white jumpers and 75 plain coloured jumpers before, compared with now?

a.£45.38 b. £45.36 c. £45.37 d. £408.39 e. £408.38

QUESTION 3

Every year, 5 people take part in a sponsored swim for charity. Below is a table showing the amount they each swam over a 5 year period (In lengths).

Person	2008	2009	2010	2011	2012
Duncan	750	760	770	780	790
James	300	320	340	360	360
Katie	500	525	550	575	550
Chris	600	580	580	540	560
Kate	700	700	700	700	710

1) If each length is 25m, how much has Kate swum in total?

a.87,500 b. 67,500 c. 87,750 d. 3,510 e. 3,500

2) If each length is 25m, how much did the group swim altogether in 2010?

a.73,250 b. 73,750 c. 73,000 d. 74,000 e. 73,500

3) **If the group raised £15,675 in 2008, and they all charged the same per length, how much were they sponsored per length?**

a.£5 b. £6 c. 55p d. 60p e. £5.50

4) **What proportion of the total lengths that year did Katie swim in 2009?**

a. 0.18 b. 0.19 c. 0.24 d. 0.25 e. 0.22

5) **If each length is 25m, what was the average amount swum in 2011?**

a. 591 b. 14,775 c. 14,750 d. 15,000 e. 590

6) **If they each asked for £6 per length in 2012, how much did they raise in total?**

a. £17,730 b. £17,760 c. £2,960 d. £17,820 e. £2,970

7) **What was the most anyone swam in the whole 5 year period?**

a. Duncan b. James c. Katie d. Chris e. Kate

8) **Who swam the least over 5 years?**

a. Duncan b. James c. Katie d. Chris e. Kate

9) **What was the percentage change in Duncan's total number of lengths from 2010 to 2012?**

a. 2.2% b. 2.3% c. 2.4% d. 2.5% e. 2.6%

10) **If each length is 25m, how much less did Chris swim in 2010 compared with 2012?**

a.1000m b. 200m c. 500m d. 50m e. 20m

QUESTION 4

Jayden is an artist. She does caricatures for fixed prices. A small caricature costs £10, whilst a large costs £16.

1) **What is the difference in price between three small and two large caricatures?**

a. £28 b. £30 c.£2 d. £32 e. £8

2) **A tourist asks Jayden to draw 5 small caricatures for his children, and 3 large ones for him, his wife, and his brother. How much does this cost the tourist in total?**

a. £48 b. £50 c. £98 d. £110 e. £194

3) **Another tourist asks Jayden to draw 4 small caricatures and 4 large ones. He decides to tip her 5%. How much does this cost the tourist in total?**

a. £109.20 b. £109 c. £104 d. £99 e. £134.40

4) Jayden uses £2 worth of material for small caricatures, and £3 for large ones. If she draws 20 small and 15 large caricatures, how much profit does she make?

   a. £440 b. £370 c. £335 d. £355 e. £85

5) Jayden uses £2 worth of material for small caricatures, and £3 for large ones. If she needs to draw 13 small and 11 large caricatures, how much will the material cost?

   a. £48 b. £72 c. £61 d. £60 e. £59

6) Jayden believes that the day will be busy, so raises her prices by £1 for small and £2 for large caricatures. She expects that she will have to draw 30 small and 20 large ones. How much money will she receive?

   a. £620 b. £690 c. £570 d. £500 e. £600

7) Jayden believes that the day will be busy, so raises her prices by £1 for small and £2 for large caricatures. On average, she draws 20 small and 15 large caricatures per day. However, due to her increased price, she only draws 15 small and 10 large caricatures. What is the difference in profit on an average day compared to today?

   a. £120 b. £145 c. £160 d. £175 e. £95

8) Jayden decides to pin some examples on a board. A small caricature is 20cm long by 15cm wide. A large caricature is 40cm by 30cm. If she wishes to pin 3 small ones side by side, how wide a board will she need?

   a. 45cm b. 60cm c. 90cm d. 120cm e. 75cm

9) Jayden decides to pin some examples on a board. A small caricature is 20cm long by 15cm wide. A large caricature is 40cm by 30cm. If she decides to pin 3 large ones side by side, and 4 small ones underneath side by side, how big will the board need to be?

   a. 90 x 60 b. 60 x 90 c. 120 x 45 d. 45 x 120 e. 45 x 90

10) Jayden gives a 20% discount to her first customer, who orders a large caricature. What will the caricature cost the customer?

   a. £14.40 b. £3.60 c. £16 d. £12.80 e. £3.20

QUESTION 5

> **Shampoo**
>
> Colour guard plus, a shampoo producer, produces a new range of shampoo with new colour protection technology. The shampoo is only available in two sizes, 250ml and 500ml. They cost £5 and £7.50 respectively

1. **What is the cheapest price value of 2750ml of this product?**

   a. £40.50 b. £55 c. £42.50 d. £51.50 e. £50

2. **Comparing 2 x 250ml bottles to 500ml what is the percentage increase of cost comparing the 250 bottles to the 500ml?**

   a. 50% b. 33% c.45% d. 26% e. 30%

3. **A local drug store offer a 2 for 1 offer on the 250ml bottles, how much would you save if you wanted 2000ml of the shampoo?**

   a. £30 b. £40 c. £35 d. £20 e. £25

4. **Another store sells 360 250ml bottles and 120 500ml bottles, what is the ratio of 250ml to 500ml bottles sold in the store?**

   a.4:1 b. 160:50 c. 3:1 d. 2.5:1 e.5:1

QUESTION 6

> **Motorcycle**
>
> Alex is a professional racer who races in the World Championships, He owns a prototype motorcycle. This motorcycle can go from 0-60mph in 3 seconds, 60-100mph in 3.5 seconds and steadily increase of 10mph per second in a linear fashion from 100-150mph and after that it takes 15seconds to reach the top speed of 180mph.

1) **How long does it take him to reach 165mph?**

   a. 19 seconds b. 11.5 seconds c. 13 seconds d. 17.5 seconds e. 21seconds

2) **He accelerates for 8 seconds, what is his speed?**

   a. 120mph b. 110mph c. 125mph d. 122.5mph e. 115mph

3) **The motorcycle is restricted to 130mph, how long will it take before the restrictions takes place?**

   a. 12seconds b. 8.5seconds c. 9.5seconds d. 10seconds e. 9seconds

4) Another motorcycle takes 5 seconds to reach 90mph how many seconds is it faster than Alex's motorcycle?

   a. 1second   b. 0.5seconds   c. 1.5seconds   d. 0.75seconds   e. Can't tell

Cafe
Joe's café is a café in Smallingham. His main sellers are the: Full English breakfast, Cheeseburgers and The Joe's special. The café makes a profit of £4 per Full English breakfast, £2.50 per Cheeseburgers and £5.50 per The Joe's special. On average the café sales 8 Full English breakfast, 15 Cheeseburgers and 7 The Joe's special per day

1) Today has been a busy day, he sales 15 Full English breakfast, 21 Cheeseburgers and 10 The Joe's special. How much profit has me made just considering these three items?

   a. £167.50   b. £155.50   c. £160.50   d. £157.50   e. £165.50

2) The owner sources a new supplier of ingredients that increase his profit of £1 per Full English breakfast, £0.50 per Cheeseburgers and £2 per The Joe's special. What is the percentage increase in profit on average per day?

   a. 28%   b. 27%   c. 25%   d. 9.30%   e. 26%

3) What this the ratio of the profit of Full English breakfast, Cheeseburger compared to The Joe's special on average per day?

   a. £32 : £37 : £38.50 b. £15 : £30.50 : £38.50 c. £38.50 : £37.50 : £32 d. £32 : £37.50 : £38.50 e. £37.50 : £32 : £38.50

4) The café excels under new management, now on average the café sales 20 Full English breakfast what is ratio compared to the previous average?

   a. 5:2 b. 2:5 c. 40:8 d. 2:1 e. 2:4

Quantitative Reasoning Answers

QUESTION 1

1) How much a holiday to the Algarve cost through Sun Tours?
d.£1179 - Flights for 2 adults + 3 children = £760. Add hotel price = £1310. Minus 10% = £1179

2) What is the cheapest price he can take his family to Rome for?
a. £1192.50 - With Sun Tours, Flights for 2 adults + 3 children = £750. Add hotel price = £1325. Minus 10% = £1192.50

3) What is the cheapest price he can get return flights to Rome if he takes only his wife?
B. £400 - With London Travel, flights for 2 adults = £400. No cash-back or discount as no hotel booking.

4) What is the difference in price if to go to Barcelona if he booked through Easyfly and Sun and Sand, compared with British Airlines and QuickFind?
e. £35 - Easyfly for 2 adults + 3 children = £590. Add to Sun and Sand hotel = £1220. British Airlines for 2 adults + 3 children = £595. Add to QuickFind Hotel = £1185. Difference is £35.

5) Easyfly are having a 15% sale on flights. What is the new price of flights to take his family to Crete?
a. £824.50 - Easyfly flights for 2 adults + 3 children = £970. Minus 15% = £824.50

6) What is the difference in price if he were to use London Travel for flights and hotels to Barcelona, compared with using London Travel for flights and QuickFind for hotels?
c. £40 - London Travel flights for 2 adults + 3 children = £600. Add London Travel hotel = £1200. Minus cashback = £1150. QuickFind hotel + London Travel Flights = £1190. Difference = £40

7) What is the cheapest price he can take his family on holiday to Crete for?
b.£1377 - Sun Tours flights for 2 adults + 3 children = £980. Add to Sun Tours hotel = £1530. Minus 10% = £1377

8) If Sun Tours reduced their discount to 5%,what would the difference between the old and new price of taking a holiday to the Algarve be?
d. £65.50 - Sun Tours flights for 2 adults + 3 children = £760. Add to hotel = £1310. 5% of £1310 = £65.50

9) What is the difference in price between Algarve and Barcelona if he books completely through London Travel?
c. £5 - Cost of flights to Algarve = £680. Add to hotel = £1205. Minus £50 = £1155. Cost of flights to Barcelona = £600. Add to hotel = £1200. Minus £50 = £1150. Difference = £5

10) What is the cheapest place he can go to with Sun Tours?
c. Barcelona - Flights for 2 adults + 3 children = £620. Add to hotel = £1220. Minus 10% = £1098

QUESTION 2

1) Someone wishes to buy 55 plain white Jumpers. How much will this cost?

b. £151.25 - Cost of 55 is £2.75 each. 55 x £2.75 = £151.25

2) A retailer wishes to buy 50 plain white Jumpers and 100 plain coloured Jumpers. How much will this cost?
a. £480 - Cost of 50 plain white jumpers is £3 each, cost of 100 plain coloured jumpers is £3.30 each. 50 x £3 = £150 + (100 x £3.30) = £480

3) Someone wishes to buy 100 plain white Jumpers with black graphics, and 100 plain white Jumpers with coloured graphics. How much will this cost?
e. £810 - Cost of white jumpers with black graphics is 100 x £3.55. Cost of white jumpers with coloured graphics is 100 x £4.55. Total = £850. The discount is eligible on the total order, which was 200 white Jumpers

4) How much profit can a retailer make on 125 coloured Jumpers, if sold at the recommended price?
c. £775 - Cost of coloured Jumpers is 125 x £3.10 = £387.50. Sold at 125 x £9.30 = £1162.50. Difference is £775

5) A retailer buys 60 plain white Jumpers, and 75 coloured Jumpers with black graphics. He sells most of the items, but has 10 white and 15 coloured Jumpers left over. What was the profit/loss?
d. £751.50
Cost of Jumpers is (60 x £2.75) + (75 x £4.80) = £525. Selling 50 plain white + 60 coloured/black graphic Jumpers = (50 x £8.25) + (60 x £14.40) = £1276.50. Difference is £751.50 profit

6) How much will it cost to buy 300 plain coloured jumpers, half with black graphics and half with coloured graphics?
d. £1470 - 300 coloured jumpers cost 300 x £2.90 = £870. Black graphics (150 x £1.50) + Coloured graphics (150 x £2.50) = £600. Total is £1470

7) A shop buys 200 plain white Jumpers, and 100 plain coloured Jumpers. However the shop goes bankrupt, and can only sell them at 1.5x the value they were bought for. What is the difference in profit made compared with if they were sold at 3x the wholesale price.
e. £1245 - Cost of 200 plain white jumpers (200 x £2.50) + 100 plain coloured jumpers (100 x £3.30) = £830. Selling at normal price would result in £830 x 2 profit = £1660. Selling at new price is £830 x 0.5 = £415. Difference is £1245

8) A retailer sells 200 white Jumpers with coloured graphics for a total of £1500 profit. How much must the retailer have been selling each Jumper for?
a. £10 - Cost of 200 white jumpers is 200 x £2.50 = £500. £1500 + £500 = £2000, so retailer must have sold total of 200 jumpers for £2000. £2000/200 = £10 each

9) What is the cost of buying 60 plain white Jumpers with coloured graphics, and 80 coloured Jumpers with black graphics?
b. £669 - Cost of 60 white jumpers with coloured graphics = 60 x £4.75 = £285. Cost of 80 coloured jumpers with black graphics = 80 x £4.80 = £384. Total = £669

10) The wholesaler places a 10% discount on all orders. What is the difference between buying 75 plain white Jumpers and 75 coloured Jumpers before, compared with now?
c. £45.37 - Before 75 white jumpers (75 x £2.75) + 75 coloured jumpers (75 x £3.30) costs = £453.75. Now, it costs 10% less = £408.38. Difference is £45.37

QUESTION 3

1) If each length is 25m, how much has Kate swum in total?

c. 87,750 - Total lengths = 700 + 700 + 700 + 700 + 710 = 3510. 3510 x 25m = 87,750m

2) If each length is 25m, how much did the group swim altogether in 2010?

e. 73,500 – Total lengths = 770 + 340 + 550 + 580 + 700 = 2,940. 2940 x 25m = 73,500m

3) If the group raised £15,675 in 2008, and they all charged the same per length, how much were they sponsored per length?

e. £5.50 - Total lengths in 2008 = 750 + 300 + 500 + 600 + 700 = 2,850. 15,675/2,850 = sponsorship per length = £5.50

4) What proportion of the total lengths that year did Katie swim in 2009?

a. 0.18 - Total lengths in 2009 = 760 + 320 + 525 + 580 + 700 = 2885. Katie swam 525, so 525/2885 = 0.18

5) If each length is 25m, what was the average amount swum in 2011?

b. 14,775 - Total lengths in 2011 = 780 + 360 + 575 + 540 + 700 = 2,955. Average = 2955/5 = 591 lengths each. 591 x 25m = 14,775m

6) If they each asked for £6 per length in 2012, how much did they raise in total?

d. £17,820 - Total lengths in 2012 = 790 + 360 + 550 + 560 + 710 = 2970 x £6 = £17,820

7) What was the most anyone swam in the whole 5 year period?

a. Duncan - Duncan swam more than anyone else each year, so it must be him.

8) Who swam the least over 5 years?

b. James - James swam less than anyone else each year, so it must be him

9) What was the percentage change in Duncan's total number of lengths from 2010 to 2012?

d. 2.5% - (790 – 770)/790 = 0.0253...x100 = 2.5%

10) If each length is 25m, how much less did Chris swim in 2010 compared with 2012?

c. 500m - In 2010, Chris swam 25 x 580 = 14,500m. In 2012, Chris swam 25 x 560 = 14,000m. The difference is 500m

QUESTION 4

1) What is the difference in price between three small and two large caricatures?

c.£2 - 3 small ones costs 3 x £10 = £30. 2 large ones cost 2 x £16 = £32. Difference is £2

2) A tourist asks Jayden to draw 5 small caricatures for his children, and 3 large ones for him, his wife, and his brother. How much does this cost the tourist in total?

c. £98 - 5 small ones costs 5 x £10 = £50. 3 large ones cost 3 x £16 = £48. Total is £98

3) Another tourist asks Jayden to draw 4 small caricatures and 4 large ones. He decides to tip her 5%. How much does this cost the tourist in total?

a. £109.20 - 4 small ones costs 4 x £10 = £40. 4 large ones costs 4 x £16 = £64. Total = £104. Add 5% = £109.20

4) Jayden uses £2 worth of material for small caricatures, and £3 for large ones. If she draws 20 small and 15 large caricatures, how much profit does she make?

d. £355 - Its costs her (20 x £2) + (15 x £3) in materials = £85. She receives (20 x £10) + (15 x £16) = £440. Difference is £355.

5) Jayden uses £2 worth of material for small caricatures, and £3 for large ones. If she needs to draw 13 small and 11 large caricatures, how much will the material cost?

e. £59 - Cost of small ones is 13 x £2 = £26. Cost of large ones is 11 x £3 = £33. Total is £59

6) Jayden believes that the day will be busy, so raises her prices by £1 for small and £2 for large caricatures. She expects that she will have to draw 30 small and 20 large ones. How much money will she receive?

b. £690 - From the small ones she will receive 30 x £11 = £330. From the large ones she will receive 20 x £18 = £360. Total is £690.

7) Jayden believes that the day will be busy, so raises her prices by £1 for small and £2 for large caricatures. On average, she draws 20 small and 15 large caricatures per day. However, due to her increased price, she only draws 15 small and 10 large caricatures. What is the difference in profit on an average day compared to today?

e. £95 - Profit due to price change is (15 x £11) + (10 x £18) = £345. Average profit is (20 x £10) + (15 x £16) = £440. Difference is £95

8) Jayden decides to pin some examples on a board. A small caricature is 20cm long by 15cm wide. A large caricature is 40cm by 30cm. If she wishes to pin 3 small ones side by side, how wide a board will she need?

a. 45cm - Each small caricature is 15cm wide, so 15 x 3 = 45cm

9) Jayden decides to pin some examples on a board. A small caricature is 20cm long by 15cm wide. A large caricature is 40cm by 30cm. If she decides to pin 3 large ones side by side, and 4 small ones underneath side by side, how big will the board need to be?

b. 60 x 90 - Width of 3 large caricatures is 3 x 30cm = 90cm. Length of one large + one small caricature is 20cm + 40cm = 60cm

10) Jayden gives a 20% discount to her first customer, who orders a large caricature. What will the caricature cost the customer?

d. £12.80 - Large caricature costs £16. £16 x 0.8 = £12.80

QUESTION 5

1) What is the cheapest price value of 2750ml of this product?

c. £42.50 – 500ml is the cheapest, 500 x 5 = 2500ml, £7.50 x 5 = £37.50, 2500ml + 250ml = 2750ml, 250ml = £5, £37.5 + £5 = £42.50

2) Comparing 2 x 250ml bottles to 500ml what is the percentage increase of cost comparing the 250 bottles to the 500ml

b. 33% - 2 x 250ml = 2 x £5 = £10, Difference in price/Price of 500ml bottle = £2.50/£7.50 = 33.3% which is rounded down to 33%

3) A local drug store offer a 2 for 1 offer on the 250ml bottles, how much would you save if you wanted 2000ml of the shampoo?

d. £20 – 2000ml, half is for free. 2000ml/2 = 1000ml. 1000ml/250ml = 4, 4 x £5 = £20

4) Another store sells 360 250ml bottles and 120 500ml bottles, what is the ratio of 250ml to 500ml bottles sold in the store?

c. **3:1** – 250ml bottles: 500ml bottles, 360:120. ÷ both by 120 to get the simplest form, 3:1

1) How long does it take him to reach 150mph?

   b. **11.5 seconds** – 165mph = 0-60 + 60-100 + 100-150 + 150-165. 3 + 3.5 + 5 = 11.5seconds

2) He accelerates for 8 seconds, what is his speed?

   e. **115mph** – 0-60 = 3seconds, 60-100 = 3.5 seconds, 0-100mph = 6.5. What's left over? 8-6.5 = 1.5. The motorcycle accelerates in the 100-150mph range in 10mph per second so 1.5 seconds = 15mph. 100+15 = 115mph

3) The motorcycle is restricted to 130mph , how long will it take before the restrictions kick in? c. **9.5 seconds** - 130mph = 0-60 + 60-100 + 30mph in the 100-150 range. This equals, 3 + 3.5 + 3 = 9.5 seconds

4) Another motorcycle takes 5 seconds to reach 90mph is it faster than Alex's motorcycle?

   e. **Can't tell** – We are only given 0-60 and 60-100 times so we do not know.

1) Today has been a busy day, he sales 15 Full English breakfast, 21 Cheeseburgers and 10 The Joe's special. How much profit has me made just considering these three items? a. **£167.50**

   - 15 x £4 = £60, 21 x £2.50 = £52.50, 10 x £5.50 = £55

   - £60 + £52.50 + £55 = £167.50

2) The owner sources a new supplier of ingredients that increase his profit of £1 per Full English breakfast, £0.50 per Cheeseburgers and £2 per The Joe's special. What is the percentage increase in profit on average per day? b. **27%**

   - Average sales = 8 Full English breakfast, 15 Cheeseburgers, 7 The Joe's special.

   - Old profit = 8 x £4 = £32, 15 x £2.50 = £37.50, 7 x £5.50 = £38.50

   - £32 + £37.50 + £38.50 = £108

   - The new profit values = Old + increase, for example for Full English breakfast £4+£1 = £5

   - New profit = 8 x £5 = £40, 15 x £3 = £45, 7 x £7.50 = £52.50

   - £40 + £45 + £52.50 = £137.50

   - Percentage increase = difference in values/ the comparing value x 100

   - £137.50 - £108 / £108 = 29.5/108 = 0.273 x 100 = 27.3%, rounded down to 27%

3) Using the original profit margins. What is the ratio of the profit of Full English breakfast, Cheeseburger compared to The Joe's special on average per day? d. **£32 : £37.50 : £38.50**

   - Old profit = 8 x £4 = £32, 15 x £2.50 = £37.50, 7 x £5.50 = £38.50

   - = £32 : £37.50 : £38.50

4) The café excels under new management, now on average the café sales 20 Full English breakfast what is this increase compared to the previous average? a. **5:2**

   - 20 : 8 simplifies to 5:2

CHAPTER 5 : ABSTRACT REASONING

ABSTRACT REASONING

Your interpretation of symbols, your planing processes and pattern recognition

This section is the Abstract Reasoning practice question, we recommend you refresh your memory on how to approach this section on pages 24 - 42

What is expected of you?

This part of the subtest assesses your ability to identify patterns among abstract shapes that are placed with several insignificant and distracting shapes. The latter exist to confuse you and could potentially lead you to draw incorrect conclusions. This subtest tests your lateral thinking ability and requires you to evaluate and think about the options critically. You need to be able to quickly identify patterns, rules and trends in a given set of data, and then apply this information to solve the question in front of you.

Candidates have 14 minutes in which 55 questions associated with sets of shapes need to be answered. There are four different item types in the UKCAT (according to the official UKCAT guide 2015).

Type 1. You will be presented with shapes labelled "Set A" and "Set B" in two sets. You will then be required to decide if a test shape belongs in Set A, Set B, or neither.
Type 2. You will have a series of shapes for which you will be required to select which shape is next in the series.
Type 3. You will be presented with a group of shapes and a statement. You will then be asked to select a shape that completes the given statement.
Type 4. These questions are similar to Type 1; but in the option you will have to select if a test shape goes into Set A or Set B.

When you look at each question, ask yourself,

'What is consistent? '
'What information can I eliminate? '
'What is the difference between the shapes in set A to those in set B?'
'What makes this particular shape stand out from the rest? '

Top tips!

1. Don't rush the answer. Look carefully at both sets A and B before trying to identify what the common theme/rule is
2. Don't simply consider each shape within a set, but try and look at an entire set and see what it has to offer (e.g. count the sides of all the shapes in Set A, rather than each shape)
3. Identify the relationship of each shape to the others in a given box for each set and remember there may be more than one rule
4. Simply flag items that you get stuck on, and come back to them at the end of the section, or else you will waste valuable time
5. Use your whiteboard to quickly note down the aspects that you can use as a checklist for each question, e.g. sides, number of shape, colour etc

Abstract Reasoning Questions

Judging from past exams approximately 80-90%of your questions might be in this format

Question 1 - Which set does it belong to? A, B or Neither?

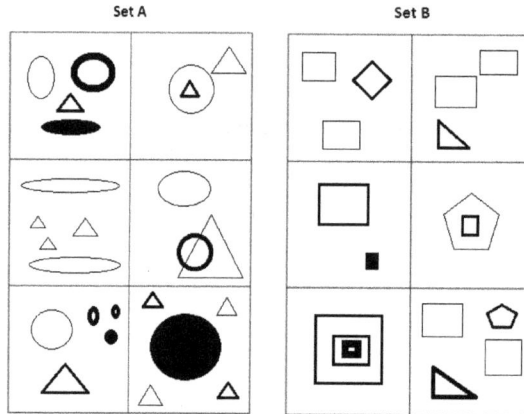

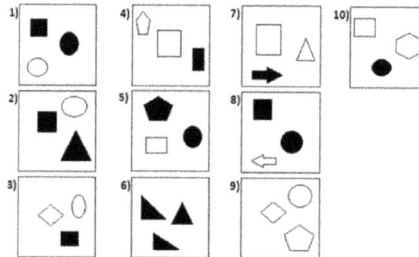

Set A   Set B

Question 2 - Which set does it belong to? A, B or Neither?

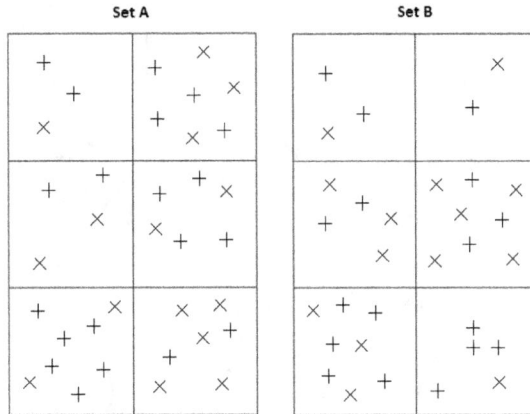

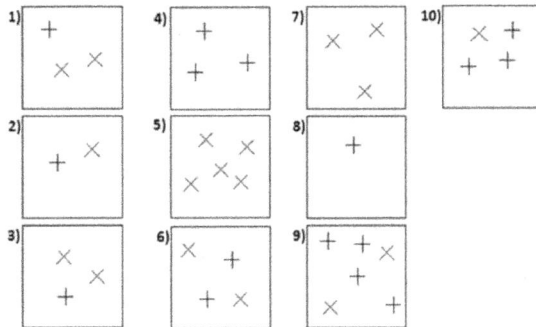

Set A   Set B

1)

4)

7)

10)

2)

5)

8)

3)

6)

9)

Question 3 - Which set does it belong to? A, B or Neither?

Set A   Set B

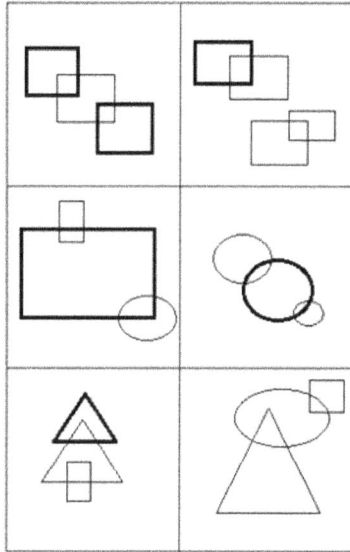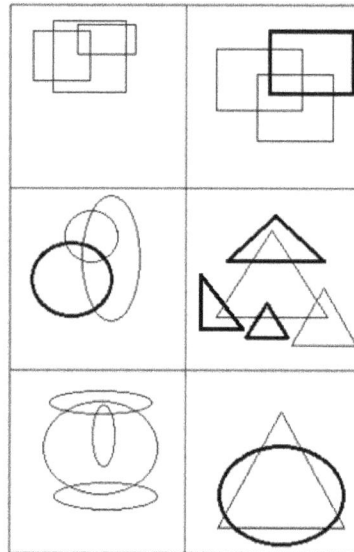

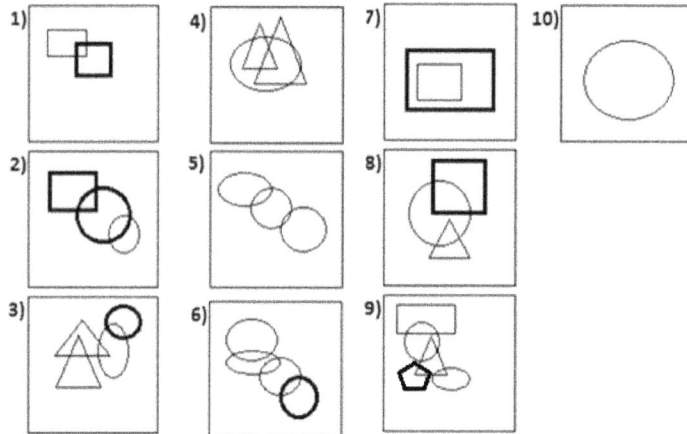

Question 4 - Which set does it belong to? A, B or Neither?

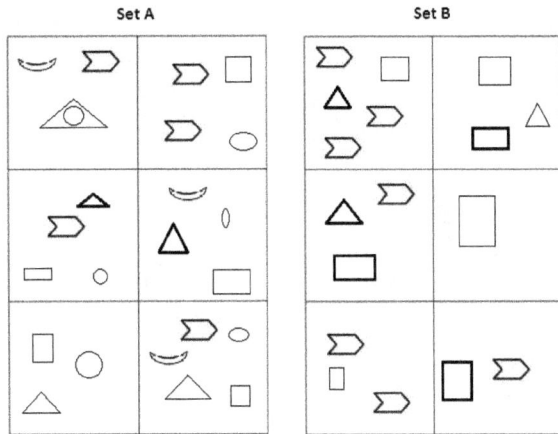

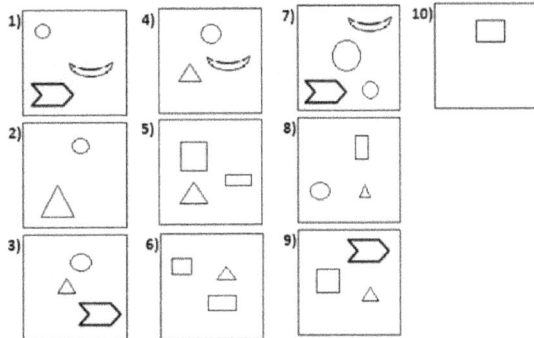

Set A

Set B

Question 5 - Which set does it belong to? A, B or Neither?

Set A   Set B

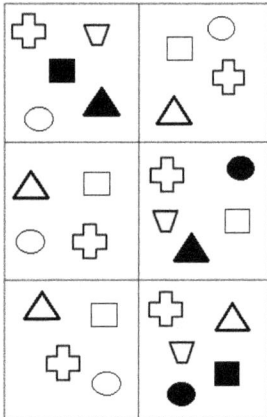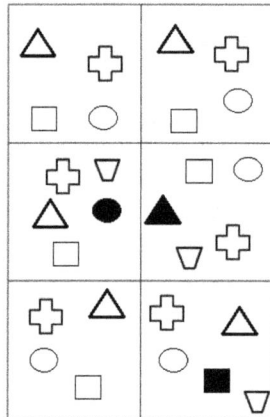

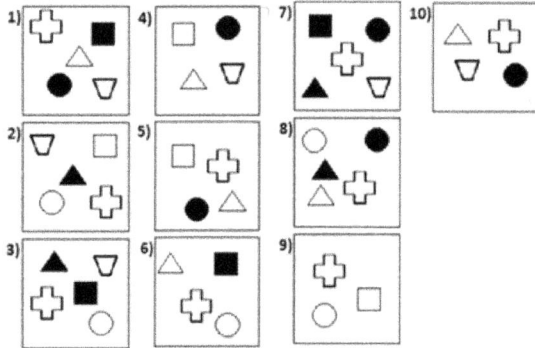

Question 6 - Which set does it belong to? A, B or Neither?

Set A   **Set B**

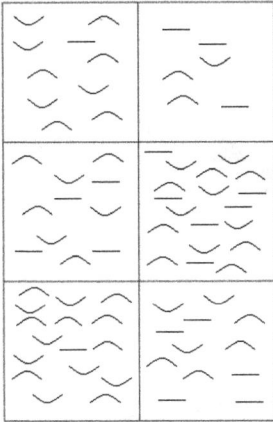 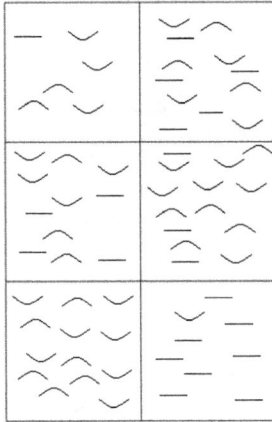

Question 7 - Which box completes the series

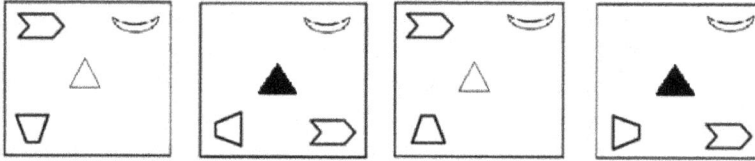

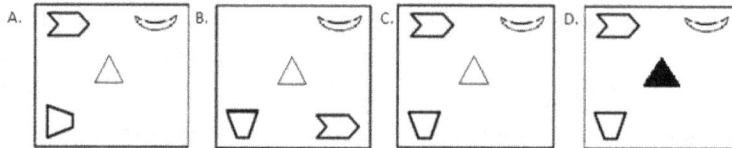

Question 8 - Which box completes the series?

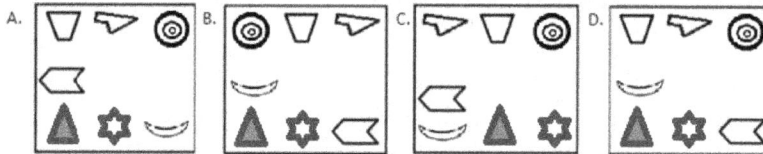

128

Question 9- Which box completes the series?

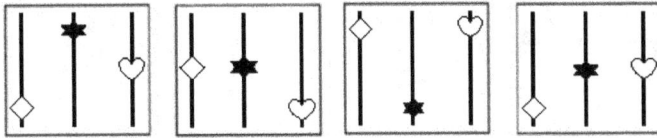

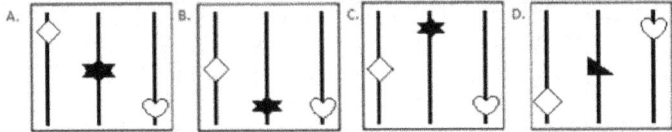

Question 10 - Which box completes the series?

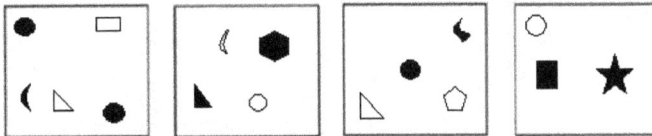

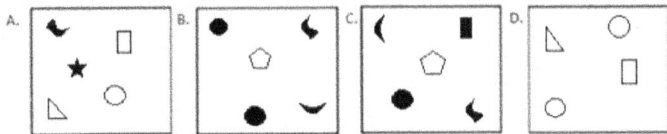

129

Question 11- Which answer completes the statement?

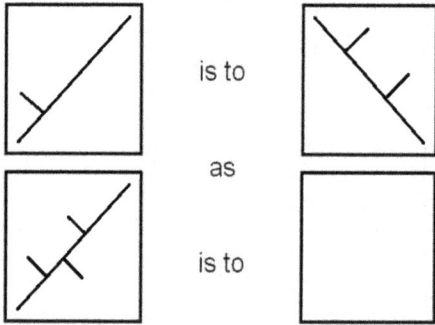

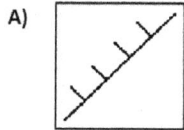

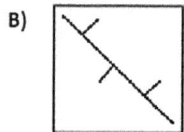

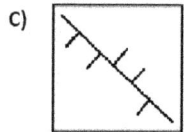

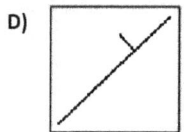

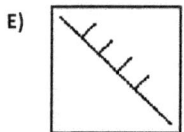

is to

as

is to

A)

B)

C)

D)

E)

Question 12 - Which answer completes the statement?

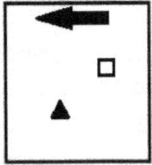 is to

as

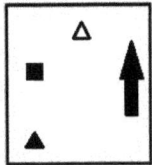 is to

A)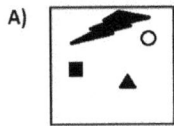

B)

C)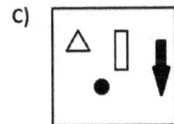

D)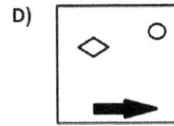

E)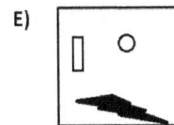

Abstract reasoning Answers

Question 1

Rule: Set A has at least one circle and one triangle, and no other shapes. Set B has only straight sided shapes.

Answers

1) **Neither** – has a four-sided shape and has a circle

2) **Neither** - has a four-sided shape and has a circle

3) **Neither** - has a four-sided shape and has a circle

4) **B** – has only straight sided shapes

5) **Neither** - has a four-sided shape and has a circle

6) **B** – has only straight sided shapes

7) **B** – has only straight sided shapes

8) **Neither** - has a four-sided shape and has a circle

9) **Neither** - has a four-sided shape and has a circle

10) **Neither** - has a four-sided shape and has a circle

Question 2

Rule: Set A has an even number of '+'s. Set B has an odd number of 'x's.

Answers

1) **Neither** – odd number of '+' and even number of 'x's

2) **B** - odd number of 'x'

3) **Neither** – odd number of '+' and even number of 'x's

4) **Neither** – odd number of '+' no 'x'

5) **B** - odd number of 'x's

6) **A** – even number of '+'s and even number of 'x's but this doesn't matter

7) **B** - odd number of 'x'

8) **Neither** - odd number of 'x'

9) **A** - even number of '+'s and even number of 'x's but this doesn't matter

10) **B** - odd number of '+' and odd number of 'x's but this doesn't matter

Question 3

Rule: Both use only a mixture of circles, triangles and four sided shape. Set A has two intersections, Set B has four intersections.

Answers

1) **Neither** – has one intersection

2) **A** – has two intersection

3) **Neither** - has three intersections

4) **Neither** - has five intersections

5) **A** – has two intersection

6) **Neither** - has three intersections

7) **Neither** - has no intersection

8) **A** - has two intersection

9) **Neither** - has four intersections but uses a five sided shape

10) **Neither** - has no intersection

Question 4

Rule: Set A has one circle. Set B has no curved edges.

Answers

1) **A** - has one circle

2) **A** - has one circle

3) **A** - has one circle

4) **A** - has one circle

5) **B** - has no curved edges.

6) **B** - has no curved edges.

7) **Neither** -- has two circles

8) **A** - has one circle

9) **B** - has no curved edges.

10) **B** - has no curved edges.

Question 5

Rule: Both have 4 shapes, Set A has a 5th quadrilateral if two are shaded. Set B has a 5th quadrilateral if one is shaded.

Answers

1) **A** – Has four shapers and a 5th four sided shape if because there are two shaded

2) **B** – Has four shapers and a 5th four sided shape if because there is one shaded

3) **A** – Has four shapers and a 5th four sided shape if because there are two shaded

4) **Neither** – Has four shapes but not a 5th one even though on is shaded

5) **B** – Has four shapers and a 5th four sided shape if because there is one shaded

6) **Neither** – Has four shapes but not a 5th one even though on is shaded

7) **Neither** – Has only three shapes

8) **Neither** - Has four shapers, two shaded and has 5th shape but it is not a four-sided shape

9) **Neither** – Has only three shapes

10) **Neither** – Has four shapes but not a 5th one even though on is shaded

Question 6

Rule: Set A has one more peak than trough, and at least one horizontal line. Set B has one less peak than trough.

Answers

1) **B** - has one less peak than trough.

2) **Neither** – has the same number of peaks and troughs

3) **A** - has one more peak than trough, and at least one horizontal line

4) **Neither**- has one more peak than trough, but no horizontal line

5) **Neither** – has the same number of peaks and troughs

6) **B** - has one less peak than trough.

7) **Neither** – has the same number of peaks and troughs

8) **A** - has one more peak than trough, and at least one horizontal line

9) **Neither** - - has one more peak than trough, but no horizontal line

10) **B** - has one less peak than trough.

Question 7

c. – First thing to take note of is that none of the shapes are changing. The triangle at the centre is changing shade consistently, On and off. In step four the triangle is shaded so it should be unshaded in the completing box. What are the other shapes doing? The crescent shape, Seems to be constantly there are, without any change at the top right hand corner for all four steps of the series so it's safe to presume that it should be present in the bow that completes the series. The trapezium shape, is at that set postion in the bottom left corner but it rotates 90° clockwise in each step regardless of the shade of the triangle. The completing box the trapezium should be on the bottom left corner rotated 90° clockwise from step four. Last but not least the arrow shape is at two positions the top left and the bottom right corner, does the postion change in relation to any other shapes? Yes it does, if the triangle is shaded the arrow is in the bottom right and if unshaded, top left.

Question 8

d. – Similar to the question before the shapes are not changing. The spaces which the shapes occupy are the same, the three in a straight line at the top and an elongated L-configuration at the bottom however, the positions seem to change from step to step. If we look closely the top three shapes move along right to left, while bottom four are moving in a clockwise fashion along the L-shape. The completing box should be the continuation of these movements from step four

Question 9

c. – At first glance you can see there are three lines and three different shapes on these lines, the shapes do not change. They move positions in a fashion that appears to be moving on the lines, but they do know move in the same manner. If you look at each shape individually you can see that the first diamond shape moves up the line. In step 3 – 4, where it reaches the top, it starts again from the bottom. Second shape, the shaded star ✪, moves down the line however in step 3-4 when it reaches the bottom, it starts moving up the line like if it was bouncing off the bottom line. The heart shape starts in the midpoint of the line and like the shaded star moved down the line. However in step 2 -3 when the shape reaches the bottom line like it was the opposite of the diamond shape but under the same rules, it starts again from top. The answer is the continuation of these movements on the line from step four.

Question 10

b. – At first glance you might be overwhelmed by the lack of obvious structure, shapes, spaces, positions, quantity of shapes changing inconsistently. You can spend a lot of time trying to make sense of chaos. A key thing to do is to focus on what is consistent not what is inconsistent. This is a takes practice. The one obvious consistent aspect is that there are always shaded shapes in the boxes. We've eliminated the effect of other shapes due their inconsistently. Most students get stuck at this point, but if you re-call from the breakdown sections, a good way to break it down is look at two steps individually. I f you take steps 1 and 2 one thing you might notice is the shapes that are shaded, in step 1 the circles are shaded but in the 2nd step it isn't. What's going on? If you then look for the circle in step 3 it changes back to shaded, there must be a link, what is it? What does a circle have in common with the other shapes? If you look overall at step 1 again, the shapes that are shaded in are not just circles but shapes without clear defined lines. What happens

to these shapes in step 2? Ah ha, the pattern emerges, the shading alternates from shaded circle shapes to shaded straight lined shapes and so on. In step 4 the shaded shapes are shapes with clear defined lines so the completing box will be of circles and shapes without clearly defined lines. This is a difficult question, do not worry if you didn't get it the first time, the key is to learn and build up from your mistakes and use the steps given to you in the breakdown section

Question 11

Rule: The diagonal line is rotated clockwise by 90 degrees. There is an addition of a branch; all branches face upwards.

Answer : E

Question 12

Rule: The position of the arrow is rotated clockwise by 90 degrees. The arrow is replaced by a lightning symbol. The shaded triangle transformed into an unshaded triangle.

Answer : B

SITUATIONAL JUDGMENT TEST

*Your ethical and moral outlook to see if
you have the qualities to become a good
medical profession*

This section is the Situational Judgment Tests practice question, we recommend you refresh your memory on how to approach this section on pages 43 - 51

What is expected of you?

This subtest encompasses the non-cognitive part of the test. It measures your capacity to understand real world situations and gauges you behaviour while dealing with them. There will be 27 minutes to get through 71 items each of which will have a range of between 3-6 response options. It consists of a series of scenarios with possible actions and considerations. Being non-cognitive, it does not require any prior knowledge or understanding of the scenarios but simply analysing the best course of action for a given scenario.

The first set of questions will require you to rate the appropriateness of a number of options in relation to the given scenario.

When considering how to respond to the scenario, an option is:
- *a very appropriate thing to do* if it applies to at least one aspect (not necessarily all aspects) of the situation
- *appropriate, but not ideal* if it could be done, but is not fundamentally a very good thing to do

- **inappropriate, but not awful** if it should not really be done, but would not be atrocious
- **a very inappropriate thing to do** if it should definitely not be done and would make the situation worse

The response in this case should not be considered as if it were the only thing that would be done. For instance, if a patient is allergic to paracetamol but is given it by accident, there are a number of steps to undertake, which include ascertaining that the patient is alright, evaluating the patient medically etc In this scenario, a response of 'ask the patient if they are ok' should still be judged as appropriate instead of seeing it as the ONLY action that will be taken.

The second set of questions will require you to rate the importance of a number of options in response to a given scenario.

. When considering how to respond to the scenario, an option is:
- **very important** if this is something that is crucial to take into account
- **important** if this is something that is imperative but not crucial to take into account
- **of minor importance** if this is something that could be taken into account, but its significance is questionable
- **not important at all** if this is something that should not be taken into account under any circumstances.

Top tips!

1. It is important to relate your responses to what an individual *should* do, rather than what they may be likely to do.
2. Response options should be considered separately. You should make a judgement as to the appropriateness or importance of a response option independent from the other options presented within the scenario. This is difficult but with practice, you'll learn how to do this.
3. The options provided do not correspond to all possible options for a given scenario. Therefore, what would have ideally been the most appropriate/most important response according to you, may not be present in the given question
4. Don't worry too much about the time frame of the response.
a) Some options may be appropriate/important in the *short term* (i.e. immediately addressing a wrong doing) and some are appropriate/important in the *long term* (discussing the implications of the wrong doing after the event). Consider response options irrelevant of the time frame. A response option may still be an appropriate thing to do even if it is not something that can be done immediately.
1. Take a moment to think before you answer and ensure that you have read the question thoroughly.
a) We advise that you learn the implications of each of the options so that it will be easier for you to answer these questions, for instance, **appropriate, but not ideal** implies that it could be done, but is not fundamentally a very good thing to do etc

1. Karthik is a junior doctor and notices on one of his shifts that there are medications going missing from the supply cupboard. One day he sees another junior doctor, Matthew, putting things from the supply cupboard in his bag

How appropriate are each of the responses by Karthik in this situation?

a. Karthik should report Matthew to the senior doctor on the team

i. A very appropriate thing to do

ii. Appropriate, but not ideal

iii. Inappropriate, but not awful

iv. A very inappropriate thing to do

b. Karthik should quietly pull Matthew aside to speak to him about what he saw

i. A very appropriate thing to do

ii. Appropriate, but not ideal

iii. Inappropriate, but not awful

iv. A very inappropriate thing to do

c. Karthik should immediately confront Matthew in front of all the other staff and patients

i. A very appropriate thing to do

ii. Appropriate, but not ideal

iii. Inappropriate, but not awful

iv. A very inappropriate thing to do

d. Karthik should report Matthew to the GMC and police for stealing prescription drugs

i. A very appropriate thing to do

ii. Appropriate, but not ideal

iii. Inappropriate, but not awful

iv. A very inappropriate thing to do

2. Katie is a medical student. On her A&E placement, she is asked to take bloods from a patient. Katie has never taken blood from a person before, however she has observed doctors taking blood and has practised the procedure several times on a model. As Katie is about to start, the patient asks her is she has done this before.

How appropriate are each of the responses by Katie in this situation?

a. Explain that she has practised taking blood on a model but has not taken it from a patient before and that her supervisor will observe

i. A very appropriate thing to do

ii. Appropriate, but not ideal

iii. Inappropriate, but not awful

iv. A very inappropriate thing to do

b. Tell the patient that she has taken blood before, omitting that this was only on a model

i. A very appropriate thing to do

ii. Appropriate, but not ideal

iii. Inappropriate, but not awful

iv. A very inappropriate thing to do

c. Ask the patient if they would prefer someone else to take their blood

i. A very appropriate thing to do

ii. Appropriate, but not ideal

iii. Inappropriate, but not awful

iv. A very inappropriate thing to do

3. On Monday morning, Sophie the medical student on the surgical ward notices that the consultant is looks very tired and unkempt, which is very unusual for this consultant.

How important to take into account are the following considerations for Sophie when deciding how to respond to the situation?

a. The consultant was on call all weekend and was in theatre all Sunday night

i. Very important

ii. Important

iii. Of minor importance

iv. Not important at all

b. This is Sophie's last week so needs her form signing by the consultant

i. Very important

ii. Important

iii. Of minor importance

iv. Not important at all

c. The consultant doesn't have a theatre list today

i. Very important

ii. Important

iii. Of minor importance

iv. Not important at all

4. Gabby is a first year medical student who has compulsory anatomy practical classes as part of her medical training on Thursday mornings. Gabby went out drinking on the Wednesday evening and wakes up feeling very unwell and still smelling of alcohol.

How appropriate are each of the responses by Gabby in this situation?

a. Tell one of her colleagues that she went out with the previous night, that she is too unwell to attend and ask them to inform the tutor

i. A very appropriate thing to do

ii. Appropriate, but not ideal

iii. Inappropriate, but not awful

iv. A very inappropriate thing to do

b. Just not turn up to the class

i. A very appropriate thing to do

ii. Appropriate, but not ideal

iii. Inappropriate, but not awful

iv. A very inappropriate thing to do

c. Arrive at the class still having not showered and despite feeling unwell

i. A very appropriate thing to do

ii. Appropriate, but not ideal

iii. Inappropriate, but not awful

iv. A very inappropriate thing to do

d. Email the tutor to report her absence and catch up the following day

i. A very appropriate thing to do

ii. Appropriate, but not ideal

iii. Inappropriate, but not awful

iv. A very inappropriate thing to do

5.   Andrew is a medical student who has been sitting in observing a GP in his clinic all week. He has noticed that every morning the GP swallows some tablets from his bag and looks a bit sleepy and spaced out during the day.

How important to take into account are the following considerations for Andrew when deciding how to respond to the situation?

a.   Andrew has seen the GP taking the medication from the medication cupboard

i.   Very important

ii.   Important

iii.   Of minor importance

iv.   Not important at all

b.   Andrew is not sure what the tablets are

i.   Very important

ii.   Important

iii.   Of minor importance

iv.   Not important at all

c.   The GP's daughter went to school with Andrew

i.   Very important

ii.   Important

iii.   Of minor importance

iv.   Not important at all

d.   Andrew knows that the GP it struggling with his marriage

i.   Very important

ii.   Important

iii.   Of minor importance

iv.   Not important at all

6.   Rowan is a medical student. He had completely forgotten about an essay that he was supposed to write and hand in before his next tutorial. He asked his friend Tom is he could look at his for some help. At the tutorial, the supervisor mentioned that both Tom's and Rowan's essays were very similar and did they write them together. Tom suspects that Rowan has copied his essay.

How important to take into account are the following considerations for Tom when deciding how to respond to the situation?

a.   Rowan's grandma died last week

i.   Very important

ii.   Important

iii.   Of minor importance

iv.   Not important at all

b.   Rowan has never asked Tom for help before

i.   Very important

ii.   Important

iii.   Of minor importance

iv.   Not important at all

c.   Rowan has a reputation for not turning up to classes and not doing his work on time

i.   Very important

ii.   Important

iii.   Of minor importance

iv.   Not important at all

7. Amedra notices during an exam that her friend Sarah, who she is sitting next to, has got some writing on her arm and it looks like she is trying to cheat.

How important to take into account are the following considerations for Amedra when deciding how to respond to the situation?

a.   This is only a formative assessment so does not count towards anything

i.   Very important

ii.   Important

iii.   Of minor importance

iv.   Not important at all

b.   Sarah's parents have just separated

i.   Very important

ii.   Important

iii.   Of minor importance

iv.   Not important at all

8. A junior doctor, Sam, is taking blood from a patient who is needle phobic and reluctant to have test. The lab call to say that they won't accept the sample as the blood was in the wrong tube. The nurse in charge of the patient's care handed Sam the blood bottle.

How appropriate are each of the responses by Sam in this situation?

a.   Sam should apologise to the patient, explain about the error and how he will have to redo the blood test

i.   A very appropriate thing to do

ii.   Appropriate, but not ideal

iii.   Inappropriate, but not awful

iv.   A very inappropriate thing to do

b.   On explaining the error to the patient, Sam should blame the nurse for the mix up

i.   A very appropriate thing to do

ii.   Appropriate, but not ideal

iii.   Inappropriate, but not awful

iv.   A very inappropriate thing to do

c.   Sam should shout at the nurse in front of the patient

i.   A very appropriate thing to do

ii.   Appropriate, but not ideal

iii.   Inappropriate, but not awful

iv.   A very inappropriate thing to do

d.   Sam decides that in the future he should double check the equipment he is using before starting a procedure

i.   A very appropriate thing to do

ii.   Appropriate, but not ideal

iii.   Inappropriate, but not awful

iv.   A very inappropriate thing to do

e.   Sam should tell the patient that the consultant has asked for another test so he needs to take another sample

i.   A very appropriate thing to do

ii.   Appropriate, but not ideal

iii.   Inappropriate, but not awful

iv.   A very inappropriate thing to do

9. A patient stops one of the medical students, Gavin, and asks him if he could find out what the results from his scan are. Gavin doesn't know the patient as he is new on the ward but looks at his notes. From reading his notes he sees that the patient has been diagnosed with pancreatic cancer but the doctors are waiting for his family to come in to tell him.

How appropriate are each of the responses by Gavin in this situation?

a. Gavin should tell the patient that the results aren't back yet

i. A very appropriate thing to do

ii. Appropriate, but not ideal

iii. Inappropriate, but not awful

iv. A very inappropriate thing to do

b. Explain the results to the patient as he has practised breaking bad news in a communication skills session

i. A very appropriate thing to do

ii. Appropriate, but not ideal

iii. Inappropriate, but not awful

iv. A very inappropriate thing to do

c. Tell the consultant in charge of the patient's care that the patient has been asking for the results and ask the consultant to speak to the patient

i. A very appropriate thing to do

ii. Appropriate, but not ideal

iii. Inappropriate, but not awful

iv. A very inappropriate thing to do

d. Gavin should tell the patient that he is unable to comment on scan results as he is only a medical student

i. A very appropriate thing to do

ii. Appropriate, but not ideal

iii. Inappropriate, but not awful

iv. A very inappropriate thing to do

10. John is a junior doctor. He was meant to be working the weekend shift but called in to say that he was ill and wouldn't be able to make it into work. Will, one of the other junior doctors that works with John, saw photos of John at the big football match from that weekend on social media.

How appropriate are each of the responses by Will in this situation?

a. Report John to the consultant in charge of him

i. A very appropriate thing to do

ii. Appropriate, but not ideal

iii. Inappropriate, but not awful

iv. A very inappropriate thing to do

b. Ignore it

i. A very appropriate thing to do

ii. Appropriate, but not ideal

iii. Inappropriate, but not awful

iv. A very inappropriate thing to do

c. On Monday ask John if he is feeling better

i. A very appropriate thing to do

ii. Appropriate, but not ideal

iii. Inappropriate, but not awful

iv. A very inappropriate thing to do

d. Ask John why he was able to attend the football match if he was too ill to work

i. A very appropriate thing to do

ii. Appropriate, but not ideal

iii. Inappropriate, but not awful

iv. A very inappropriate thing to do

e. Wait and see if it happens again

i. A very appropriate thing to do

ii. Appropriate, but not ideal

iii.   Inappropriate, but not awful

iv.   A very inappropriate thing to do

11.   Hassal is a junior doctor. Every afternoon she leaves Maria, another junior doctor, to do all the boring paperwork on the ward whilst she teaches the medical students.

How appropriate are each of the responses by Maria in this situation?

a.   Tell the med students they are too busy to teach

i.   A very appropriate thing to do

ii.   Appropriate, but not ideal

iii.   Inappropriate, but not awful

iv.   A very inappropriate thing to do

b.   Tell the consultant that Hassal is not doing her fair share of the work

i.   A very appropriate thing to do

ii.   Appropriate, but not ideal

iii.   Inappropriate, but not awful

iv.   A very inappropriate thing to do

c.   Talk to Hassal about alternating who teaches the students and who does the paperwork

i.   A very appropriate thing to do

ii.   Appropriate, but not ideal

iii.   Inappropriate, but not awful

iv.   A very inappropriate thing to do

d.   Tell Hassal that she doesn't want to be left to do all the paperwork

i.   A very appropriate thing to do

ii.   Appropriate, but not ideal

iii.   Inappropriate, but not awful

iv.   A very inappropriate thing to do

12.   Sophie and Hannah are part of a group of students that need to do a group presentation as part of their medical studies. They are all meant to come up with ideas and split the work between them. Sophie has noticed that Hannah doesn't seem to be contributing to the work and is sitting very quietly in the corner.

How appropriate are each of the responses by Sophie in this situation?

a.   Ask everyone in the group to present their ideas to the rest of the group

i.   A very appropriate thing to do

ii.   Appropriate, but not ideal

iii.   Inappropriate, but not awful

iv.   A very inappropriate thing to do

b.   Call Hannah out for not pulling her weight in front of the rest of the group

i.   A very appropriate thing to do

ii.   Appropriate, but not ideal

iii.   Inappropriate, but not awful

iv.   A very inappropriate thing to do

c.   Privately mention to Hannah that she doesn't seem to be doing her fair share of the work, and find out if Sophie can help her in any way

i.   A very appropriate thing to do

ii.   Appropriate, but not ideal

iii.   Inappropriate, but not awful

iv.   A very inappropriate thing to do

d.   Report Hannah to the tutor in charge of the presentation for not contributing to the assignment

i.   A very appropriate thing to do

ii.   Appropriate, but not ideal

iii.   Inappropriate, but not awful

iv.   A very inappropriate thing to do

13. Sally is a medical student on placement at a GP. She notices that one of her friends from university (Anna) is sitting in the waiting room, but Anna has not seen her.

How appropriate are each of the responses by Sally in this situation?

a. Ask Anna why she was seeing her doctor

i. A very appropriate thing to do

ii. Appropriate, but not ideal

iii. Inappropriate, but not awful

iv. A very inappropriate thing to do

b. Ask the GP why Anna had come into the practice

i. A very appropriate thing to do

ii. Appropriate, but not ideal

iii. Inappropriate, but not awful

iv. A very inappropriate thing to do

c. Look up Anna's notes on the system

i. A very appropriate thing to do

ii. Appropriate, but not ideal

iii. Inappropriate, but not awful

iv. A very inappropriate thing to do

d. Pretend she didn't see Anna, unless Anna mentions it

i. A very appropriate thing to do

ii. Appropriate, but not ideal

iii. Inappropriate, but not awful

iv. A very inappropriate thing to do

14. Ed is a patient that has been waiting a long time for an operation. He is very anxious about the procedure and has been psyching himself up for it for a while. Katie is one of the junior doctors working with the surgical team and has been told by her consultant that they are going to have to cancel Ed's operation as they have no beds free today and that they will try and do it first thing the next day. The consultant has asked Katie to tell Ed. Ed's operation is not urgent so he will not be harmed waiting another day.

How appropriate are each of the responses by Katie in this situation?

a. Ask the medical student to tell the patient

i. A very appropriate thing to do

ii. Appropriate, but not ideal

iii. Inappropriate, but not awful

iv. A very inappropriate thing to do

b. Explain the reasons why the operation has been cancelled and that they will try their best to do it first thing tomorrow

i. A very appropriate thing to do

ii. Appropriate, but not ideal

iii. Inappropriate, but not awful

iv. A very inappropriate thing to do

c. Explain to the Ed that waiting another day will not alter his safety

i. A very appropriate thing to do

ii. Appropriate, but not ideal

iii. Inappropriate, but not awful

iv. A very inappropriate thing to do

d. Tell him that she is too busy to answer any questions he has now and that she will speak to him properly tomorrow

i. A very appropriate thing to do

ii. Appropriate, but not ideal

iii. Inappropriate, but not awful

iv. A very inappropriate thing to do

e.   Promise Ed she will speak to the consultant and make him do his operation today

i.   A very appropriate thing to do

ii.   Appropriate, but not ideal

iii.   Inappropriate, but not awful

iv.   A very inappropriate thing to do

15.   Kevin and Radhika are medical students who are both under the same consultant. They are both sitting in on consultations in clinic when Radhika notices that Kevin is using his phone whilst the consultation is going one.

How important to take into account are the following considerations for Radhika when deciding how to respond to the situation?

a.   The patient has noticed and looks frustrated but the consultant hasn't seen.

i.   Very important

ii.   Important

iii.   Of minor importance

iv.   Not important at all

b.   The patient and consultant haven't seen Kevin on his phone

i.   Very important

ii.   Important

iii.   Of minor importance

iv.   Not important at all

c.   Kevin is texting his family about a family emergency at home

i.   Very important

ii.   Important

iii.   Of minor importance

iv.   Not important at all

d.   Kevin is using his phone to look up information about the condition that the patient suffers from

i.   Very important

ii.   Important

iii.   Of minor importance

iv.   Not important at all

16.   A new technology system has been installed in the hospital where Dr Woods is working. He doesn't like using the new systems and ways of doing things now that this has been installed so he continues to use the old methods. One of the other doctors complains to Dr Woods about the difficulties caused by him not using the new system.

How appropriate are each of the responses by Dr Woods in this situation?

a.   Apologise to the other doctor and ask to be shown how to use the new system

i.   A very appropriate thing to do

ii.   Appropriate, but not ideal

iii.   Inappropriate, but not awful

iv.   A very inappropriate thing to do

b.   Tell the other doctor that he will continue to use the old system as that it takes him 3 times longer to use the new system so he can see more patients not using it

i.   A very appropriate thing to do

ii.   Appropriate, but not ideal

iii.   Inappropriate, but not awful

iv.   A very inappropriate thing to do

c.   Tell the other doctor that he is retiring in a year so he doesn't see the point in trying to learn how to use the new system

i.   A very appropriate thing to do

ii.   Appropriate, but not ideal

iii.   Inappropriate, but not awful

iv.   A very inappropriate thing to do

17. Jen is a junior doctor working at a GP. She is just about to take the next patient into the consulting room when she notices a young toddler by herself crying out for her mum.

How appropriate are each of the responses by Jen in this situation?

a. Ask the receptionist to look after the toddler until the mother appears

i. A very appropriate thing to do

ii. Appropriate, but not ideal

iii. Inappropriate, but not awful

iv. A very inappropriate thing to do

b. Comfort the toddler and reassure her that she will find her mother

i. A very appropriate thing to do

ii. Appropriate, but not ideal

iii. Inappropriate, but not awful

iv. A very inappropriate thing to do

c. Ask the patient to wait whilst she finds the toddler's mother and then come back and see the patient next.

i. A very appropriate thing to do

ii. Appropriate, but not ideal

iii. Inappropriate, but not awful

iv. A very inappropriate thing to do

d. Distract the toddler with toys whilst she sees the next patient

i. A very appropriate thing to do

ii. Appropriate, but not ideal

iii. Inappropriate, but not awful

iv. A very inappropriate thing to do

e. Pretend she didn't see the toddler crying

i. A very appropriate thing to do

ii. Appropriate, but not ideal

iii. Inappropriate, but not awful

iv. A very inappropriate thing to do

18. A medical student, Sophie, sees that one of her friends from medical school has posted a picture of an x-ray from a patient on social media with the caption "an interesting case I saw in the hospital today. Great case to learn from". It also had a brief description of the history from the patient, which was anonymised. However the X-ray had the patient's hospital number on it.

How important to take into account are the following considerations for Sophie when deciding how to respond to the situation?

a. The identity of the hospital has not been revealed

i. Very important

ii. Important

iii. Of minor importance

iv. Not important at all

b. The student had not intended to disclose any identifiable information

i. Very important

ii. Important

iii. Of minor importance

iv. Not important at all

c. Negative consequences for the patient as a result of posting this

i. Very important

ii. Important

iii. Of minor importance

iv. Not important at all

d. The patient has given consent for it to be used for this purpose

i. Very important

ii. Important

iii. Of minor importance

iv. Not important at all

e.   The condition is very uncommon and a good learning point for all doctors

i.   Very important

ii.   Important

iii.   Of minor importance

iv.   Not important at all

19.   Mina is a medical student. She hears two junior doctors talking loudly about a patient in the hospital lift.

How important to take into account are the following considerations for Radhika when deciding how to respond to the situation?

a.   There are other members of the public in the lift

i.   Very important

ii.   Important

iii.   Of minor importance

iv.   Not important at all

b.   The doctors do not mention the patient's name

i.   Very important

ii.   Important

iii.   Of minor importance

iv.   Not important at all

c.   Mina doesn't know the patient that they are talking about

i.   Very important

ii.   Important

iii.   Of minor importance

iv.   Not important at all

20.   Bill is a medical student. On his first week of placement he is stuck in theatre helping with a case over a teaching session. The next week, he is ill so cannot attend the teaching session. How appropriate are the following responses of Bill in dealing with the situation.

How appropriate are each of the responses by Bill in this situation?

a.   Not attend any more teaching sessions as the tutor won't notice that he is meant to be there

i.   A very appropriate thing to do

ii.   Appropriate, but not ideal

iii.   Inappropriate, but not awful

iv.   A very inappropriate thing to do

b.   Apologise to the tutor about not attending for the previous 2 weeks and say that he will catch up on the work

i.   A very appropriate thing to do

ii.   Appropriate, but not ideal

iii.   Inappropriate, but not awful

iv.   A very inappropriate thing to do

c.   Get his friends to explain why he has not shown up to the sessions

i.   A very appropriate thing to do

ii.   Appropriate, but not ideal

iii.   Inappropriate, but not awful

iv.   A very inappropriate thing to do

d.   Catch up on the work he has missed and join in next week

i.   A very appropriate thing to do

ii.   Appropriate, but not ideal

iii.   Inappropriate, but not awful

iv.   A very inappropriate thing to do

21.   A GP walks into the waiting room of the surgery that she works in and is approached by a patient that she does not know. The patient starts shouting at her that he has been waiting for hours and that this place is a shambles and that it is unacceptable making people wait so long for an appointment that they booked weeks ago.

How appropriate are each of the responses by the GP in this situation?

a.   Ask one of the reception staff to find out when the patient will be seen

i.   A very appropriate thing to do

ii.   Appropriate, but not ideal

iii.   Inappropriate, but not awful

iv.   A very inappropriate thing to do

b.   Invite the patient to sit down and have a chat with him

i.   A very appropriate thing to do

ii.   Appropriate, but not ideal

iii.   Inappropriate, but not awful

iv.   A very inappropriate thing to do

c.   Ask the patient not to shout, and explain his concerns to the GP

i.   A very appropriate thing to do

ii.   Appropriate, but not ideal

iii.   Inappropriate, but not awful

iv.   A very inappropriate thing to do

d.   Ignore the patient and continue with her work

i.   A very appropriate thing to do

ii.   Appropriate, but not ideal

iii.   Inappropriate, but not awful

iv.   A very inappropriate thing to do

e.   Try and find out what the delay is and try to explain any reasons for it

i.   A very appropriate thing to do

ii.   Appropriate, but not ideal

iii.   Inappropriate, but not awful

iv.   A very inappropriate thing to do

22.   Adam is a medical student who has signed up to a shift in A&E on a Saturday evening. It is compulsory for their course that they must attend a shift at the weekend but they can select which one. After having signed up, Adam realises that he has his Grandfather's 80th birthday celebrations that weekend which he does not want to miss

How appropriate are each of the responses by Adam in this situation?

a.   Swap with another student to a different shift and tell the consultant in charge of the rotation

i.   A very appropriate thing to do

ii.   Appropriate, but not ideal

iii.   Inappropriate, but not awful

iv.   A very inappropriate thing to do

b.   Make excuses as to why you can't make it

i.   A very appropriate thing to do

ii.   Appropriate, but not ideal

iii.   Inappropriate, but not awful

iv.   A very inappropriate thing to do

c.   Pretend he is ill on Saturday so cannot come in for his shift

i.   A very appropriate thing to do

ii.   Appropriate, but not ideal

iii.   Inappropriate, but not awful

iv.   A very inappropriate thing to do

d.   Explain to the consultant in charge that he has this clash and ask if he could come on a different Saturday night to do the shift instead.

i.   A very appropriate thing to do

ii.   Appropriate, but not ideal

iii.   Inappropriate, but not awful

iv.   A very inappropriate thing to do

e.   Get one of the other students working on Saturday to explain why he hasn't turned up

i.   A very appropriate thing to do

ii.   Appropriate, but not ideal

iii.   Inappropriate, but not awful

iv.   A very inappropriate thing to do

23.   Sally and Ian are both medical students placed on the same ward. Ian is always late arriving in the morning for the ward round or teaching. This is starting to annoy Sally, as she always has to explain to the doctors that he is running late again.

How important to take into account are the following considerations for Sally when deciding how to respond to the situation?

a.   Ian lives 30 minutes away from the hospital and there is always traffic

i.   Very important

ii.   Important

iii.   Of minor importance

iv.   Not important at all

b.   The medical school has a code of conduct that states that tardiness is not professional

i.   Very important

ii.   Important

iii.   Of minor importance

iv.   Not important at all

c.   Ian works very hard once he has arrived

i.   Very important

ii.   Important

iii.   Of minor importance

iv.   Not important at all

d.   Ian has permission to drop his child off at school before arriving and stays late

i.   Very important

ii.   Important

iii.   Of minor importance

iv.   Not important at all

e.   Ian is her best friends boyfriend

i.   Very important

ii.   Important

iii.   Of minor importance

iv.   Not important at all

24.   **Angus is a junior doctor who is wearing a watch on the ward. The infection control nurse sees and asks him to remove it and not wear it again in clinical areas as it contravenes the bare below the elbow rules. The next day, Ben, the medical student on the ward, sees Angus wearing his watch again.**

How important to take into account are the following considerations for Ben when deciding how to respond to the situation?

a.   Angus is new and hasn't had his induction yet

i.   Very important

ii.   Important

iii.   Of minor importance

iv.   Not important at all

b.   Angus also doesn't wash his hands between patients

i.   Very important

ii.   Important

iii.   Of minor importance

iv.   Not important at all

c.   Everyone has a responsibility to ensure that infection control protocols are followed

i.   Very important

ii.   Important

iii.   Of minor importance

iv.   Not important at all

d.   They have all just had a lecture by the infection control team on the ward

i.   Very important

ii.   Important

iii.   Of minor importance

iv.   Not important at all

25. **Ed is a medical student who has been asked by one of the doctors to take blood. The doctor gets the equipment ready for Ed to use. Just as Ed is about to start he notices there aren't any gloves. He asks the doctor for gloves. The doctor responds by saying you don't need to use gloves. Ed feels uncomfortable because he has been told to always wear gloves when taking blood from a patient.**

How important to take into account are the following considerations for Ed when deciding how to respond to the situation?

a.   The medical school say that they should always wear gloves

i.   Very important

ii.   Important

iii.   Of minor importance

iv.   Not important at all

b.   Other doctors don't wear gloves

i.   Very important

ii.   Important

iii.   Of minor importance

iv.   Not important at all

c.   The patient doesn't mind

i.   Very important

ii.   Important

iii.   Of minor importance

iv.   Not important at all

d.   Ed feels uncomfortable taking blood without gloves

i.   Very important

ii.   Important

iii.   Of minor importance

iv.   Not important at all

e.   The result is needed urgently as the patient is going to theatre

i.   Very important

ii.   Important

iii.   Of minor importance

iv.   Not important at all

26.   Emma is a medical student taking a history from a patient in a GP. The patient mentions that they have been put on a new medication and they were wondering why and what the side effects of it might be. Emma has never heard of the drug before.

How appropriate are each of the responses by Emma in this situation?

a.   Google the drug and then answer the patient's questions

i.   A very appropriate thing to do

ii.   Appropriate, but not ideal

iii.   Inappropriate, but not awful

iv.   A very inappropriate thing to do

b.   Ask the patient to speak to his doctor about this

i.   A very appropriate thing to do

ii.   Appropriate, but not ideal

iii.   Inappropriate, but not awful

iv.   A very inappropriate thing to do

c.   Tell the patient that she do not know much about the drug

i.   A very appropriate thing to do

ii.   Appropriate, but not ideal

iii.   Inappropriate, but not awful

iv.   A very inappropriate thing to do

27.   John is a junior doctor. At the end of the day he asks his colleague Matt to finish off all the paperwork, investigation requests and discharge letters, so that he can leave early.

How important to take into account are the following considerations for Matt when deciding how to respond to the situation?

a.   John has been asking Matt to do this everyday

i.   Very important

ii.   Important

iii.   Of minor importance

iv.   Not important at all

b.   John has a doctors appointment that he has asked for permission to leave early for

i.   Very important

ii.   Important

iii.   Of minor importance

iv.   Not important at all

c.   John produced a list of tasks to be done in order of priority

i.   Very important

ii.   Important

iii.   Of minor importance

iv.   Not important at all

d.   John and Matt don't get on

i.   Very important

ii.   Important

iii.   Of minor importance

iv.   Not important at all

28.   Lucy is a junior doctor. She is on social media one day when a former patient that she recognises contacts her to ask her out on a date.

How appropriate are each of the responses by Lucy in this situation?

a.   Ignore the request

i.   A very appropriate thing to do

ii.   Appropriate, but not ideal

iii.   Inappropriate, but not awful

iv.   A very inappropriate thing to do

b.   Block the patient from contacting her

i.   A very appropriate thing to do

ii.   Appropriate, but not ideal

iii.   Inappropriate, but not awful

iv.   A very inappropriate thing to do

c.   Accepting his request as he is no longer a patient of hers

i.   A very appropriate thing to do

ii.   Appropriate, but not ideal

iii.   Inappropriate, but not awful

iv.   A very inappropriate thing to do

d.   Explain to the patient that it would be inappropriate for them to go on a date

i.   A very appropriate thing to do

ii.   Appropriate, but not ideal

iii.   Inappropriate, but not awful

iv.   A very inappropriate thing to do

29.   Miriam and Luke are medical students paired on the ward together. Miriam notices that Luke always looks as though he hasn't brushed his hair and that he often looks scruffy.

How important to take into account are the following considerations for Miriam when deciding how to respond to the situation?

a.   No one else has mentioned anything to Luke

i.   Very important

ii.   Important

iii.   Of minor importance

iv.   Not important at all

b.   The medical school gives strict guidelines about appearance on the wards

i.   Very important

ii.   Important

iii.   Of minor importance

iv.   Not important at all

c.   Luke's parents have just split up

i.   Very important

ii.   Important

iii.   Of minor importance

iv.   Not important at all

d.   The students have signed a code of conduct that includes making sure that they are dressed appropriately for the wards

i.   Very important

ii.   Important

iii.   Of minor importance

iv.   Not important at all

e.   Miriam knows that Luke struggles financially

i.   Very important

ii.   Important

iii.   Of minor importance

iv.   Not important at all

30.   A medical student Felicity hears a group of other students discussing their weekend activities at the nurses station on the ward

How appropriate are each of the responses by Felicity in this situation?

a.   Ignore them as long as they aren't talking too loudly

i.   A very appropriate thing to do

ii.   Appropriate, but not ideal

iii.   Inappropriate, but not awful

iv.   A very inappropriate thing to do

b.   Join in

i.   A very appropriate thing to do

ii.   Appropriate, but not ideal

iii.   Inappropriate, but not awful

iv.   A very inappropriate thing to do

c.   Ask them to discuss this in a more appropriate place

i.   A very appropriate thing to do

ii.   Appropriate, but not ideal

iii.   Inappropriate, but not awful

iv.   A very inappropriate thing to do

31.   Yoseph is a junior doctor at the ward handover, about to start a night shift. Josefine, the junior working the day shift, asks him if he can go and see one of her patients urgently because she has to rush off to a meeting. Yoseph knows that Josefine has difficult handwriting to read and worries about not understanding the previous notes that she has written.

How appropriate are each of the responses by Yoseph in this situation?

a.   Ask the ward clerk to try and read them

i.   A very appropriate thing to do

ii.   Appropriate, but not ideal

iii.   Inappropriate, but not awful

iv.   A very inappropriate thing to do

b.   Ask Josefine to give a quick verbal summary before she leaves

i.   A very appropriate thing to do

ii.   Appropriate, but not ideal

iii.   Inappropriate, but not awful

iv.   A very inappropriate thing to do

c.   Try to work it out and if he can't restart from the beginning

i.   A very appropriate thing to do

ii.   Appropriate, but not ideal

iii.   Inappropriate, but not awful

iv.   A very inappropriate thing to do

d.   Ask another doctor is go and see the patient who may be able to understand better

i.   A very appropriate thing to do

ii.   Appropriate, but not ideal

iii.   Inappropriate, but not awful

iv.   A very inappropriate thing to do

32. Vicky is a trainee surgeon who is not feeling very well. She is considering going home as she feels that she would have difficulty performing the tasks of the day but is worried about leaving her colleagues in the lurch.

How important to take into account are the following considerations for Vicky when deciding how to respond to the situation?

a. She has a whole list of operations to do that afternoon

i. Very important

ii. Important

iii. Of minor importance

iv. Not important at all

b. She only has paperwork to do in the afternoon

i. Very important

ii. Important

iii. Of minor importance

iv. Not important at all

c. Other colleagues have left in similar circumstances

i. Very important

ii. Important

iii. Of minor importance

iv. Not important at all

d. She has already discussed this with her team and produced a list of things that still need to be done

i. Very important

ii. Important

iii. Of minor importance

iv. Not important at all

e. There isn't another doctor on call to take over her work and all the others are in surgery

i. Very important

ii. Important

iii. Of minor importance

iv. Not important at all

33. Arjun is a junior doctor having to consent a patient for procedure. The patient is alert but not responding verbally to Arjun's questions. She seems to be nodding and smiling but he's not sure whether to take that as consent or not.

How appropriate are each of the responses by Arjun in this situation?

a. Check whether the patient speaks English

i. A very appropriate thing to do

ii. Appropriate, but not ideal

iii. Inappropriate, but not awful

iv. A very inappropriate thing to do

b. Go ahead with the procedure as it is only minor

i. A very appropriate thing to do

ii. Appropriate, but not ideal

iii. Inappropriate, but not awful

iv. A very inappropriate thing to do

c. See if the patient seems to understand better if the information if written down

i. A very appropriate thing to do

ii. Appropriate, but not ideal

iii. Inappropriate, but not awful

iv. A very inappropriate thing to do

d. Wait for the family to come in to consent the patient

i. A very appropriate thing to do

ii. Appropriate, but not ideal

iii. Inappropriate, but not awful

iv. A very inappropriate thing to do

e.   Go and seek advice from a senior colleague as to the best approach

i.   A very appropriate thing to do

ii.   Appropriate, but not ideal

iii.   Inappropriate, but not awful

iv.   A very inappropriate thing to do

34.   Ian is a medical student who is examining a patient on a ward when the patient asks to speak to the consultant in charge of his care regarding his treatment plan. Ian knows that the consultant is away today on a conference.

How appropriate are each of the responses by Ian in this situation?

a.   Tell the patient that it won't be possible as everyone is too busy

i.   A very appropriate thing to do

ii.   Appropriate, but not ideal

iii.   Inappropriate, but not awful

iv.   A very inappropriate thing to do

b.   Ian should try and answer the patients questions

i.   A very appropriate thing to do

ii.   Appropriate, but not ideal

iii.   Inappropriate, but not awful

iv.   A very inappropriate thing to do

c.   Explain to the patient that the consultant is away and will be back tomorrow and could speak to him then

i.   A very appropriate thing to do

ii.   Appropriate, but not ideal

iii.   Inappropriate, but not awful

iv.   A very inappropriate thing to do

d.   Ask another senior doctor to come and speak to the patient and try and answer his questions

i.   A very appropriate thing to do

ii.   Appropriate, but not ideal

iii.   Inappropriate, but not awful

iv.   A very inappropriate thing to do

e.   Tell the junior doctor in charge of the patient and hope he sorts it out

i.   A very appropriate thing to do

ii.   Appropriate, but not ideal

iii.   Inappropriate, but not awful

iv.   A very inappropriate thing to do

35.   Laurence is a junior doctor. Whilst on the ward round he remembers that he has forgotten to order a chest X-ray for the next patient that the consultant asked him to do yesterday as a non-urgent request. He knows that the consultant will ask today about the results of the x-ray

How appropriate are each of the responses by Laurence in this situation?

a.   Pretend he has ordered it and they are delayed in radiology

i.   A very appropriate thing to do

ii.   Appropriate, but not ideal

iii.   Inappropriate, but not awful

iv.   A very inappropriate thing to do

b.   Apologise to the consultant before the reach the patient and order it as soon as possible

i.   A very appropriate thing to do

ii.   Appropriate, but not ideal

iii.   Inappropriate, but not awful

iv.   A very inappropriate thing to do

c.   Blame another doctor for not doing it

i.   A very appropriate thing to do

ii.   Appropriate, but not ideal

iii.   Inappropriate, but not awful

iv.   A very inappropriate thing to do

d.   Make excuses as to why he didn't do it

i.   A very appropriate thing to do

ii.   Appropriate, but not ideal

iii.   Inappropriate, but not awful

iv.   A very inappropriate thing to do

e.   Explain to the patient that it doesn't need to be done urgently but they will try and get it done as soon as possible today

i.   A very appropriate thing to do

ii.   Appropriate, but not ideal

iii.   Inappropriate, but not awful

iv.   A very inappropriate thing to do

36.   Sophie is a junior doctor on her paediatrics rotation. She is doing a consultation with a 6- year old girl. During the examination of the girl's chest the carer steps out of the room to answer and phone call. When listening to her chest, Sophie notices that there are bruises on the girl under her clothes. The child seems quiet and reserved and seems upset that Sophie has noticed these.

How appropriate are each of the responses by Sophie in this situation?

a.   Ask the child what happened

i.   A very appropriate thing to do

ii.   Appropriate, but not ideal

iii.   Inappropriate, but not awful

iv.   A very inappropriate thing to do

b.   Ask the carer for consent to examine the bruises on the child

i.   A very appropriate thing to do

ii.   Appropriate, but not ideal

iii.   Inappropriate, but not awful

iv.   A very inappropriate thing to do

c.   Speak to the carer outside the consulting room about the

cause

i.   A very appropriate thing to do

ii.   Appropriate, but not ideal

iii.   Inappropriate, but not awful

iv.   A very inappropriate thing to do

d.   Ignore the bruises

i.   A very appropriate thing to do

ii.   Appropriate, but not ideal

iii.   Inappropriate, but not awful

iv.   A very inappropriate thing to do

e.   Get advice from a senior colleague about what to do

i.   A very appropriate thing to do

ii.   Appropriate, but not ideal

iii.   Inappropriate, but not awful

iv.   A very inappropriate thing to do

37. Alan and Tom are both medical students. They were at the same party at the weekend. Early in the evening, Alan heard Tom and some of his friends talking about taking recreational drugs and then later noticed that Tom seemed to be high.

How important to take into account are the following considerations for Alan when deciding how to respond to the situation?

a. Medical school has a strict policy about taking recreational drugs

i. Very important

ii. Important

iii. Of minor importance

iv. Not important at all

b. The party was at the weekend, so Tom wont have been going into the hospital under the influence

i. Very important

ii. Important

iii. Of minor importance

iv. Not important at all

c. It is an illegal activity

i. Very important

ii. Important

iii. Of minor importance

iv. Not important at all

d. Tom doesn't have a reputation for doing this sort of thing

i. Very important

ii. Important

iii. Of minor importance

iv. Not important at all

e. Alan wasn't 100% sure that he was correct in what he saw

i. Very important

ii. Important

iii. Of minor importance

iv. Not important at all

38. Whilst Matthew, a medical student, is scrubbing up to assist in theatre he notices that the surgeon's breath smells of alcohol and that he is a bit shaky. Matthew is concerned that the surgeon has been drinking

How appropriate are each of the responses by Matthew in this situation?

a. Ask the surgeon if he has been drinking loudly in front of all the other members of staff

i. A very appropriate thing to do

ii. Appropriate, but not ideal

iii. Inappropriate, but not awful

iv. A very inappropriate thing to do

b. Mention the concerns to the sister in charge of the theatre

i. A very appropriate thing to do

ii. Appropriate, but not ideal

iii. Inappropriate, but not awful

iv. A very inappropriate thing to do

c. Pretend he hasn't noticed anything

i. A very appropriate thing to do

ii. Appropriate, but not ideal

iii. Inappropriate, but not awful

iv. A very inappropriate thing to do

d. Watch to see if he seems ok when performing the operation

i. A very appropriate thing to do

ii. Appropriate, but not ideal

iii. Inappropriate, but not awful

iv. A very inappropriate thing to do

39. Kandathil is a medical student. He gets a phone call from his parents to say that his Grandma is ill in hospital and could he come and visit her urgently. Kandathil wants to leave as soon as possible to see his Grandma but has a tutorial that afternoon.

How important to take into account are the following considerations for Kandathil when deciding how to respond to the situation?

a.   He is able to the email the tutor to explain why he will be missing the session

i.   Very important

ii.   Important

iii.   Of minor importance

iv.   Not important at all

b.   The medical school say that students are able to miss teaching sessions if there is a family emergency

i.   Very important

ii.   Important

iii.   Of minor importance

iv.   Not important at all

c.   Whether the tutor would mind if Kandathil missed the session if he explained the absence

i.   Very important

ii.   Important

iii.   Of minor importance

iv.   Not important at all

40. Dr Smith is a junior doctor who is approached by a man who says that he is the son of a patient that Dr Smith is looking after. He wants to know what has been going on with his father and how long it will be until he can go home. Dr Smith's consultant will be busy all day and Dr Smith knows that the patient is very sick and has been diagnosed with terminal cancer. The patient has asked the consultant to inform his family for him.

How appropriate are each of the responses by Dr Smith in this situation?

a.   Tell the man that he is too busy

i.   A very appropriate thing to do

ii.   Appropriate, but not ideal

iii.   Inappropriate, but not awful

iv.   A very inappropriate thing to do

b.   Tell the man that he cannot tell him anything about the patient

i.   A very appropriate thing to do

ii.   Appropriate, but not ideal

iii.   Inappropriate, but not awful

iv.   A very inappropriate thing to do

c.   Confirm that this man is the son of the patient and then take the man to the relatives room to wait for the consultant

i.   A very appropriate thing to do

ii.   Appropriate, but not ideal

iii.   Inappropriate, but not awful

iv.   A very inappropriate thing to do

d.   Suggest that the man waits for the consultant to speak to him later in the day and explain that this was the patient's wishes

i.   A very appropriate thing to do

ii.   Appropriate, but not ideal

iii.   Inappropriate, but not awful

iv.   A very inappropriate thing to do

41. Sally is a GP who is in the middle of a consultation with a patient when the receptionist walks into the consulting room without knocking and interrupts the consultation. Sally is very annoyed with the receptionist.

How important to take into account are the following considerations for Sally when deciding how to respond to the situation?

a. Sally was in the middle of an intimate exam

i. Very important

ii. Important

iii. Of minor importance

iv. Not important at all

b. Sally's clinic was running late

i. Very important

ii. Important

iii. Of minor importance

iv. Not important at all

c. The receptionist was trying to relay a message that someone had collapsed in the waiting room

i. Very important

ii. Important

iii. Of minor importance

iv. Not important at all

d. Receptionist had received a phone call that Sally needed to pick up her child from school

i. Very important

ii. Important

iii. Of minor importance

iv. Not important at all

42. Dr Davis is a GP. Before calling the next patient into his consulting room he quickly checks the notes from previous visits to find that one of his colleagues had requested a blood test from the patient 6 months earlier. The results showed an abnormal result but there was no record of anyone contacting the patient to let them know or any follow up from then.

How important to take into account are the following considerations for Dr Davis when deciding how to respond to the situation?

a. The test result was only slightly abnormal

i. Very important

ii. Important

iii. Of minor importance

iv. Not important at all

b. Coincidental finding and not related to any of the symptoms that the patient had been experiencing at the time of the request

i. Very important

ii. Important

iii. Of minor importance

iv. Not important at all

c. The other doctor had been under a lot of stress at that time

i. Very important

ii. Important

iii. Of minor importance

iv. Not important at all

d. The patient had actually had a follow up appointment but had not attended

i. Very important

ii. Important

iii. Of minor importance

iv. Not important at all

e. The patient was known to be a frequent attender; often with trivial complaints

i. Very important

ii. Important

iii. Of minor importance

iv. Not important at all

43.   Tom is a nurse working in clinic. He notices that there are still 2 patients waiting to be seen by Dr Singh but his last patient left a while ago and he hasn't called anyone else in since. Tom knocks on the door of the consulting room that Dr Singh is using and enters to find Dr Singh asleep on the desk.

How important to take into account are the following considerations for Tom when deciding how to respond to the situation?

a.   Dr Singh had been on call and up all night

i.   Very important

ii.   Important

iii.   Of minor importance

iv.   Not important at all

b.   Dr Singh had been at his sisters 21st party that weekend

i.   Very important

ii.   Important

iii.   Of minor importance

iv.   Not important at all

c.   The patients waiting were only routine follow ups

i.   Very important

ii.   Important

iii.   Of minor importance

iv.   Not important at all

d.   Tom has found Dr Singh asleep on his desk every week for over a month

i.   Very important

ii.   Important

iii.   Of minor importance

iv.   Not important at all

44.   Will is a junior doctor working within the same medical team as Sam, another one of the doctors. Will notices that Sam is writing in the notes of a patient whom he saw last week and is writing in the entry dated from the previous week.

How important to take into account are the following considerations for Will when deciding how to respond to the situation?

a.   Sam had written today's date and time next to the edited entry

i.   Very important

ii.   Important

iii.   Of minor importance

iv.   Not important at all

b.   Sam was adding that he had examined the patient's abdomen

i.   Very important

ii.   Important

iii.   Of minor importance

iv.   Not important at all

c.   The patient was admitted to hospital yesterday

i.   Very important

ii.   Important

iii.   Of minor importance

iv.   Not important at all

d.   Sam had just got off the phone with the patient

i.   Very important

ii.   Important

iii.   Of minor importance

iv.   Not important at all

45. Anna is one of the partners at a GP surgery. One of her other partner colleagues, Ben, is considering entering the practice into a clinical trial for a new drug to treat Asthma. Ben is asking all of the doctors at the practice to send any patients with asthma who would be interested in joining the trial to see him so that he can ask them to join the trial.

How important to take into account are the following considerations for Anna when deciding how to respond to the situation?

a. The practice is receiving £100 for each patient entered

i. Very important

ii. Important

iii. Of minor importance

iv. Not important at all

b. Ben believes that the drug is wonderful and everyone should be on it

i. Very important

ii. Important

iii. Of minor importance

iv. Not important at all

c. Patients have been asking to try the drug after reading about it in the papers

i. Very important

ii. Important

iii. Of minor importance

iv. Not important at all

d. They have had a lot of patients at the practice not responding to the current therapies

i. Very important

ii. Important

iii. Of minor importance

iv. Not important at all

46. Conor, a junior doctor, approaches Andy, another junior doctor, and asks Andy to take over the care of a patient he has been assigned to look after. Andy asks why and Conor replies that he can't deal with 'another person who eats their own body weight in food'. When Andy asks Conor to explain himself, Conor says that he can't stand having to look after people who inflict their own health problems on themselves by eating too much and not doing enough activity.

How important to take into account are the following considerations for Andy when deciding how to respond to the situation?

a. Conor's mother is overweight

i. Very important

ii. Important

iii. Of minor importance

iv. Not important at all

b. Whether there are any patients or staff nearby

i. Very important

ii. Important

iii. Of minor importance

iv. Not important at all

c. Conor has never made comments similar to this to Andy before

i. Very important

ii. Important

iii. Of minor importance

iv. Not important at all

d. Conor has recently helped Andy out when he was having a difficult time

i. Very important

ii. Important

iii. Of minor importance

iv. Not important at all

47. **Maddie and Rebecca are both medical students who are assigned to the same group to prepare a presentation. The group will be assessed together for their work. This is a compulsory piece of work for their course. At the beginning of the first group meeting, Maddie receives a message from Rebecca stating that she has a punctured tyre on her bike so won't be able to come and could Maddie cover for her.**

How important to take into account are the following considerations for Maddie when deciding how to respond to the situation?

a. There is a private area where Maddie could call Rebecca

i. Very important

ii. Important

iii. Of minor importance

iv. Not important at all

b. Maddie knows that Rebecca lives 1 mile out of town where there is no bus route

i. Very important

ii. Important

iii. Of minor importance

iv. Not important at all

c. The have been told that they must all contribute to the presentation

i. Very important

ii. Important

iii. Of minor importance

iv. Not important at all

d. Both Maddie and Rebecca play Netball for the same team

i. Very important

ii. Important

iii. Of minor importance

iv. Not important at all

e. Rebecca had done a lot of preparatory work which she had already e-mailed to the team

i. Very important

ii. Important

iii. Of minor importance

iv. Not important at all

48. **Daniel and Alastair are junior doctors. Daniel catches Alastair putting bandages and syringes into his bag when he walks into the supplies room. Daniel realises that Alastair has taken the last of a particular syringe. Alastair asks Daniel not to tell anyone.**

How important to take into account are the following considerations for Daniel when deciding how to respond to the situation?

f. Alastair was a refugee and says that he is sending the supplies to a charity in his home town

i. Very important

ii. Important

iii. Of minor importance

iv. Not important at all

g. Daniel needs the syringe to give a medication to his patient

i. Very important

ii. Important

iii. Of minor importance

iv. Not important at all

h. Alastair is on his final warning from the medical school because of his previous unprofessional behaviour

i. Very important

ii. Important

iii. Of minor importance

iv. Not important at all

i. Ali and Daniel have previously fallen out and they do not like each other

i. Very important

ii. Important

iii. Of minor importance

iv. Not important at all

j.   Ali shows a letter from Management that allows him to take out-of-date stock

i.   Very important

ii.   Important

iii.   Of minor importance

iv.   Not important at all

49.   Colin, a junior consultant, has been asked to present a case at the monthly mortality and morbidity meeting. He has picked the case of a young woman who was admitted to hospital with a large haemorrhage in her brain and who died the following day. He discovers that she had been seen in A&E 10 days previously with a severe headache and sent home. In retrospect he is certain that this was a warning bleed and if admitted she could have had life-saving surgery.

How important to take into account are the following considerations for Colin when deciding how to respond to the situation?

a.   It is clear from the notes that the second team did not know about the A&E visit.

i.   Very important

ii.   Important

iii.   Of minor importance

iv.   Not important at all

b.   The case that he is reviewing actually happened 2 years ago.

i.   Very important

ii.   Important

iii.   Of minor importance

iv.   Not important at all

c.   It was actually Colin's best friend who saw the young lady in the A&E

i.   Very important

ii.   Important

iii.   Of minor importance

iv.   Not important at all

d.   Colin finds out that the husband of the woman who died is one of his patients

i.   Very important

ii.   Important

iii.   Of minor importance

iv.   Not important at all

e.   A&E was very busy that time and there was huge pressure from management not to breach the 4 hr target

i.   Very important

ii.   Important

iii.   Of minor importance

iv.   Not important at all

50.   Mark is the educational supervisor of Krishna, a trainee doctor. Mark receives a complaint from a consultant colleague that Krishna has shared his IT login and password with another trainee.

How important to take into account are the following considerations for Mark when deciding how to respond to the situation?

a.   The trust has a clear policy, which does not allow any sharing of computer logins.

i.   Very important

ii.   Important

iii.   Of minor importance

iv.   Not important at all

b.   Krishna informs Mark that other people in surgery share logins.

i.   Very important

ii.   Important

iii.   Of minor importance

iv.   Not important at all

c.   Krishna feels that the consultant who complained is racially bullying him.

i.   Very important

ii.   Important

SJT Answers

1a. (A) - If he thinks that something is going on then it would be good to escalate the problem to a senior member of staff who can try and find out what he was taking and why. It may be that Karthik doesn't feel comfortable dealing with this situation himself, so asking a senior colleague to help is very appropriate.

1b. (A) - This is very appropriate, as before making any judgements it is a good idea to speak to the person involved to find out from them what was going on and it is always best to this in a private manner. Once Karthik has found out from Matthew what was happening then he can decide what is appropriate to do next

1c. (C) - This response is inappropriate but not awful. Ideally you should not confront other people in front of other colleagues and the patients, this should be done in a more private manner.

1d. (D) - This would be very inappropriate, as Karthik doesn't have hard evidence that Matthew was stealing the drugs and why he was doing it, therefore it would be inappropriate to escalate the situation to that level immediately.

2a. (A) - Accurately describes her level of experience whilst reassuring the patient of her supervisor's support. This therefore gives the patient the information to be able to make an informed choice as to whether they consent to Katie proceeding with the blood test.

2b. (D) - Highly inappropriate to imply that you have taken blood before from a living person, not just from a model. It is a serious violation of medical professionalism for a student or doctor to suggest or state that they have more experience than they actually do.

2c. (C) – It would be inappropriate for Katie to suggest that someone else can do it before explaining her own level of experience as she has been asked to do this by her supervisor. Once she has explained then it may be appropriate to suggest this if the patient has questions about her expertise to undertake the blood taking. This is not awful as it is clear that the patient is questioning her level of experience.

3a. (A) – This is very important, as this seems to be a one off episode that may be due to the consultant being very busy all weekend working on call. If he has been in theatre all night the night before he will almost certainly be very tired and this is probably therefore not a situation that needs to be escalated.

3b. (D) – This is not important, as it shouldn't matter who the person is or whether they are responsible for signing you off at the end of the placement, it should not affect how you deal with a situation that arises.

3c. (A) – This is very important because if the consultant surgeon is only coming in to check on the patients from the night before and isn't going to be dealing with delicate operations then his tiredness will be much less of a worry.

4a. (D) – This is very inappropriate, as not attending a practical session that is compulsory is inappropriate and then asking one of your friends to lie for you, is highly inappropriate

4b. (D) – this is very inappropriate as the class is compulsory to complete her course so not attending will impact on her learning

4c. (C) – This is inappropriate, as the medical school will have strict guidelines about appearance at practical classes, especially at anatomy ones where there may be human tissue. This is not awful, as she is at least attempting to attend the compulsory class.

4d. (B) - Letting one of the tutors know that you are not able to attend is appropriate but not ideal as she shouldn't have really got into the state where she was not feeling well enough to attend this compulsory class. Also by catching up the work at least she isn't going to impact her learning too much.

5a. (A) - This indicates that the GP is taking something that they have not been prescribed and that they should probably not be taking. Also it is illegal to steal medications so this just escalates the issue further meaning Andrew will need to respond to this.

5b. (C) - This is of minor importance as if Andrew feels that the GP is spaced out in clinic therefore not performing to his best ability this is a problem that needs to be addressed, no matter what the tablets are that the GP is taking

5c. (D) – This is not important at all as this has no relevance to the issue at hand. IF the GP is struggling and not giving his patients the best quality of care this issue needs to be dealt with and knowing his family should not influence how this is done.

5d. (B) – This is important as it may mean that the GP needs some help with the issues that he is facing. This shouldn't mean that you ignore the situation but that when you deal with the situation he is able to get any help or speak to the correct people about what has been going on.

6a. (C) - This is a factor that may explain why Rowan hadn't done his essay on time, however it is of minor importance when suspecting that someone has copied your work and passed it off as his or her own. Tom may feel more sympathetic towards Rowan as to why he hasn't done his essay on time which to help him out but it isn't really a factor for cheating.

6b. (C) – Whether he is a regular for asking for help or not shouldn't is not an important factor when deciding what to do about someone coping your work and passing it off as his own.

6c. (A) – This is important as this may be one more factor that the tutors need to know about and they may need to assess his learning and if there is anything going on that they need to help him with to get him back on track with his work.

7a. (D) – This is not important as cheating in all exams is inappropriate and dishonest and taking no action when it is just a formative assessment may make Sarah think that it is ok to cheat in more important summative exams.

7b. (D) – This is not important in this situation as cheating for whatever reason is dishonest and should not be allowed. If she is struggling because of this factor then Sarah should seek help from someone who may be able to get her help with her studies if that is what she needs.

8a. (A) – This is very appropriate as it is best to be open and honest to patients about mistakes and errors, especially when you will need to redo a test that they do not like. It is also important to apologise for any errors that have happened, whether they are specially Sam's

fault or not, it is appropriate for him to apologise to the patient because he will have to redo the test.

8b. (D) – It would be very inappropriate to blame the nurse as the final responsibility for checking the equipment falls to the person taking the blood from the patient, which was Sam. Also blaming other members of staff is highly inappropriate, instead he should apologise for the error but not blame anyone for it.

8c. (D) – It is very inappropriate and unprofessional to shout at other members of staff at any time, especially in front of other colleagues or patients.

8d. (A) – This is a very appropriate response. This shows that Sam reflected well on what had happened to cause the error and will hopefully ensure that this sort of mistake won't happen again. This is a very professional response to an error.

8e. (D) – It is very dishonest and unprofessional to lie to patients to cover up mistakes that have been made. Telling the patient this would be very inappropriate, as it would be lying to get away from having to explain the truth.

9a. (C) – This is inappropriate as it is a dishonest statement. It is not awful ass it wouldn't harm the patient by telling him this, until one of the doctors can come and explain the results at a later stage.

9b. (D) – This is very inappropriate. Although Gavin may have practiced in a safe environment how to deliver this sort of information, he is only a medical student and therefore is not experienced or qualified enough to do this. It would also be inappropriate as Gavin would not be able to answer all of the patient's questions.

9c. (A) – This would be very appropriate, as this would pass the message along to the doctor who is able to deliver this sort of information and answer any relevant questions that the patient may have as a result of this diagnosis.

9d. (A) – Explaining that as a medical student he is not able to comment on results of tests is a very appropriate thing to do as it is honest and professional as he is not trying to do anything outside of his level of experience or expertise.

10a. (B) – It would be appropriate to raise this issue with a senior if he had been lying about being sick to have time off work. However, this is not ideal, as Will has not attempted a local solution to the problem by asking John what had been going on before risking damaging his reputation with the consultant. As Will doesn't know for sure that John was lying.

10b. (D) – This is inappropriate as if John has been lying to get out of contractual work then this is very dishonest and unprofessional and he should not be allowed to get away with it.

10c. (D) – This response is very inappropriate as it is evasive and not a direct way of dealing with this issue. It seems like Will is hoping that John he will confess, which seem unlikely.

10d. (B) – This response is would be good in that it gives John a chance to explain his actions, however it sounds a bit confrontational and therefore may hinder a successful conversation about the events at the weekend.

10e. (D) – This is a very inappropriate this to do as this is a serious probity issue, therefore it would not be appropriate to allow it to potentially happen again before doing anything about it.

11a. (D) – This is very inappropriate as it is not the medical students faults that she is left to do all the paperwork. Also if they shared out the paperwork then they would have time to teach the medical student who are there to learn in a clinical environment.

11b. (C) – This is inappropriate but not awful, as Maria should try to speak to Hassal about this and try to come up with a solution together before escalating it to their senior colleague.

11c. (A) – This would be very appropriate, as this would give them both equal opportunities to teach and do the paperwork.

11d. (B) – This would be appropriate it would open a discussion about the division of responsibilities. However, this is not ideal as it may be seen as confrontational and may not facilitate a discussion on how to split the responsibilities in a fair and professional way.

12a. (B) – This response would allow everyone in the group to be able to show the rest of the group how much they have done towards the group project, so may enable the rest of the group to work out if Hannah has not been pulling her weight. IT may also make Hannah think that she needs to contribute more so as to be able to explain what she has achieved, however this is not ideal as it may be putting Hannah on the spot in front of the other members of the group and isn't the most delicate way of dealing with this situation.

12b. (D) – This would be very inappropriate as Sophie is not sure how much Hannah has done already, she also should try and deal with this situation in a private manner and not accuse her of not pulling her weight in front of the other members of the group as this is a very confrontational way of dealing with the situation.

12c. (A) – This would be a very appropriate response as it would be local solution and would be a private way of finding out if there were any issues that Hannah could use some help with. It is also very useful to offer support to someone in a situation, as it would hopefully be more likely to start a discussion about distribution of workload rather than be confrontational.

12d. (D) – This would not be appropriate to do as the first response as this does not give Hannah a chance to explain or change her ways. It would be much more appropriate to speak to Hannah first about the issue before potentially getting her into trouble with the tutor.

13a. (D) - Anna seems to be a patient therefore she would expect a certain level of privacy and discretion. As a result it would be very inappropriate for Sally to ask her why she is there.

13b. (D) – This is highly inappropriate as her friend Anna has come in as a patient therefore, the GP needs to maintain patient confidentiality.

13c. (D) – This is also highly inappropriate for the similar reason, as Sally should not be looking at notes of people who are not patients of hers or the team that she has been allocated under to maintain confidentiality.

13d. (A) – As it seems likely that Anna has come to the GP as a patient, and does not seem to have seen Sally, it is best that she pretends not to have seen her, unless she brings it up later.

14a. (D) – This would be highly inappropriate as Katie has been asked by the consultant to do this and should not delegate this to someone else. Also the medical student would also not have the expertise nor experience to be able to do this sort of thing, therefore it would be very inappropriate to ask them to do it instead of her.

14b. (A) – This would be the best response as under the duty of candor, doctors are expected to be open and honest with patients, so it would be very appropriate to explain honestly the reasons for the cancellation. Also by telling the patient that they will try their best to do it tomorrow, Katie is not promising that it will definitely happen which is something that she has no control over.

14c. (B) – This is would be appropriate as it may help calm the patient, however, it is not ideal, as it may seem patronizing to the patient. It would be better to apologise, explain the reason for the cancellation and then reassure the patient.

14d. (D) – This is not appropriate as the patient is known to be very anxious and so it would be in his best interests to try and at least answer some of his questions today not leave him to worry about it all night. Also Katie has been asked by her consultant to speak to the Ed, therefore, it would be inappropriate to tell him that she is too busy.

14e. (D) – This would be highly inappropriate as this is something that is completely out of the control of Katie, also she does not have the power to be able to make the operation happen today. IT would also be very unprofessional to tell her consultant what to do.

15a. (A) – It is very rude and unprofessional for students and/or doctors to be on their phones when in consultations, whether or not they are just observing. Having observed this, the patient may leave the consultation very unsatisfied about the experience; therefore Kevin needs to be told to put his phone away and to not do it again.

15.b (D) - This is of minor importance, as stated above, it is very unprofessional therefore whether anyone has seen or not, it should not be allowed to happen again.

15c. (D) - If Kevin was trying to sort out a family emergency then he should excuse himself from the consultation to do this and should not be on his phone within the consulting room.

15d. (C) - Kevin should not really be using a phone, even if it is for academic reasons without checking first with the consultant and patient that this would be ok, as

it may be misinterpreted as him just texting his friends and therefore be seen as rude and unprofessional.

16a. (A) – This would be very appropriate as it would accepting that you need to learn but that you could do with some additional help. Asking for help shouldn't be seen as sign of weakness, rather a very responsible and professional response to not knowing how to do something.

16b. (D) – This would not be appropriate as it is impeding other people's work and may even have negative consequences on patient care if their notes/tests are not all unified on the one new system. Even though he may be able to see more patients using the old system, care may be slowed at other points by Dr Woods refusing to switch over, also once he's learnt to use the new system he will probably speed up again, so it will only be a temporary lull. It is also not very professional to refuse to use a new system that everyone has been asked to use now.

16c. (D) – This is also highly inappropriate as he is still impeding others in that time and being near retirement should not be an excuse to not learn new systems.

17a. (C) - It would not be that appropriate to pass on the responsibility of this lost child to the receptionist, however it is not awful because at lest Jen is acknowledging that this child needs to be looked after until her mother is found.

17b. (A) – It would be a very good idea to try and comfort and reassure this child who is obviously very upset, therefore this response would be very appropriate.

17c. (A) – Most patients' would understand and be happy to wait for a little bit longer whilst Jen goes and tries to find the child's mother. As long as she comes back and sees the patient next, this is a very appropriate response.

17d. (D) – this would be a very inappropriate response as the child should not be left unattended in case something happens to the child whilst no one is looking after her.

17e. (D) – It would be unprofessional to leave a crying child that you believe to be alone and pretend you didn't see her. As already stated, it would be inappropriate to leave the child unattended and also it would be wrong to make no attempt to find her mother.

18a. (D) – This is not important as there are very strict rules from both medical schools and the GMC about putting patient identifiable information on social media without their consent, so even though the identity of the hospital has not been revealed it could be worked out and then the patient may be identifiable which is seen as a serious breach of confidentiality.

18b. (C) - This is would be of minor importance because even though they had not meant to post identifiable information, they are very aware of the rules about posting confidential information or pictures on social media without consent which is a serious issue. The student shouldn't be posting pictures of patients that are identifiable or not without their consent.

18c. (A) – The consequences for the patient as a result of this breach of confidentiality are very important to consider.

18d. (A) – This is important to consider, because if the patient has given full consent to this use of the image then the student hasn't done anything wrong. It would have to be clear that the patient had consented to the hospital number still being present on the image.

18e. (D) - This of no importance to the issue because even if this was the only case in the world, if the student hadn't got consent from the patient to have this picture, put it on social media or disclose any identifiable information then it is a breach of confidentiality to do it.

19a. (A) – This is very important to consider, as members of the public would not like to think that their personal details were being discussed in such a public place, even if they weren't specifically mentioned by name.

19b. (C) - This makes the actions of the doctors slightly less serious, but still doesn't make it that important as the patient may be recognizable from other details.

19c. (D) – This is unimportant, as the principles of professionalism and patient confidentiality must apply in all circumstances.

20a. (D) – This is very inappropriate for Bill to do, as he will be seriously impacting his learning by not attending the teaching sessions. Also assuming that the tutor wont notice a very foolish thing to think as they are likely to have a list of student who are supposed to attend each week and may even have to notify the medical school if people frequently do not attend.

20b. (A) – This is a very appropriate response as he is acknowledging that he should have been at the previous sessions but will catch up on the work so will hopefully have not missed out too much by not being able to attend.

20c. (D) – This is not appropriate, as he should explain to the tutor himself, why he hasn't shown up. It is not very polite to ask his colleagues to explain on his behalf.

20d. (B) – This is appropriate, as he will be ensuring that he hasn't missed out too much by not attending the previous sessions. However, this isn't ideal as he should also apologise and explain to the tutor as to why he had missed the sessions.

21a. (B) – Finding out when the patient will be seen is an appropriate response as it may be useful to be able to explain the situation, however it is not ideal as if the GP doesn't talk to the patient about what his concerns are then this may not fully diffuse the situation.

21b. (A) – This response would give the GP as chance to understand the patient's exact concerns and trying to do this immediately and discreetly would be very appropriate,

21c. (A) – This would be an appropriate response as it would be an immediate, discreet and calm response.

21d. (D) – This would be highly inappropriate as he would not be doing anything to address the patient's agitation and as the anger of the patient was directed at the GP, the GP should try to assist the patient in a calm manner immediately.

21e. (B) – This would be an appropriate response as the GP would be trying to deal with the concern of the patient that they have had to wait for a long time, however it is not ideal as it may not be an immediate response and should maybe be a secondary response once the GP has calmed the patient.

22a. (A) – Doing the shift in A&E is compulsory therefore it is important that Adam undertakes this experience as part of his course. Therefore swapping with another student, if possible, is a highly appropriate thing to do, especially if he lets the team know that is what he is going to do.

22b. (D) – Lying is highly inappropriate and unprofessional and doing this would also meant hat Adam missed this opportunity which is compulsory for his course, which would impact his training.

22c. (D) – As stated above pretending to be ill is dishonest and he would still be missing the shift, so this would be very inappropriate

22d. (A) – This is very appropriate, as he will be informing the team that he will not be attending and also ensures that he does this compulsory shift at a later date.

22e. (D) – This is also very inappropriate as he is still missing the shift and has not informed the team that he will not be turning up.

23a. (C) - This is minor importance as if this was a one off occasion then you could forgive Ian for getting stuck in traffic that may have been greater than usual, however if it is regular problem then Ian should really give extra time to get into the hospital in the morning as constantly turning up late is unprofessional.

23b. (A) – This is very important as the students should be acting within the rules of the medical school's code of conduct and they may feel that being constantly late is an issue that needs addressing.

23c. (B) – This is important as it shows that he is a hard working student and tries to make up for his tardiness, however it is not very important as he should try his best to arrive on time.

23d. (A) – this is very important factor, as Ian has asked for special permission to be late, however he should maybe have informed Sally and the team about this agreement.

23e. (D) – This is not important at all, as it is not relevant and should not affected Sally's decision on how to respond to this situation.

24a. (D) - This is of no importance as all doctors and medical students are should be aware of the bare below the elbow policies that are in all trusts within the NHS, therefore this should not be an excuse to not abide by the rules.

24b. (A) – This is very important as this shows that Angus is not abiding by more than one infection control policy and this needs to be addressed as these policies were introduced for patient safety and are compulsory for all members of staff to abide by.

24c (A) – This is very important as this means that Ben has a responsibility to do something about Angus not following the policy on infection control by wearing his watch.

24d. (A) – This is also very important as it means that both Ben and Angus have both been given the information about the rules and therefore Angus has no excuse for not knowing the rules and for breaking them. It also means that Ben knows that Angus is breaking them and possibly even what to do if someone is seen to be breaking the rules.

25a. (A) – This is very important to consider because if the medical school tell them to do something then they have no excuse for not doing it and this is almost certainly an expectation from the medical school that all students should always wear gloves.

25b. (B) – This is not important because Ed should not be doing anything that makes him feel uncomfortable even if everyone else does it.

25c. (D) - This is not important. As stated above Ed should not be doing something that he feels uncomfortable doing, even if the patient doesn't mind. Also the patient may not be aware of the reason that the doctor should wear gloves when doing this procedure.

25d. (A) – This is a very important factor as he should not do the procedure unless he feels comfortable doing it and if this means he needs to wear gloves then he should wear them.

25e. (C) - This is of minor importance, as it would only take a tiny bit longer for Ed to go and get some gloves before taking the blood, therefore wearing gloves would not significantly delay the taking of the blood.

26a. (D) – This is very inappropriate as Emma doesn't have the knowledge to answer the patient's questions properly and she is also not using a reliable source for the information that she is trying to gather about the drug. As a medical student it is not appropriate for her to answer questions about medications that she doesn't know.

26b. (A) – Asking the patient to speak to their doctor who may have put them on the medication or at least know more about it than Emma does is a very appropriate response. 26c. (B) – This response is appropriate as Emma is being honest about her lack of knowledge about the drug and therefore making the patient aware that she cannot answer his questions. However this is not ideal, as she is not giving him the opportunity to ask his doctor who could answer the questions. A more ideal response would be to tell the patient that you don't know much about the drug but tell the patient to ask the doctor.

27a. (A) – This is very important to consider as if John has been asking Matt to do more than his fair share of work everyday so that John can leave early this is a serious issue as this implies that John is not completing the work that he is contracted to do on a regular basis.

27b (A) – If John has had permission to leave work early on a one off occasion then the response to the situation would be very different from if he is just trying to skive work.

27c. (B) – This is an important factor to consider as it highlights that he is trying to help Matt out with the work that is left, making sure that he is aware of the tasks that urgently need to be done so Matt could concentrate on them.

27d. (C) - This is of minor importance because relationships with other colleagues shouldn't affect your work relationships and responses to situations. However, if the reason that they don't get on is due to John doesn't do his fair share of the work then this would have some importance.

28a. (A) – This would be a very appropriate response as it will not escalate the situation further and will ensure that Lucy doesn't engage in inappropriate social contact with a patient. It is very unprofessional for Lucy to go on a date with a patient and could lead to serious professional consequences for her.

28b. (A) – This would be highly appropriate so that the patient cannot engage in any more contact with Lucy. Having conversations with the patient on social media may have serious professional consequences for Lucy.

28c. (C) – This would be inappropriate as he may still come back to the hospital as a patient, also it would be unprofessional for Lucy to date him if he has recently been her patient. However it would not be awful as you can date one of your old patients as long as you make sure that he would not be a patient again.

28d. (B) - This would be an inappropriate response as although she would be telling him that she doesn't think its appropriate for them to date, she will potentially be starting a conversation over social media which could ultimately have consequences for Lucy.

29a. (D) – This is of no importance as if Miriam believes that Luke is not dressed appropriately for the wards then she should try to resolve the situation before someone else has to say something to him.

29b. (A) – If the medical school has made it clear to students that they are expected to be presentable when on the wards, then this is a very important factor to consider, as they should therefore obey these instructions. If students are not smartly presented then this reflects badly on the medical school and the hospital.

29c. (D) – This is not important at all, as Luke needs to maintain a smart, professional appearance when he is at the hospital, not matter what is happening at home

29d. (A) – This is very important to consider, because if they have had to sign an agreement then that means that Luke has no excuse for not knowing what is expected of them and not following the rules whilst he is in hospital, which he has agreed to.

29e. (D) – This is not important at all, as you can make yourself look presentable without spending any money. If he is struggling financially, then he could go apply to the university for a grant to be able to buy smart clothes. It is very easy to look presentable and it is very important to gaining trust and respect of patients.

30a. (B) – As long as they are being quiet and only talk about their social activities for a short period of time this would be an appropriate response. However if it went only for long or they weren't being quiet then they should really talk about this somewhere else that is more appropriate. Therefore it may be more ideal to ask them to continue the conversation somewhere more appropriate.

30b. (D) – This is a very inappropriate response. As stated above it is not appropriate or professional for the students to be talking about their social activities whilst on the ward so it would be highly inappropriate for Felicity to join in.

30c. (A) – This would be a very appropriate response as it would be letting them know that it is not appropriate to discuss this on the ward and they should be discussing this elsewhere.

31a. (D) – This is a very inappropriate; as there is no guarantee that the ward clerk will be able to read Josefine's handwriting. There is also a risk that the ward clerk may misinterpret the notes and this may compromise patient safety as a result.

31b. (A) – This is a very appropriate response as it is a very quick and easy solution to the problem and will ensure that Yoseph can look after the patients appropriately.

31c. (B) - Although, Yoseph is trying to work it out by himself, it is not a very appropriate this to do as having to restart from the beginning with the patients may impact on their care and will slow down their management which is really not ideal. You shouldn't have to do this but if you are left in this situation then you need to do your best.

31d. (D) – This is a very inappropriate response as Yoseph is the doctor in charge of the patients care once Josefine has left so he should not be trying to get other doctors to see them for him. Also there is no guarantee that they will be able to read her handwriting.

32a. (A) – This is very important to consider as it may mean that she leaves a whole list of patients not being able to have their operations. However, if she doesn't feel up to doing it and thinks that she may have difficulty performing the operations then it is important that she considers this for the safety of the patients.

32b. (B) – This is important to consider as it may mean that it is easier for Vicky to go home as she could always leave the paperwork to do another day when she is feeling better. This would not be such an important factor when worrying about leaving her colleagues in the lurch unless it is urgent and would need to be done by someone else that day.

32.c (D) – This is not important to consider, as others doing something that may be wrong is not a justification for you also doing it. Vicky should still tell the other members of the team that she is going to leave and make arrangements for the work that still needs to be done.

32d. (A) – This is highly important to consider, because if she has been open and honest with her team about what has to still be done and how she is feeling then this will help her team and they will be more supportive with her going home.

32e. (A) – This is a very important thing to consider as she will have to make sure that the patients are properly looked after and that her tasks are handed over to another appropriate member of staff before she could leave.

33a. (A) – This is a very appropriatee thing to do. This is definitely a reason why the patient may not be responding to Arjun, as they don't understand what he is saying to them.

33b. (D) – This would be highly inappropriate, as the patient has not given consent for the procedure. It doesn't matter how minor the procedure is it is highly unprofessional to proceed with a treatment that the patient hasn't consented to. This may result in serious professional consequences for Arjun.

33c. (A) – This is a very appropriate response as it may be that the patient hasn't understood due to hearing difficulties or poor English, therefore is would be appropriate to try and see if they could understand better giving the information in a different format.

33.d (B) – This would be appropriate as the family may be able give the doctor advise on what the exact reason for the patient not responding may be and may be able to help get the patient to understand. However, it is not ideal, as this relies on them coming in that day to see the patient, therefore if this is not the case then this may delay treatment for the patient. Also the patient may not want the doctor to speak to his family.

33e. (A) – It is always very appropriate for a doctor to seek advise from a senior colleague

34.a (D) – This is not appropriate as the patient will not get his questions answered and it can't be possible that everyone on the team is too busy to talk to the patient.

34b. (D) – This would be inappropriate as Ian is only a medical student and is unlikely to be able to answer the patient's questions correctly. The patient has also asked to speak to the consultant, so it would be appropriate for him to speak to a doctor.

34c. (B) – it would be appropriate to let the patient know that the consultant is away and not available to speak to the patient until tomorrow. However it is not ideal as this is not a quick and local solution to the problem, and it would be more ideal to offer another doctor to come and speak to the patient today.

34d. (A) – this would be very appropriate and an ideal solution to ensure that the patient's questions are answered.

34e. (C) – This would be inappropriate but not awful, as this does not necessarily ensure that the patients' questions will get answered.

35a. (D) – This would be a very inappropriate response as it would be dishonest and would be putting the blame for it not being done onto someone else which would be unprofessional. A much better response by Laurence would be to be honest about the mistake and apologise for any inconvenience.

35b. (A) – This would be highly appropriate, as it would involve Laurence being honest and apologetic about his error before being caught out and would also mean that the X-ray would be done as soon as possible to try and not affect the patients management any more than it may have already been so far.

35c. (D) – This is highly unprofessional and dishonest and would be very inappropriate.

35d. (D) – This would be inappropriate as it may compromise the dynamic of the team if he makes excuses as to why he hasn't done his work on time, as it is not very professional to make excuses for your mistakes. It would be a much better idea to apologise and be upfront about the mistake.

35e. (A) – This would be a very appropriate thing to do, as it would reassure the patient that it won't affect his treatment or management by waiting another day for it to be done, but that they will try and organize it as soon as possible.

36a. (A) – This is a very appropriate response, as it is an open and neutral question that the child, with no possible negative consequences for the child.

36b. (A) – If Sophie wants to examine the bruises on the child, then it would be very appropriate to ask for consent from the child's carer first.

36c. (B) – Asking the carer about the cause of the bruises away from the child would be an appropriate thing to d, however it is not ideal to speak to the carer outside of the consulting room in a possibly public space as this requires a discrete conversation

36d. (D) – Even if she isn't sure what caused the bruises, Sophie should still examine them and document about them in the child's notes and from this investigation she can then work out what to do next. Therefore it would be highly inappropriate to ignore them in case they are because of something serious, such as child abuse.

36e. (A) - Getting advice from a senior colleague is always highly appropriate, especially in a situation in which you are unsure how to proceed.

37a. (A) – If the medical school has a strict policy about the use of recreational drugs then it is very important that this taken into account when trying to deal with this situation.

37b. (D) – This is not important at all. Although it is a good thing that he wont be potentially under the influence of recreational drugs whilst in the hospital, it is still not acceptable to be taking recreational drugs even in your spare time as a medically student or doctor and it is taken very seriously be medical schools and the GMC, who see it as a fitness to practice issue.

37c. (A) – This is very important, as there are very strict rules about not undergoing illegal activities whilst a medical student as this is seen as a very serious issue by the medical schools and the GMC and is deemed extremely unprofessional.

37d. (D) – This is not important, as his reputation should not interfere with Alan's decision in how to deal with this current situation, as this is potentially a very serious issue.

37e. (A) – This is a very important factor, as this is potentially such a serious issue that could cause very negative consequences for Tom, Alan needs to take into account how sure he was that he saw what he thought he did.

38a. (D) – This is a very inappropriate response. It is not a discrete way of dealing with the situation and could have very negative implications for the surgeon and potentially ruin his reputation if he is accused of this behaviour in front of his colleagues. A much more appropriate response would be to speak to him privately.

38b. (A) – This would be a very appropriate thing to do, as this would be a discrete and local solution to the problem and the sister in charge would be able to deal with the situation in a way that may be difficult for a medical student.

38c. (D) – This is a highly inappropriate thing to do. If the surgeon has been drinking and is not up to doing his job then there could be very serious consequences for the patient's.

38d. (D) – This is also highly inappropriate, as by the time the surgeon is already operating he may be doing something that is not safe for the patients in his care. Therefore it is very inappropriate to allow the surgeon to start operating if you have any concerns about his capability to perform his job satisfactorily.

39a. (A) – This is an important factor, as the tutor will expect Kandathil to notify him for the reason for his absence before the tutorial starts. If he can email the tutor, then he can explain the circumstances and try and make arrangements to catch up on anything that he will miss.

39b. (A) – This is very important as people are understanding and if there is an emergency at home then the medical school would be happy for someone to miss some teaching, within reason, to be able to be with their family at that time.

39c. (C) - This is of minor importance as it doesn't really matter whether the tutor would mind if Kandathil missed the tutorial, as long as he explains his absence and arranges to catch up on the work, it shouldn't matter

whether the tutor is happy or not about him missing the session for such a reason.

40a. (D) – This is a very inappropriate thing to do, as the patient has given consent for the family to be informed of his condition and it is likely that his son has come for that very purpose. The doctor should make time to speak to him, even if only briefly to explain that he would be better off speaking to the consultant.

40b. (D) – This would be very inappropriate as the patient has given consent for his family to be told about his condition and this would be going against his wishes.

40c. (A) – This would be a very appropriate response, as it confirms the relationship to the patient and offers the relative someone more appropriate to wait for the consultant, who the patient wished to explain his condition to his family.

40d. (A) – This is a very appropriate response, as it ensures that the consultant explains the patient's condition to the relative, which is what the patient asked to happen. Whilst explaining to the relative why he is asking him to wait to for the consultant to be free.

41a. (A) – This is a very important factor to consider, as it would be highly inappropriate for someone to come into a consulting room without permission if an intimate exam was being undertaken

41.b (C) - This is of minor importance. The receptionist interrupting the clinic is a reason why Sally would be slightly annoyed with the receptionist. However, the clinic running late is of not an important reason for a receptionist to interrupt a clinic without knocking.

41c. (A) – This is very important to consider as the receptionist may have only interrupted because of the emergency and therefore was not meaning to be rude and therefore this should be taken into consideration when Sally responds to this situation.

41d. (D) – This is not important at all, as this is no reason for the receptionist to interrupt Sally's clinic without knocking. The receptionist should have privately messaged or spoken to Sally in a break in clinic about such a matter.

42a. (C) - This is of minor importance as it shouldn't really matter how abnormal the result is, all abnormal results should be told to the patient and appropriately followed up, however there may have been a factor at the time that would have accounted for a slight abnormality and therefore may explain why it looks like it was ignored.

42b. (B) – This is an important factor to consider as it may have been overlooked if it was coincidental and not causing any problems, however there should have probably been some record made of this thought process.

42c. (C) – This is of minor importance as this should not be an excuse for not appropriately following up test results that you requested for patients, however it may make Dr Davis more sensitive in how he deals with the present situation.

42d. (A) – This is very important to consider as this may explain why there seems to be no follow up. This may have been attempted by the doctor through asking the patient to make a follow up appointment, which the patient did not attend for whatever reason. However if the result had been very abnormal, them this should have still been followed up.

42e. (D) – This is not important at all, as this should not affect the care of the patient in any way. The same protocols should be followed for all patients and if there is one that states that patients should be informed of abnormal results and they should be followed up, then this should happen no matter who the patient is.

43a. (A) – This is a very important factor to consider as this would be a perfectly good explanation for Dr Singh being so tired during clinic and Tom should try and be as sympathetic as possible about this and see if there is anything he can do to help Dr Singh.

43b. (B) – This is important to consider, because if it was that Dr Singh was falling asleep in clinic because he had been partying at the weekend then this is an issue that needs to be addressed, as it is not really professional or appropriate.

43c. (D) – This is not important at all, as it should make no difference to how Tom deals with the situation who the patients are or why they are there as no patients should be made waiting unnecessarily and patients should be treated the same no matter what the reason for them being there.

43d. (A) – This is very important to consider as this implies that this is a chronic not just a one off problem that needs to be addressed. It may be a sign that Dr Singh is unwell or not coping and may need help with this.

44a. (A) – This is a very important factor as this implies that Sam is editing the notes with some new information but making it clear that this is a new edition and that he isn't trying to tamper with old notes which could have very serious professional consequences for Sa,

44b. (A) – This is very important to consider, because if he is adding this information to old notes without making it clear that this is new information then he could be tampering with the patient's record which is a very serious offence and could have some serious consequences for him.

44c. (A) – this is also very important to consider as it may also imply that Sam is trying to tamper with the patient's record now that something else has happened to him.

44d. (A) – This is also very important to consider, as it may be that Sam is just adding to the old notes having just spoken to the patient, and if he makes it clear that this is a new addition to the old record then there is nothing wrong in doing that.

45a. (D) – It is irrelevant if the practice is getting any money. It shouldn't matter to Anna's decision to enter patients to a trial if her practice is receiving money for this, unless she feels that Ben is behaving inappropriately.

45.b (A) – This is very important to consider as it implies that Ben might not be following trial protocol and also this is very unethical. If a person running a trial doesn't have clinical equipoise they shouldn't be involved in the trial. If he thinks that the drug is wonderful then he should be offering it to all his patients not involving then in a trial that may mean that they only receive a placebo.

45c. (B) – This is important to consider as the patients are interested and want to be involved trial. It should also be considered as it may mean that patients need to be made aware that by joining the trial they may not necessarily be receiving the new drug, as some will be given the placebo.

45d. (A) – This is very important to consider as if they do have lots of patients not responding to the current treatments then this is a very god reason to get involved with a trial to find new better drugs. If all the patients were doing well on the current treatment then there would not be much point in doing a trial.

46a. (C) – This factor is of minor importance, as it doesn't really mitigate Conor's unprofessional comments about the patient, however it may serve as a constructive point about prejudging people in Andy's response to Conor.

46b. (A) – This is a very important factor to consider, as it would help Andy decide whether to deal with the situation immediately or move the conversation to a more private area where they can speak freely.

46c. (D) – This is not important at all, as Conor's comments are unprofessional so Andy should deal with them directly and discretely, even if Conor has never made comments lie this before.

46d. (C) - This is of minor importance, as it would make Andy more sensitive when dealing with Conor's remarks, but it does not reduce the need to address Conor's behaviour in any way.

47a. (A) – This is very important as Maddie could call Rebecca to ask her if she needs any help. She could find out if Rebecca could still get to the session, even if she was late, or if this wont be possible, has she let the tutor know that she cannot attend.

47b. (C) – This is of minor importance, as Rebecca should make every attempt to attend the meeting about the compulsory work. She should not ask Maddie to cover for her and should inform the course tutor herself if she cannot make it.

47c. (A) – This is very important, as they have all been informed about the rules by the medical school. Therefore, Rebecca should not ask Maddie to cover for her but should contact her tutor herself if she cannot attend.

47d. (D) – This is not important at all as it is irrelevant.

47e. (A) – This is important as this shows that Rebecca has shown some commitment to the project and has already done some work towards it, therefore has contributed something to the group project already. However, she should still not really ask Maddie to cover for her.

48a. (D) – This is not important, as it is not an excuse for stealing and he should not ask Daniel to pretend that nothing is happening.

48b. (B) – This is important as the patients should always come first and their care should be a priority, therefore if Alastair is taking equipment that is needed for a patient then this means that it is even more essential that Daniel responds to this immediately and efficiently.

48c. (D) – This is not important, as his previous behaviour shouldn't impact the current issue, whether this is in a negative or positive way.

48d. (D) – This is not important, as not liking someone or not getting on with them shouldn't influence your judgement about how to deal with situations.

48e. (A) – This is important, as if Alastair can demonstrate that the equipment that she is taking is out of date then if he has permission to take it then it is not such a serious issue.

49a. (A) – This is very important as Colin will need to inform the second team about what he has discovered so that they know what the relatives were told at the time of the first A&E visit.

49b. (C) – This is of minor importance. It shouldn't matter how long ago the incident happened, it is of minor importance as a factor to be considered when trying to decide what to do to ensure that things like things don't happened again if possible. The hospital still has a duty to found out what happened and to out in place any protocols or guidance to make sure it won't happen again.

49c. (D) – This is not important at all. Just because his best friend may have made an error this should not influence how Colin deals with the situation.

49d. (C) – This is of minor importance, as it should not influence his judgement other than the fact that he may offer to speak to the relatives, as he may already know them.

49e. (B) – This is important to consider, as it may be a factor that was involved in why the error was made on the day. It is not an excuse for a mistake to happen but it may have been a factor in what happen, therefore it should be considered.

50a. (A) – This is very important to consider, as Mark has to ensure that all trainees that he is responsible for adhere to all Trust policies.

50b. (B) – This is important to consider. Even though it is not an excuse for Krishna to have done it, it may mean that Mark needs to inform the relevant staff that this is a widespread problem throughout the trust that needs to be dealt with.

50c. (A) – This is very important to consider, as there are very strict rules regarding harassment and bullying and this needs to be investigated, alongside the problem of sharing logins.

MOCK TEST

*Highlight your obstacles to success, work
on them.*

Time allowed 120 minutes

Mock exam questions
Verbal Reasoning – 22 minutes

Stem 1

Below is an extract from a study review:

This review has sought to evaluate all existing research concerning health care professionals' perspectives regarding telehealth. Several common beliefs, namely "Quality of Patient Care", "Implementation and Resistance to Change", "Face to Face Interaction", "Healthcare Professional Benefits", and "Locality and Convenience" have emerged from the literature. The majority of these provoked mixed opinions, with HCPs often divided on the issue.

One notable omission is the issue of cost. Very few researchers asked about cost perceptions, and the two that did only asked about remuneration procedures. The response was that they were undeveloped and would remain as barriers to the utilisation of telehealth until resolved. This lack of discussion of overall cost implications can perhaps be explained be noting that this issue would be more concerning to managers or policy makers, and not one considered by HCPs.

In addition to simply elucidating these perceptions, this review has discussed the potential reasons why HCPs hold these views. A factor potentially explaining why HCPs hold these beliefs could be age. Several of the papers identified that an age difference could explain the disparity between beliefs regarding telehealth. Younger doctors (or those with less experience) were found to have more positive opinions than older ones (or those with more experience).

Future work could perhaps seek to ascertain more conclusively what underlying factors, be they demographical or otherwise, contribute to these perceptions.

A major limitation of this review is that the identification and appraisal of the literature may not have been as thorough as that of an experienced researcher. Secondly, only published literature was considered (see appendix). Similarly, due to resource constraints, only articles with readily available access were appraised, limiting the scope of the analysis.

Questions

1) There are 5 common beliefs.

     True   **False**   **Can't Tell**

2) HCP stands for health care professional.

     True   **False**   **Can't Tell**

3) HCPs seem to be less concerned about financials compared to policy makers.

     True   **False**   **Can't Tell**

4) The more experienced doctors should be listened to according to the author.

True   **False**   **Can't Tell**

5)The author believes that the differing perceptions between doctors need to be examined to determine why they exist.

True   **False**   **Can't Tell**

6)The review is not very good due to its limitations.

True   **False**   **Can't Tell**

7)Younger doctors were more positive about telehealth than older doctors because they had less experience.

True   **False**   **Can't Tell**

8)Older doctors have less negative views on telehealth than younger doctors.

True   **False**   **Can't Tell**

9)Telehealth costs too much.

True   **False**   **Can't Tell**

1) Which is least likely to be true :
    a. Younger doctors have less experience
    b. The review could have been better in its analysis
    c. Policy makers are involved in the financials of medicine
    d. Older doctors tend to be against telehealth as they have more experience

Stem 2

Below is a list of phases used by a group in a study on patient comments.

The six phases of Thematic analysis that we used include:
Phase 1: Familiarising yourself with your data
    Patient comments were typed up electronically, and then re-read several times by each member to ensure thorough familiarisation with the content. Initial ideas for codes were generated (for example, the prevalence of negative comments on transport, positive comments in relation to the service provided etc.)and noted down persisting with an inductive approach.
Phase 2: Generating initial codes
    Once all members were familiar with the content, interesting features of the data were coded manually. A code is defined by Boyatzis (1998) as being "the most basic segment, or element, of the raw data or information that can be assessed in a meaningful way …" Codes were formed in relation to information prevalence as well as their relative importance; if comments written by at least two patients revealed a significant finding relating to our research question, these were applied to generate a code. Consideration was taken to keep codes brief while still retaining the full meaning intended by the data.
Phase 3: Searching for themes
    After fully coding the data set, the codes were collated into potential themes which at times involved the

occurrence of cognitive conflict within the group, demonstrating the flexibility of thematic analysis to yield rich, varied analyses of data. When conflicting ideas emerged, each member justified their views which were considered equally among the entire group. Themes were derived using a quantitative approach based on their prevalence, and were also included based on their importance and relevance of each code to our overall research question.

Phase 4: Reviewing themes

A thematic map was produced and potential themes identified in phase 3 were reviewed. Some themes were redefined and some codes reallocated, illustrating the iterative process involved.

Phase 5: Defining and naming themes

Ongoing analysis lead to the refinement of the thematic map and members debated among the optimal name of each theme. The final themes agreed upon were: evaluation of the service at NPSDU; efficiency of sponsored transport; facilities at NPSDU; and the quality of care provided by the staff. Care was taken to avoid pitfalls described by Braun and Clarke (2006) by ensuring to fully analyse the data rather than simply paraphrasing the content.

Phase 6: Producing the report

The final step entailed producing a report which included a carefully selected compelling set of examples from the patient comments and a finalised thematic map in order to convey a clear and analytical understanding of the data to our reader.

Questions

1)The six phases involve production, defining, generation, reviews, familiarising and searching.

True   **False**   **Can't Tell**

2)There was one person in the team that wrote the report.

True   **False**   **Can't Tell**

3)A code involves changing the information into numbers or single letters.

True   **False**   **Can't Tell**

4)Codes were kept to a maximum of a few words.

True   **False**   **Can't Tell**

5)Themes were put together to form ideas.

True   **False**   **Can't Tell**

6)The work done in phases 2, 3 and 4 were revisited and occasionally changed.

True   **False**   **Can't Tell**

7)There were 4 themes.

True   **False**   **Can't Tell**

8)We can assume a report was produced.

True   **False**   **Can't Tell**

9)We can infer that Braun and Clarke suggested that simple paraphrasing was not the right way to analyse.

True   **False**   **Can't Tell**

10)The final thematic map will be clear.

True   **False**   **Can't Tell**

Stem 3

Below is an extract from a recent study:

A vast amount of data was collected but due to resource constraints, principally time, the depth of our research and post-collection analysis were bounded. This provides opportunities for future research, further delving into the complex relationships affecting patient experience at satellite dialysis units.

The most obvious example of this would be to focus on another facet of patient experience, other than waiting times, as established by the NHS National Quality Board (NQB, 2011).

Apart from measuring a different aspect of patient experience, future research could investigate waiting times more comprehensively, either by increasing the quantity of data collected or by increasing the depth of analysis. The increased data collection would result in a higher likelihood of obtaining normal distributions, which we failed to collect; this would enable parametric tests to be run, which hold more statistical weight than the non-parametric tests we were restricted to.

Additionally, nurses could be interviewed or administered a questionnaire to gauge a multi-stakeholder perspective on patient experience within NPSDU. This would lead to a deeper understanding about how the identified factors relate to waiting times, and provide a strong qualitative basis to inform possible areas of improvements.

As well as nurses, future work could also involve carers or family members who transport the patient to and from the unit, or accompany the patient during their dialysis treatment. Questionnaires could be administered to find out what they think could be improved, as they are also affected by the way the unit is run.

This study focuses on service quality solely from a patient experience perspective; however, future work could explore the cost-effectiveness and economic feasibility of each of the recommendations to ensure that efficiency savings are maximised, working towards the NHS Nicholson challenge.

Furthermore, interventional studies should be carried out to test the applicability and 'real-time' benefits of each of the proposed recommendations. This will reveal whether the recommendation in question actually has the scope to reduce waiting times or improve patient satisfaction prior to a longer term commitment of financial and human resources.

Based on the limitations of the questionnaire, quantitative questionnaires with a five- or seven-point Likert scale could be used to more accurately gauge patient satisfaction. If multiple significant relationships are found with satisfaction, a multiple regression analysis could be carried out to elicit the contributory role each independent variable plays on the dependent variable, patient satisfaction.

Further work should involve the use of both sequential and hierarchical process maps at NPSDU to guarantee that all aspects of the process are captured, as advised by Colligan et al. (2010).

To test the validity of the results, this study should be repeated at another satellite dialysis unit based around the hub of Hammersmith hospital, to study the differences in patient experience when the hub unit is kept constant, as well as other satellite dialysis units around the country. Confirmation of results would aid generalisability of findings to other satellite dialysis units on a national scale.

Questions

1) The analysis in the study was restricted.
   True   **False**   **Can't Tell**

2) The NQB is studying other aspects of patient experience.
   True   **False**   **Can't Tell**

3) The author says that the statistical tests in this study were not accurate.
   True   **False**   **Can't Tell**

4) If nurses had been interviewed, all the stakeholders would have been included in the study.
   True   **False**   **Can't Tell**

5) If nurses and family members/carers had been interviewed, all the stakeholders would have been included in the study.
   True   **False**   **Can't Tell**

6) The study has given ideas on how to improve patient experience.
   True   **False**   **Can't Tell**

7) It is better to adopt a recommendation for a short period of time to see its effectiveness before committing.
   True   **False**   **Can't Tell**

8) The results of the study cannot be said to be valid until further studies have been conducted.
   True   **False**   **Can't Tell**

9) We can assume that the results are only applicable to satellite units.
   True   **False**   **Can't Tell**

10) When was this paper written?
   a. 2010
   b. 2011
   c. 2012
   d. Unknown

Stem 4

Below is an extract from a study's Findings:

This study evaluated the service at NPSDU by measuring waiting times and satisfaction, two components of patient experience. The rising provision of dialysis treatment at satellite dialysis units, coupled with a lack of existing literature exploring patient experience in this setting, makes the results of this study particularly valuable.

Factors found to significantly affect waiting times were: mobility, transport, shift of the day, mode of vascular access and the area of the unit where a patient is dialysed. These factors were not found to have an association with satisfaction with overall care, with the single exception of area of the unit. We were able to speculate why these relationships may exist; however due to the inability to negate confounding factors, resulting from the obligatory use of non-parametric tests, we were unable to draw conclusions with greater statistical power.

The generalisability of these findings is limited by the unique characteristics of NPSDU. However, in multiple cases such as AVF, transport, unit area and mobility, we were able to draw somewhat generalisable conclusions on their effects on waiting times.

In general, patients who completed the questionnaire expressed a high level of satisfaction with the care. This, along with the limited significant results in the final satisfaction model, reveals that the associations between these factors and patient satisfaction are complex in nature, providing scope for future research. Thematic analysis of patient comments received from the questionnaires revealed four recurrent themes which helped guide our speculative discussion.

Based on our findings, a number of recommendations have been suggested to help reduce waiting times due to these factors. Most of the proposed recommendations are generalisable to other satellite dialysis units, and therefore, have the potential to improve patient experience with haemodialysis in a wider setting. These revolve around smoothing demand, improving patient flow and encouraging the use of Tesio.

All in all, this paper fulfilled the function of providing a stepping stone into evaluating the additional dimensions of patient experience within satellite dialysis units.

Questions

1) The study was conducted to measure waiting times and satisfaction.
   True   **False**   **Can't Tell**

2) The study was conducted to evaluate waiting times and satisfaction.
   True   **False**   **Can't Tell**

3) Waiting time differences did not correlate with overall care satisfaction.
   True   **False**   **Can't Tell**

4) It may have been better to use parametric tests if this had been possible.
   True   **False**   **Can't Tell**

5) There will be recommendations on how to improve satisfaction at satellite dialysis units.

True **False** **Can't Tell**

6) The reason for the paper could be said to help explore different areas of patient experience.
   True **False** **Can't Tell**

7) NPSDU stands for Northwick Park Satellite Dialysis Unit.
   True **False** **Can't Tell**

8) Not much research has been done in this area.
   True **False** **Can't Tell**

9) The paper can be used by other satellite dialysis units.
   True **False** **Can't Tell**

10) There are three main recommendations, and one minor one.
    True **False** **Can't Tell**

Quantitative reasoning – 23 minutes

i. **Below is a table showing repair claims for various makes of phone.**

Make	Requests per 1000	Average cost per claim (£)
Blueberry	66	33
myPhone	75	45
Mockia	24	40
Clamshell	31	41
JYV	44	26

1) Which make has the highest cost per 1000?

   a. Blueberry b. myPhone c. Mockia d. Clamshell e. JYV

2) Which make has the lowest requests per 1000?

   a. Blueberry b. myPhone c. Mockiad. Clamshell e. JYV

3) myPhone release a new phone, but the requests for repairs doubles. How many requests is this per 100 phones?

   a. 15 b. 150 c. 75 d. 7.5 e. 9

4) myPhone decide to include a compulsory insurance scheme in their phone charges. If they wish to break even on repair costs, how much should they charge per phone?

   a. Can't Tell b. £4.00 c. £4.50 d. £3.37 e. £3.38

5) Clamshell reduces the cost per claim by 20%. How much is the total cost of repair per 1000 now?

   a. £3276.80 b. £2540.20 c. £1,016.80 d. £820.20 e. Can't Tell

6) Mockia have an increase of 25% in the number of requests. How many more requests are there per 100?

   a. 0.6 b. 31 c. 0.3 d. 6 e. Can't Tell

7) What is the difference in costs of repair per 1000 between Blueberry and JYV?

   a. £720 b. £1,034 c. £1.03 d. £7,000 e. Can't Tell

8) What is the average cost per claim across all the makes?

   a. 48 b. 47 c. 34 d. 37 e. Can't Tell

9) What is the average number of claims across all the makes?

   a. 49 b. 46 c. 47 d. 48 e. Can't Tell

10) What is the range in cost per 1000 phones?

   a. £960 b. £3,375 c. £2,415 d. £2,231 e. Can't Tell

2. Below is a table showing exchange rates across various fictional currencies.

Currency	Curling	Roller	Puro	Jen	Juan	Keso	Filling	Skand	Corona
Amount	1	1.6	1.23	500	4509	62	107	98	118

1) How many Puros would someone get for 250 Curlings

   a. 307.50 b. 250 c. 300 d. 207.50 e. 400

2) How many Rollers would someone get for 1000 Juans?

   a. Can't Tell b. 0.34 c. 7.2 d. 7.3 e. 0.35

3) What is the exchange rate from Jens to Kesos?

   a. 4,032 b. 0.182 c. 0.124 d. 8.06 e. Can't Tell

4) What is the exchange rate from Fillings to Coronas?

   a. 0.92 b. 1.11 c. 1.1 d. 0.91 e. Can't Tell

5) If someone changes 100 Curlings into Rollers, with a 5% commission charge, how many Rollers would they receive?

   a. 160 b. 168 c. 59.4 d. 152 e. Can't Tell

6) If someone changes 100 Curlings into Puros, and then half of those Puros into Kesos, how many Kesos would they receive if the commission was 4% on each transaction?

   a. 2,856.96 b. 5,713.92 c. 5,952 d. 3,224 e. Can't Tell

7) The rate changes so that you can get 10% more Jen for the same amount of Filling. How much extra Jen would someone get for 856 Fillings?

   a. Can't Tell b. 400 c. 4,000 d. 8 e. 80

8) Someone wants to swap 100 Curlings, 100 Rollers and 150 Puros into Skand. How much Skand should they receive if there is no commission?

   a. 27, 875 b. 27,880 c. 43,561 d. 27,876 e. Can't Tell

9) The rate changes so you can now get 100 Skand for the same amount of Corona. How many Skand would you receive from 649 Corona if there was no commission?

   a. 18 b. 18.2 c. 550 d. 5.5 e. Can't Tell

10) The rate changes so you can get 65 Keso for the same amount of Puro. How many Keso would you receive from 13.53 Puro if there was 5% commission?

a. 752.63 b. 753 c. 79.95 d. 750.95 e. 679.25

3. 112 people were interviewed with the following results. 70 people followed a football team, 38 people regularly went to the gym and 11 people were vegetarian.

1) What percentage of people were not vegetarian?

   a. Can't Tell b. 11% c. 9.9% d. 10% e. 90%

2) What percentage of people followed a football team?

   a. Can't Tell b. 37% c. 38% d. 63% e. 62%

3) How many people followed a football team and regularly went to the gym?

   a.Can't Tell b. 38 c. 19 d. 24 e. 20

4) How many people regularly went to the gym and were vegetarian?

   a. Can't Tell b. 11 c. 10 d. 5 e. 4

5) If 2 people fell into all three categories, how many people fell into only one category?

   a. Can't Tell b. 107 c. 110 d. 108 e. 100

6) If 1 person fell into all three categories, how many people fell into only one category?

   a. Can't Tell b.106 c. 107 d. 111 e. 110

Water treatment

Water treatment is essential in converting polluted water to provide drinking water. The current waterworks converts 100 litres of polluted water to 50 litres of drinking water per hour, using 50units of energy in the process. One unit of energy costs £25

---

4)

1) How much does it cost to convert 1,000 litres of polluted water?

   a. £11,500   b. £12,000 c. £11,750 d. £12,500 e. £12,250

2) The demand from the city is 800litres of drinking water per hour. How many waterworks are needed to supply this demand?

   a. 14 waterworks b. 10 waterworks c. 12 waterworks d. 18 waterworks e. 16 waterworks

3) One new design offers to convert the same amount of water but using only 40 units of energy, with an initial cost of £2,000,000 how long will it take before the company breaks even in terms of the current design? Give your answers in hours

a. 8000 hours b. 8250 hours c. 8125 hours d. 7875 hours e. 7500 hours

4) The cost of energy has gone up by 25%. What is the cost of one waterwork working at maximum capacity for one day?

a. £36,000 b. £37,500 c. £32,000 d. £38,500 e. £37,250

5)

The garden

Andy is an avid gardener and he want to redesign his garden. He goes to the local plant retailer where a rose plant cost £5, a daffodil plant costs £4, a tomato plant costs £6 and an apple plant £15.

---

1) How would it cost for Andy to redesign his garden using 5 rose plants and 2 apple plants?

a. £47.50   b. £55 c. £65 d. £52.50 e. £50

2) His wife disagrees, she wants to redesign it using 10 rose plants and 3 daffodil plants, what is percentage increase of this redesign compared to his budget of £40?

a. 50% b. 45% c. 55% d. 58% e. 60%

3) The retailer sells 165 rose plants, 55 daffodil plants, 132 tomato plants and 22 apple plants. What is the ratio of the rose, daffodil and tomato plants sales compared to the apple plants?

a. 15:5:12:2 b. 12:5:15:1 c. 17:12:2 d. 15:7:12 e. 20:9:12:3

4) The retailer is in a seasonal sale, which is 25% off everything in store, what is price to resign his garden using, 12 tomato plants, 7 rose plants and an apple plant?

a. £87.50   b. £105 c. £92.50 d. £91.25 e. £90

6)

```
                    Car Journey

Jane owns a car, she is going from London to Dover today, which is 77miles. She has to catch a
ferry to Calais at 10am and her car gives her 40miles per imperial gallon. We presume that
60miles are on the motorway where the speed limit is 70mph and 17miles is in the city where
the speed limit is 30mph
```

1) What time does Jack have to leave her house to catch is ferry? Providing she sticks to the speed limit

   a. 9am   b. 8.30am   c. 8am   d. 9.15am   e. 8.45am

2) How many gallons of petrol will be used for the journey?

   a. 1 gallon   b. 1.5 gallon   c. 2.5 gallons   d. 3 gallons   e. 2 gallons

3) The price of petrol is £1.30 per litre, 1litre is = 0.22 imperial gallons, how much does the journey cost?

   a. £10   b. £10.75   c. £11.70   d. £11   e. £11.75

4) There is road works on 20miles of the motorway and she is limited to 30mph, what time does she have to leave his house to catch the ferry? Providing she sticks to the speed limit

   a. 9am   b. 8.16am   c. 8am   d. 8.06am   e. 7.45am

Abstract Reasoning – 14 minutes

Question 1 - For each question - does the box fit into A, B or neither.

Set A   Set B

189

Question 2 - For each question - does the box fit into A, B or neither.

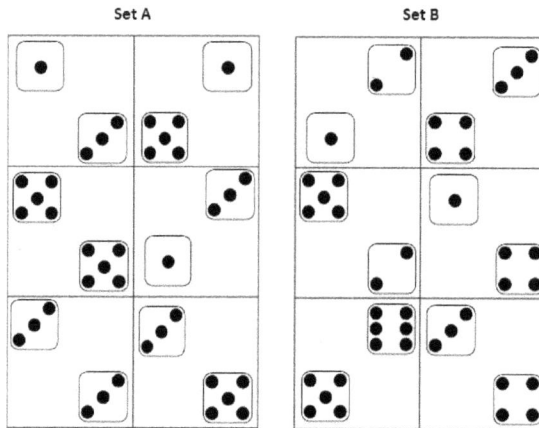

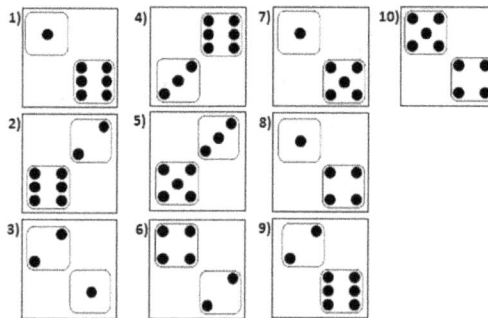

Set A

Set B

Question 3 - For each question - does the box fit into A, B or neither.

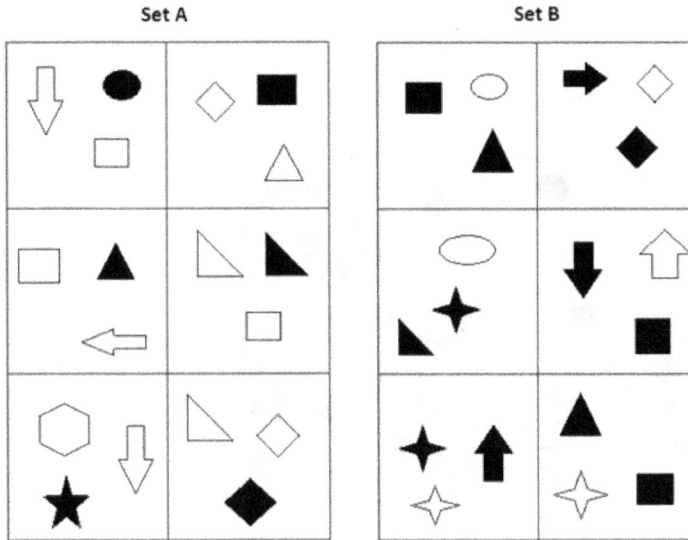

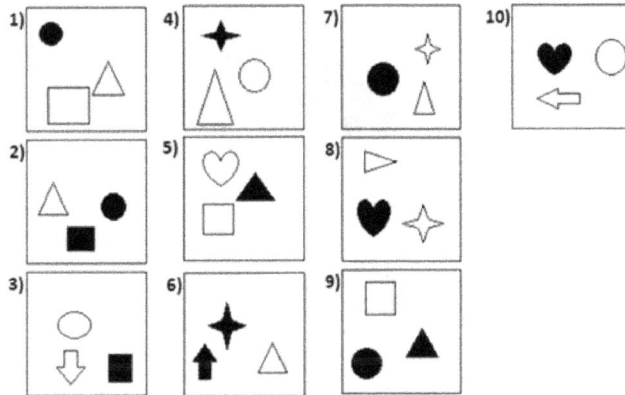

Set A

Set B

1)

2)

3)

4)

5)

6)

7)

8)

9)

10)

191

Question 4 - For each question - does the box fit into A, B or neither.

Set A   Set B

Question 5 - For each question - does the box fit into A, B or neither.

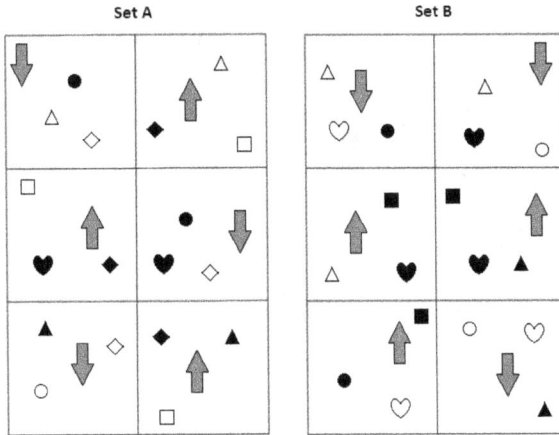

Set A

Set B

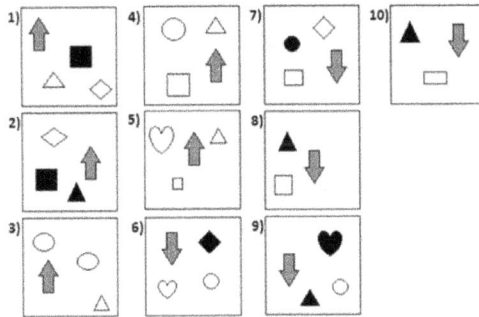

Question 6 - For each question - does the box fit into A, B or neither.

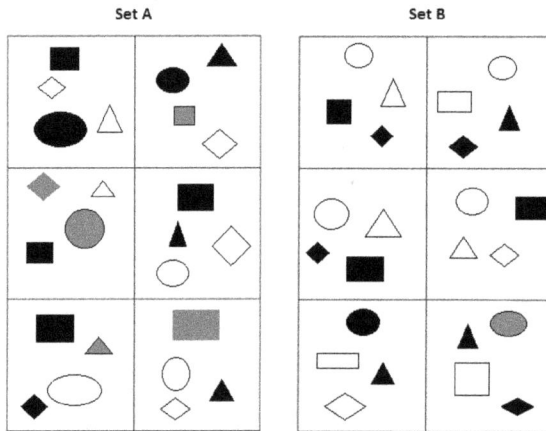

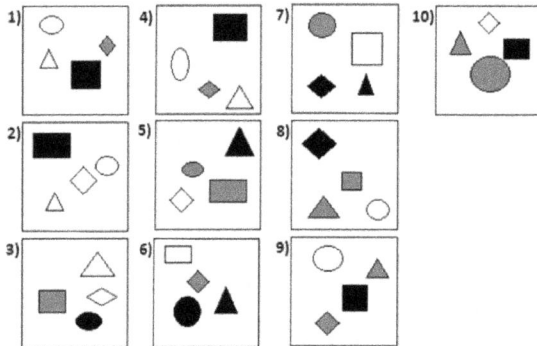

Set A

Set B

1)
4)
7)
10)

2)
5)
8)

3)
6)
9)

194

Question 7 - Which box comes next

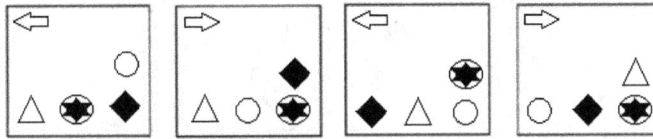

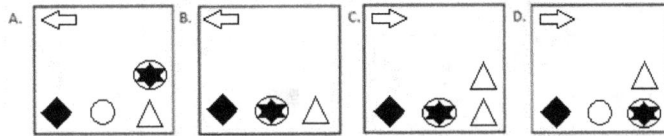

Question 8 - Which box comes next

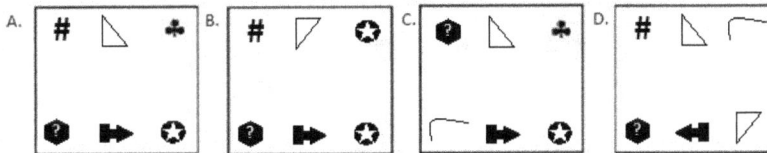

Question 9 - Which box comes next

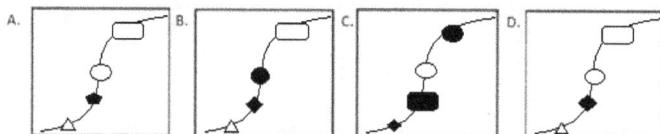

Question 10 - Which box comes next

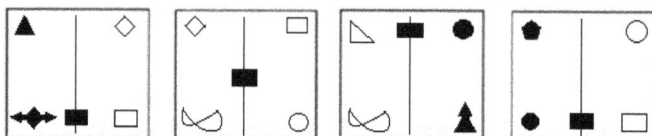

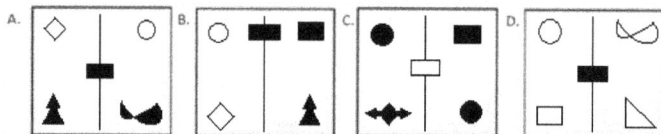

Question 11 - Which answer completes the statement?

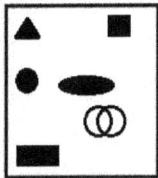 is to

as

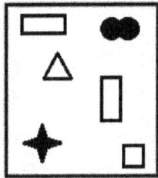 is to

A)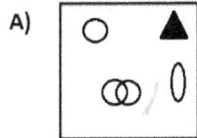

B)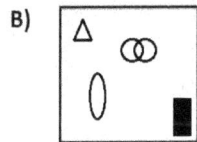

C)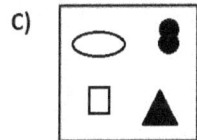

D)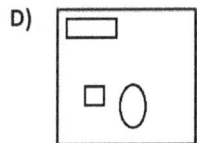

E)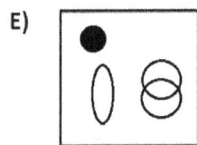

Question 12 - Which answer completes the statement?

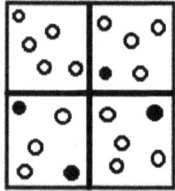 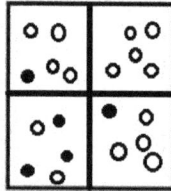

is to

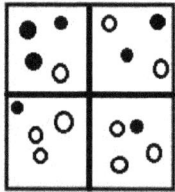 as

is to

is to

A)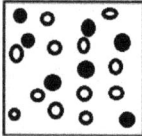

B)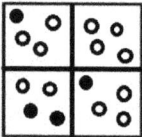

C)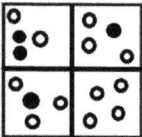

D)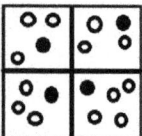

E)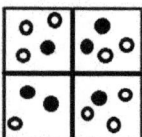

Question 13 - Which answer completes the statement?

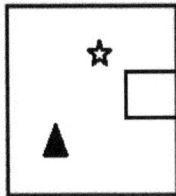

is to

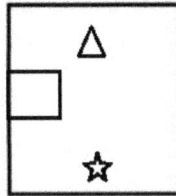

as

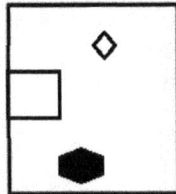

is to

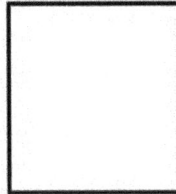

A)

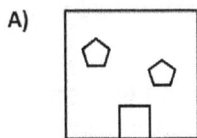

B)

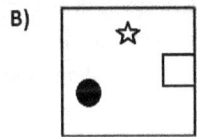

C)

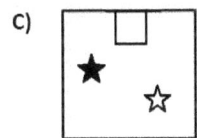

D)

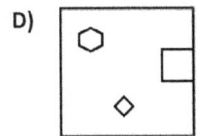

E)

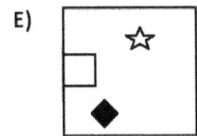

Situational Judgment Test –

27 minutes

1. **A woman comes into A&E with bruising. The triage nurse recognises her as she has been to A&E several times recently. She suspects domestic violence, and informs the doctor. The woman says she has fallen down the stairs. How appropriate are each of the following responses.**

1) The doctor calls the police to report the abuse

A very appropriate thing to do

Appropriate, but not ideal

Inappropriate, but not awful

A very inappropriate thing to do

2) The doctor says that he does not believe the injury has resulted from a fall, and asks her if anything else has happened

A very appropriate thing to do

Appropriate, but not ideal

Inappropriate, but not awful

A very inappropriate thing to do

3) The doctor asks the patient to report the abuse

A very appropriate thing to do

Appropriate, but not ideal

Inappropriate, but not awful

A very inappropriate thing to do

4) The doctor does nothing as the patient says she has fallen down stairs

A very appropriate thing to do

Appropriate, but not ideal

Inappropriate, but not awful

A very inappropriate thing to do

5) The doctor refuses to treat the patient until she admits what has really happened

A very appropriate thing to do

Appropriate, but not ideal

Inappropriate, but not awful

A very inappropriate thing to do

2. **A doctor is in a consultation with a teenager in a psychiatric clinic. They have struck up a good rapport. The teenager asks the doctor if he is on Facebook, and whether he will accept her friend request. How important to take into account are the following considerations when deciding how to respond to the situation?**

1) The vulnerability of the teenager

Very important

Important

Of minor importance

Not important at all

2) The doctor-patient relationship

Very important

Important

Of minor importance

Not important at all

Of minor importance

Not important at all

3) The doctor's professional boundaries

Very important

2) The confidentiality of the patients

Important

Very important

Of minor importance

Important

Not important at all

Of minor importance

Not important at all

4) The intentions of the teenager

Very important

3) The scope for learning via this medium

Important

Very important

Of minor importance

Important

Not important at all

Of minor importance

Not important at all

5) How active he is on Facebook

Very important

4) The fact that Facebook is a social networking site

Important

Very important

Of minor importance

Important

Not important at all

Of minor importance

Not important at all

3. A group of medical students have set up a group on Facebook that allows them to discuss patients that they have seen on their separate placements. A fellow student suggests that this may not be appropriate. How important to take into account are the following considerations when deciding how to respond to the situation?

5) The fact that the fellow student is not yet a member of the group on Facebook

Very important

Important

Of minor importance

Not important at all

1) The privacy level of the group to the wider public

Very important

Important

4. An elderly man comes in to the see his GP about his wife, who is also a patient at the practice. He is worried about some signs she has been exhibiting. A week or so later, the wife comes in having been in an accident that may have been caused by some of the things that her husband had been worried about. The doctor pursues a line of enquiry based around this, at which point the wife asks if her husband has come in to talk about her to the doctor. How important to take into account are the following considerations when deciding how to respond to the situation?

1) The husband's confidentiality

Very important

Important

Of minor importance

Not important at all

2) The health of the wife

Very important

Important

Of minor importance

Not important at all

3) The likelihood that the husband is correct about the wife

Very important

Important

Of minor importance

Not important at all

4) Whether the wife and husband have a good relationship

Very important

Important

Of minor importance

Not important at all

5. A patient is suffering from a condition that impairs her ability to drive. The doctor has advised the patient that legally, he must inform the DVLA of the change in circumstances. However at the next appointment, the patient admits he is still driving and has not informed the DVLA. The doctor has to decide whether to inform the DVLA. How important to take into account are the following considerations when deciding how to respond to this situation?

1) The confidentiality of the patient

Very important

Important

Of minor importance

Not important at all

2) The safety of the patient

Very important

Important

Of minor importance

Not important at all

3) The safety of the public

Very important

Important

Of minor importance

Not important at all

4) The law

Very important

Important

Of minor importance

Not important at all

5) The severity of the condition

Very important

Important

Of minor importance

Not important at all

6. A patient suffering from a mental health disorder comes in to the GP after a recent stay in hospital to review his medication. During the consultation, a conversation develops around the issue of who would make decisions on his behalf if he was no longer able to. The patient decides that he wants to officially name his son as that person, even though his daughter is the one who looks after him. How important to take into account are the following considerations when deciding how to respond to the situation?

1) The view of the daughter

Very important

Important

Of minor importance

Not important at all

2) The view of the patient

Very important

Important

Of minor importance

Not important at all

3) The capacity of the patient currently to make such a decision

Very important

Important

Of minor importance

Not important at all

4) The doctor's own view

Very important

Important

Of minor importance

Not important at all

5) The likelihood that a situation will arise where this decision will come into action

Very important

Important

Of minor importance

Not important at all

7. Dr. Sellers, a senior doctor, is approached by a nurse who has been working with one of the trainee doctors on the ward. He complains to Dr. Sellers about the doctor's attitude on the ward, primarily to the nursing staff, as well as the patients. He says that the trainee doctor does not respect the nurses, and it causing problems

within the team. How important to take into account are the following considerations when deciding how to respond to the situation?

1) The nurse's feelings

Very important

Important

Of minor importance

Not important at all

2) The view of the trainee doctor

Very important

Important

Of minor importance

Not important at all

3) Patient feedback

Very important

Important

Of minor importance

Not important at all

4) The availability of extra training in communication

Very important

Important

Of minor importance

Not important at all

5) The view of the university

Very important

Important

Of minor importance

Not important at all

8. A patient is being treated in A&E for a stab wound to his leg. The patient insists to the nurse that the stab was accidental, but the nurse does not believe him as there have been similar incidents reported recently. He informs the doctor, and suggests that the doctor contact the police due to the suspicious nature of the incidence. How important to take into account are the following considerations when deciding how to respond to the situation?

1) The safety of the public

Very important

Important

Of minor importance

Not important at all

2) The safety of the patient

Very important

Important

Of minor importance

Not important at all

3) The patient's opinion

Very important

Important

Of minor importance

Not important at all

4) The confidentiality of the patient

Very important

Important

Of minor importance

Not important at all

5) Where the patient was found after the incident

Very important

Important

Of minor importance

Not important at all

9. **A patient comes in to see her doctor about a developing complaint. The doctor reviews her condition and suggests prescribing her a specific medication that is relatively new on the market. The patient is unsure, and asks the doctor what he would do in her position. How important to take into account are the following considerations when deciding how to respond to the situation?**

1) The clinical guidelines

Very important

Important

Of minor importance

Not important at all

2) The doctor's own personal view

Very important

Important

Of minor importance

3) The doctor's professional view

Very important

Important

Of minor importance

Not important at all

4) The reasons for the patient's anxiety

Very important

Important

Of minor importance

Not important at all

5) The risk to the patient

Very important

Important

Of minor importance

Not important at all

10. **A patient comes into the clinic for a regular check-up. Her doctor knows she has been subject to domestic abuse in the past, and finds out that her husband attacked her a few days ago. The doctor suggests that she contact the police, but the patient refuses. How important to take into account are the following considerations when deciding how to respond to the situation?**

1) The safety of the patient

Very important

Important

Of minor importance

Not important at all

2) The confidentiality of the patient

Very important

Important

Of minor importance

Not important at all

3) The patient's opinion

Very important

Important

Of minor importance

Not important at all

4) The level of abuse

Very important

Important

Of minor importance

Not important at all

5) The likelihood the husband will attack her again

Very important

Important

Of minor importance

Not important at all

11. An elderly patient has been hospitalised with a serious complaint. The only treatment option available is surgery, which carries high risk. The doctors believe that it may not be in his interests to undergo surgery, and that they should discuss palliative care. The patient is unable to make the decision for himself, and his son and daughter disagree with how to proceed. How important to take into account are the following considerations when deciding how to respond to the situation?

1) Any previous indications of the patient on the issue (or similar issues)

Very important

Important

Of minor importance

Not important at all

2) Whether anyone has power of attorney

Very important

Important

Of minor importance

Not important at all

3) Who the patient's primary carer is

Very important

Important

Of minor importance

Not important at all

4) The amount of risk involved in the surgery

Very important

Important

Of minor importance

Not important at all

5) The views of the medical team

Very important

Important

Of minor importance

Not important at all

12. A junior doctor has come to see her senior consultant about some basic failings of care on the ward. He has noticed other people making several mistakes recently. Although there are no specific staff members at fault, the junior doctor is concerned that eventually one of these mistakes could lead to a severe incident. How important to take into account are the following considerations when deciding how to respond to the situation?

1) The timings of the mistakes

Very important

Important

Of minor importance

Not important at all

2) The type of mistakes –

Very important

Important

Of minor importance

Not important at all

3) Whether there are any specific personnel involved

Very important

Important

Of minor importance

Not important at all

4) Whether anyone else has noticed the mistakes

Very important

Important

Of minor importance

Not important at all

5) The competence of the junior doctor

Very important

Important

Of minor importance

Not important at all

13. A GP is in a consultation with a patient who has had a recent fall. The doctor is worried about the patient's ability to cope at home, as she has no support from friends or family. However the patient does not want to involve the social services as she wants to maintain her independence. How important to take into account are the following considerations when deciding how to respond to the situation?

1) The safety of the patient

Very important

Important

Of minor importance

Not important at all

2) The patient's personal preference

Very important

Important

Of minor importance

Not important at all

3) The level of intrusion that social services may inflict on the patient's life

Very important

Important

Of minor importance

Not important at all

4) The tasks that the patient will need to carry out at home

Very important

Important

Of minor importance

Not important at all

5) The patient's proximity to local amenities

Very important

Important

Of minor importance

Not important at all

14. Dr. Mellor has recently been diagnosed by epilepsy. Although there is treatment for the condition, he has admitted to having a brief seizure in the operating room that was missed by the rest of the staff. The doctor who is treating Dr. Mellor has to decide whether to inform the hospital of Dr. Mellors condition. How important to take into account are the following considerations when deciding how to respond to the situation?

1) The confidentiality of Dr. Mellor

Very important

Important

Of minor importance

Not important at all

2) The safety of the patient's where Dr. Mellor works

Very important

Important

Of minor importance

Not important at all

3) The severity of Dr. Mellor's condition

Very important

Important

Of minor importance

Not important at all

4) The fact that Dr. Mellor's condition is treatable

Very important

Important

Of minor importance

Not important at all

5) The type of work Dr. Mellor does

Very important

Important

Of minor importance

Not important at all

15. A patient with a terminal illness is admitted to hospital after attempted suicide. The attempt has left her severely brain damaged, and she is on a ventilator. The medical team have to decide whether to keep her on the ventilator. How important to take into account are the following considerations when deciding how to respond to the situation?

1) The ability of the patient to make a decision at this point

Very important

Important

Of minor importance

Not important at all

2) The fact that removing her from a ventilator may class as suicide or assisted suicide

Very important

Important

Of minor importance

Not important at all

3) The views of her next of kin

Very important

Important

Of minor importance

Not important at all

4) The patient's quality of life

Very important

Important

Of minor importance

Not important at all

5) The view of the medical team

Very important

Important

Of minor importance

Not important at all

16. Two patients require an organ transplant. One is aged 33, the other aged 60. The medical team have to decide who to give the organ to. How important to take into account are the following considerations when deciding how to respond to the situation?

1) The age of the patients

Very important

Important

Of minor importance

Not important at all

2) Which patient will gain the most from the treatment

Very important

Important

Of minor importance

Not important at all

3) The clinical need of each patient

Very important

Important

Of minor importance

Not important at all

4) The view of the hospital ethics board

Very important

Important

Of minor importance

Not important at all

5) The views of the patients families

Very important

Important

Of minor importance

Not important at all

Mock exam answers

Verbal reasoning

Stem 1

1) **True**. "Quality of Patient Care", "Implementation and Resistance to Change", "Face to Face Interaction", "Healthcare Professional Benefits", and "Locality and Convenience".
2) **Can't Tell**. The full wording for HCP is not given in the text.
3) **True**. The text says that the issue of cost is more concerning to policy makers.
4) **False**. The author does not give a personal opinion.
5) **True**. The author says that future work could seek to find out why the differences occur.
6) **Can't Tell**. There is no information on how 'good' the review is.
7) **Can't Tell**. This is not a conclusion that can be drawn. All that is said in the text is that the younger doctors have less experience.
8) **False.** They have more negative views.
9) **Can't Tell**. The text says that renumeration is undeveloped and therefore a barrier, but does not say it overall costs too much.
10) **Older doctors tend to be against telehealth as they have more experience.** The article does not say that – it says that older doctors are more experienced, and they have tend to be more negative about telehealth. There is no causal link identified.

Stem 2

1) **True**. These are a description of the 6 phases (although in a different order).
2) **False**. There are references to members (plural) and each member, so we know there was more than one person in the team.
3) **False**. A code has been defined in the text as something else.
4) **Can't Tell**. We do not know what the author means by 'brief'.
5) **True**. Themes were put together for analysis.
6) **False**. The work done in phase 3 was the primary area that was revisited.
7) **True**. Evaluation of the service at NPSDU, efficiency of sponsored transport, facilities at NPSDU, and the quality of care provided by the staff.
8) **False**. We do not know whether the rest of the report was completed.
9) **True**. We can infer this as the author says that they avoided pitfalls that Braun and Clarke described by not simply paraphrasing.
10) **Can't Tell**. We do not know if the finished version will be as intended.

Stem 3

1) **True**. The post-collection analysis was 'bounded'.
2) **Can't Tell**. The text suggests the NQB is involved in this area of research, but it is not clear what exactly they have (or are) studying.

3) **False**. The author says the statistical tests would provide better results if there were larger sample sizes. This does not mean the tests performed were not accurate.
4) **False**. The text talks about carers/family members who were not involved.
5) **Can't Tell**. We do not know which of the other stakeholders have/have not been involved.
6) **True**. Recommendations have been made.
7) **Can't Tell**. This is the authors suggestion, but we do not know this for fact.
8) **Can't Tell.** We do not know if the results are valid. The author says that the validity can be tested.
9) **False.** Satellite dialysis units.
10) **Unknown**. There is no date given.

Stem 4

1) **False.** The study was conducted to evaluate service.
2) **False.** The study was conducted to evaluate service.
3) **False.** One aspect (area of unit) had an association.
4) **True**. The author writes that they could not negate confounding factors as they had to use non-parametric tests. This implies that parametric tests would have solved this problem.
5) **Can't Tell**. The text only talks about recommendations for waiting times. We do not know about satisfaction.
6) **True** The last sentence says the paper fulfilled the function of providing a stepping stone into evaluating the additional dimensions of patient experience.
7) **Can't Tell**. There is no information in this text about what NPSDU stands for.
8) **True**. There is a lack of existing literature.
9) **True**. The author says some of the recommendations are generalisable to other units, so this is true.
10) **Can't Tell**. It's not stated in the text which of the three recommendations are major and which are minor.

Quantitative reasoning

QUESTION 1

1) Which make has the highest cost per 1000?

   b. myPhone

   myPhone costs £45 per claim (highest) and 75 requests (also highest)

2) Which make has the lowest requests per 1000?

   c. Mockiad

   Mockia has 24 requests per 1000, which is the lowest value in the table.

3) myPhone release a new phone, but the requests for repairs doubles. How many requests is this per 100 phones?

a. 15

Total new requests is 75 x 2 = 150. This is 15 per 100

4) myPhone decide to include a compulsory insurance scheme in their phone charges. If they wish to break even on repair costs, how much should they charge per phone?

e. £3.38

Total costs of repairs is 75 x £45 = £3,375 per 1000 phones. £3,375/1000 = £3.375, so £3.38

5) Clamshell reduces the cost per claim by 20%. How much is the total cost of repair per 1000 now?

c. £1,016.80

New cost per claim is £41 x 0.8 = £32.80. £32.80 x 31 = £1,016.80.

6) Mockia have an increase of 25% in the number of requests. How many more requests are there per 100?

a. 0.6

Extra number of requests is 24 x 0.25 = 6 per 1000. This is 0.6 per 100.

7) What is the difference in costs of repair per 1000 between Blueberry and JYV?

b. £1,034

Cost for Blueberry is 66 x £33 = £2,178. Cost for JYV is 44 x £26 = £1,144. £2,178 - £1,144 = £1,034

8) What is the average cost per claim across all the makes?

d. 37

Total cost is 33 + 45 + 40 + 41 + 26 = £185. £185/5 = £37

9) What is the average number of claims across all the makes?

d. 48

Total number of claims is 66 + 75 + 24 + 31 + 44 = 240. 240/5 = 48

10) What is the range in cost per 1000 phones?

c. £2,415

Lowest cost per 1000 is by Mockia = 24 x £40 = £960. Highest cost per 1000 is by myPhone = 75 x £45 = £3,375. Difference is £2,415

QUESTION 2

1) How many Puros would someone get for 250 Curlings

a. 307.50

250 x 1.23 = 307.50

2) How many Rollers would someone get for 1000 Juans?

e. 0.35

1000/4509 = 0.221...x 1.6 = 0.35

3) What is the exchange rate from Jens to Kesos?

c. 0.124

Kesos/Jens = 62/500 = 0.124

4) What is the exchange rate from Fillings to Coronas?

c. 1.1

Coronas/Fillings = 118/107 = 1.10

5) If someone changes 100 Curlings into Rollers, with a 5% commission charge, how many Rollers would they receive?

d. 152

Curlings to Rollers is 100 x 1.6 = 160. Minus 5% commission is 160 x 0.95 = 152

6) If someone changes 100 Curlings into Puros, and then half of those Puros into Kesos, how many Kesos would they receive if the commission was 4% on each transaction?

a. 2,856.96

Curlings into Puros, including commission is 100 x 1.23 x 0.96 = 118.08. Half of this into Kesos is 59.04/1.23 x 62 x 0.96 = 2,856.96.

7) The rate changes so that you can get 10% more Jen for the same amount of Filling. How much extra Jen would someone get for 856 Fillings?

b. 400

Before, 856 Fillings would give 856/107 x 500 = 4,000. 10% of this is 400.

8) Someone wants to swap 100 Curlings, 100 Rollers and 150 Puros into Skand. How much Skand should they receive if there is no commission?

d. 27,876

100 Curlings is 100 x 98 = 9,800 Skand. 100 Rollers is 100/1.6 x 98 = 6,125 Skand. 150 Puros is 150/1.23 x 98 = 11,951. Total is 27,876

9) The rate changes so you can now get 100 Skand for the same amount of Corona. How many Skand would you receive from 649 Corona if there was no commission?

c. 550

100Sk to 118Co. 649/118 = 5.5 x 100 = 550Sk

10) The rate changes so you can get 65 Keso for the same amount of Puro. How many Keso would you receive from 13.53 Puro if there was 5% commission?

e. 679.25

65Ke to 1.23Pu. 13.53/1.23 = 11 x 65 = 715Ke. Minus 5% commission is 715 x 0.95 = 679.25

QUESTION 3

1) What percentage of people were not vegetarian?

   e. 90%

   112 – 11 = 101 not vegetarian. 101/112 = 0.901 x 100 = 90.1%

2) What percentage of people followed a football team?

   d. 63%

   70/112 = 0.625 x 100 = 62.5%

3) How many people followed a football team and regularly went to the gym?

   a.Can't Tell

   We have no information on the overlap between the two answers

4) How many people regularly went to the gym and were vegetarian?

   a. Can't Tell

   We have no information on the overlap between the two answers

5) If 2 people fell into all three categories, how many people fell into only one category?

   b. 107

   (70+38+11) – 112 = 7 'extra people'. 7 – 4 = 3 (subtract 4 for people in all 3 categories who have all been counted twice extra) 3 is the amount of extra people that don't fall into all three categories (two categories). 3 + 2 = 5 (total amount of people who fall into two or three categories). 112 – 5 = 107

6) If 1 person fell into all three categories, how many people fell into only one category?

   b.106

   (70+38+11) – 112 = 7 'extra people'. 7 – 2 = 5 (subtract 2 for people in all 3 categories who have all been counted twice extra) 6 is the amount of extra people that don't fall into all three categories (two categories). 5 + 1 = 6 (those who fall into two or three categories). 112 – 6 = 106

Question 4

1) How much does it cost to convert 1,000 litres of polluted water? **d. £12,500**

   - 1,000 litres ÷ 100 litres per hour = 10hours

   - 10 hours x 50units = 500 units

   - 500 units x £25 = £12,500

   - The demand from the city is 800 litres of drinking water per hour. How many waterworks are needed to supply this demand? **e. 16 waterworks**

   - 800 litres ÷ 50 litres = 16

   - 16 waterworks

2) One new design offers to convert the same amount of water but using only 40 units of energy, with an initial cost of £2,000,000 how long will it take before the company breaks even in terms of the current design? Give your answers in hours **a. 8000 hours**

   - Difference in the two designs = 10 units, 10 x £25 = £250 per hour

   - £2,000,000 ÷ £250 per hour = 8000 hours

3) The cost of energy has gone up by 25%. What is the cost of one waterwork working at maximum capacity for one day? **b. £37,500**

   - New cost of one energy unit, Increase in 25% = 1.25, £25 x 1.25 = £31.25

   - Total energy used in one day = 50 x 24 = 1200units

   - Cost = 1200 x £31.25 = £37,500

Question 5

1) How would it cost for Andy to redesign his garden using 5 rose plants and 2 apple plants? **b. £55**

   - 5 x £5 = £25

   - 2 x £15 = £30

   - Total = £55

2) His wife disagrees, she wants to redesign it using 10 rose plants and 3 daffodil plants, what is percentage increase of this redesign compared to his budget of £40? **c. 55%**

   - 10 x £5 = £50

   - 3 x £4 = £12

   - Total = £62

   - Percentage increase = difference in values/ the comparing value x 100

   - £62-£40/£40 = £22/£40 x 100 = 55%

3) The retailer sells 165 rose plants, 55 daffodil plants, 132 to-
    mato plants and 22 apple plants. What is the ratio of the
    rose, daffodil and tomato plants sales compared to the apple
    plants? **a. 15:5:12:2**

    -   Rose:Daffodil:Tomato:Apple

    -   165:55:132:22 all can be divided by 11

    -   Simplest form = 15:5:12:2

Question 6

1) What time does Jack have to leave her house to catch is
    ferry? Providing she sticks to the speed limit **b. 8.30am**

    -   17miles ÷ 30mph = 0.566hours = 0.6 hours

    -   60 miles ÷ 70mph = 0.857hours = 0.9 hours

    -   0.9 + 0.6 = 1.5hours, 0.5 is a proportion of 60mintutes in
        a hour, the time is 0.5 x 60 = 30minutes = 1hour and
        30minutes

    -   10am – 1 hour and 30mintues = 8.30am

2) How many imperial gallons of petrol will be used for the jour-
    ney? **e. 2 gallons**

    -   77 miles ÷ 40 miles per gallon = 1.925 gallons = 2 gallons

3) The price of petrol is £1.30 per litre, 1litre is = 0.22 imperial
    gallons, how much does the journey cost? **c. £11.70**

    -   77 ÷ 40 = 1.925 gallons = 2 gallons

    -   2 ÷ 0.22 = 9.09 litres = 9 litres

    -   9 x 1.30 = £11.70

4) There is road works on 20miles of the motorway and she is
    limited to 30mph, what time does she have to leave her
    house to catch the ferry? Providing she sticks to the speed
    limit **d. 8.06am**

    -   Total motorway miles = 60miles, 60miles – 20 limited
        miles = 40miles of unlimited miles.

-   17 miles ÷ 30mph = 0.566hours = 0.6 hours

-   40 miles ÷ 70mph = 0.571hours = 0.6 hours

-   20 miles ÷ 30mph = 0.666hours = 0.7 hours

-   0.6 + 0.6 + 0.7 = 1.9hours, 0.9 is a proportion of 60min-
    tutes in a hour, the time is 0.9 x 60 = 54minutes

-   Total time = 1hour 54 minutes, 10am - 1hour 54 minutes
    = 8.06am

Abstract reasoning

Question 1

Rule: In Set A, each matching pair of shapes is the same size. In
Set B, one matching pair of shapes is of differing size, but the
rest are of the same size.

Answers

1) Neither

2) B

3) A

4) B

5) A

6) Neither

7) Neither

8) B

9) Neither

10) Neither

Question 2

Rule: Set A has odd numbers on each die. Set B has one odd and
one even number.

Answers

1) B

2) Neither

3) B

4) B

5) A

6) Neither

7) A

9) Neither

10) B

Question 3

Rule: Set A has one white shape with an odd number of sides, one white shape with an even number of sides, and one black shape. Set B has one black shape with an odd number of sides, one black shape with an even number of sides, and one white shape.

Answers

1) A

2) B

3) Neither

4) Neither

5) Neither

6) B

7) A

8) A

9) Neither

10) Neither

Question 4

Rule: Set A has an odd number of black quadrilaterals. Set B has an even number of black circles.

Answers

1) A

2) A

3) A

4) B

5) Neither

6) B

7) A

8) Neither

9) B

10) Neither

Question 5

Rule: In Set A, a circle means a downward facing arrow. No circle means the arrow faces upwards. In Set B, one black shape means a downward facing arrow. If more than one, the arrow faces upwards. Both sets have at least one shaded shape

Answers

1) A

2) B

3) Neither

4) Neither

5) Neither

6) A

7) A

8) B

9) A

10) B

Question 6

Rule: In Set A, the upper most shape is shaded. In Set B, the uppermost shape is a circle. There are always four different shapes.

Answers

1) B

2) A

3) Neither

4) A

5) A

6) Neither

7) B

8) A

9) B

10) Neither

Question 7

Box a.

What is consistent? There are the same five shapes consistently in each step, there is always an arrow in the top left corner.

Let's focus on step 1-2, the bottom four shapes in a L-configuration seams to move positions in an inconsistent manner. The arrow seams to rotate at 180º.

Does this pattern stay the same for step 2-3? Yes. We have identified the pattern, the rotation of the arrow at the top left and the same four shapes at the bottom.

Question 8

Box a.

What is consistent? There are the same seven shapes in the step they occupy the same space, along the top and bottom line.

Let's focus on step 1-2, The top three shape move in a left to right fashion, the club doesn't change, the right angle triangle seem to rotate 90° and the number sign seems to disappear, replaced by a curve shape. None of the bottom three shapes change however, they seem to move positions from right to left.

Let's see if step 2-3 follows are proposed pattern? Yes it does we have found the pattern.

Question 9

Box d.

What is consistent? There is a curve running from the bottom left corner to the top right, there are four symbols that lie on this line. There is constant unshaded circle in the middle of the curve, and there are a total of five shape shapes used in each step.

Let's focus on step 1-2, the rectangular looking shape seems to change shading but remains in the same position. In step 1, underneath the unshaded circle there seem to be a shaded diamond shape that moves down a position in step 2. The unshaded triangle disappears and a shaped circle appears where the shaded diamond was in step 1. The unshaded circle in the centre doesn't change.

Let's look at step 2-3, the shaded rectangle goes back to being unshaded like in step 1. We can make a pattern that it changes shade each step. Below the unshaded circle, the diamond shaded appears to change positions again, back to where it was in step 1. Along with this change in position of the shaded diamond the shaded circle disappears and the unshaded triangle appears again in the same position. Whether they appear or disappear must be dependent on the position of the shaded diamond.

Now we have made a pattern let's look at step 3-4 so see if it's correct. Yes it is.

Question 10

Box d.

What is consistent? There is a line in the middle with a shaded rectangle on it. The shaded rectangle seems to be moving in an upward motion on the line. There are shapes present on the four corners and these shapes appear to be random.

Let's focus on step 1-2, the shaped rectangle moves up, in step 1 the shapes to the left of the line are shaded and to the right of the line, unshaded. In step 2 the shaded rectangle is in the middle and there are no other shaded patterns. No obvious pattern yet.

Let's focus on step 2-3. The shaded rectangle is now at the top of the line, the shapes to the right of the line are shaded and to the left of

the line unshaded. There is still no obvious pattern but we can start to suspect the position of the shaded rectangle box has something to do with the shading of the other shapes.

Let's have a look at step 3-4. The shaded rectangle starts again from the bottom, now, we can see the shading of the shapes, is exactly the same as step 1. The shapes on the left are shaded and the shapes on the right are unshaded. We have a pattern. The shading of the shapes split by the line depends on the position of the shaded rectangle.

Rule: There is an odd number of straight edged shapes, before and after the statement. There is one less shaded shape.

Answer : A

Rule: The number of circles in each quadrant does not change. There is an addition of a shaded circle in the bottom left quadrant and one shaded circle in the bottom right.

Answer : B

Rule: The straightened U shape on the vertical edges of the square is reflected in the vertical midline. The position of shapes is swapped in relation to the U shape. Shaded shapes are unshaded.

Answer : D

Situational judgment tests

1. A woman comes into A&E with bruising. The triage nurse recognises her as she has been to A&E several times recently. She suspects domestic violence, and informs the doctor. The woman says she has fallen down the stairs. How appropriate are each of the following responses.

1) The doctor should try and get the information from the patient first **A very inappropriate thing to do**

2) This allows the patient to come forward and explain what has really happened **A very appropriate thing to do**

3) The doctor should not make assumptions, and should get the patient to explain what has happened first **Appropriate, but not ideal**;

4) If a different reason is suspected, especially one that puts the patient's safety at risk, the doctor should not just accept the reason **A very inappropriate thing to do**

5) The doctor should do what is in the patient's best interests, as well as doing the least harm **A very inappropriate thing to do**

2.A doctor is in a consultation with a teenager in a psychiatric clinic. They have struck up a good rapport. The teenager asks the doctor if he is on Facebook, and whether he will accept her friend request. How important to take into account are the following considerations when deciding how to respond to the situation?

1) This is extremely important as the doctor needs to be sensitive in however he responds. The doctor must respect professional boundaries. **Very important**

2) It is important to maintain the relationship as it is, as the patient needs to understand the role of the doctor. **Very important**

3) The doctor should be wary of getting close to the patient especially as she is vulnerable. **Very important**

4) If the teenager merely wishes to be friends on Facebook, a different response is needed to if she wishes to strike up a close relationship with the doctor. **Very important**

5) Regardless of how active he is on Facebook, the doctor should maintain certain boundaries. **Of minor importance**

3. A group of medical students have set up a group on Facebook that allows them to discuss patients that they have seen on their separate placements. A fellow student suggests that this may not be appropriate. How important to take into account are the following considerations when deciding how to respond to the situation?

1) If the group is private, the medical students may not be doing anything wrong. However with sites like Facebook, site administrators have access to a lot of material so the group may never be completely private.**Important**

2) Patient confidentiality should never be sacrificed for the sake of a learning opportunity. **Very important**

3) There are other ways to learn, so even if this is a particularly effective way to learn, other issues such as confidentiality are more important. **Of minor importance**

4) This does not play a factor in any decision. **Not important at all**

5) The student has a valid concern, so her reasons for speaking up are immaterial. **Not important at all**

4. An elderly man comes in to the see his GP about his wife, who is also a patient at the practice. He is worried about some signs she has been exhibiting. A week or so later, the wife comes in having been in an accident that may have been caused by some of the things that her husband had been worried about. The doctor pursues a line of enquiry based around this, at which point the wife asks if her husband has come in to talk about her to the doctor. How important to take into account are the following considerations when deciding how to respond to the situation?

1) The husband has come to see the GP in confidence. By breaking confidentiality, the GP loses his trust. **Very important**

2) The health of the wife is the main problem here, so this is of utmost importance. The GP should look to do the least harm. **Very important**

3) It does not matter whether he is right or wrong, just that he is worried. **Not important at all**

4) The GP should try not to deceive any patient, however there are ways to protect the husband's confidentiality as well as not lying to the wife. **Of minor importance**

5. A patient is suffering from a condition that impairs her ability to drive. The doctor has advised the patient that legally, he must inform the DVLA of the change in circumstances. However at the next appointment, the patient admits he is still driving and has not informed the DVLA. The doctor has to decide whether to inform the DVLA. How important to take into account are the following considerations when deciding how to respond to this situation?

1) The GP should try to make sure the patient does not lose trust by respecting her confidentiality. However there are ways around this.**Important**

2) The patient's safety and health should be at the forefront of the GP's mind at all times.**Very important**

3) The safety of the public is just as important as the patient – by driving around she is risking other people's safety**Very important**

4) The law is there for a reason, and the GP should respect this wherever possible. **Very important**

5) The fact that the condition impairs her ability to drive means that regardless of the severity, the DVLA should be informed. However, this could inform the urgency with which the GP should act.**Of minor importance**

6. A patient suffering from a mental health disorder comes in to the GP after a recent stay in hospital to review his medication. During the consultation, a conversation develops around the issue of who would make decisions on his behalf if he was no longer able to. The patient decides that he wants to officially name his son as that person, even though his daughter is the one who looks after him. How important to take into account are the following considerations when deciding how to respond to the situation?

1) The daughters view should be taken into account as she is the patient's primary carer. **Of minor importance**

2) As this decision is about the patient, the patient should have the ultimate decision, so his view is the most important. **Very important**

3) If the patient is currently not competent to make a decision, then any decision he does make cannot be accepted.**Very important**

4) The doctor should have no say as this is a personal/family issue rather than a health issue. **Not important at all**

5) .The likelihood that the situation will arise does not matter. **Not important at all**

7. Dr. Sellers, a senior doctor, is approached by a nurse who has been working with one of the trainee doctors on the ward. He complains to Dr. Sellers about the doctor's attitude on the ward, primarily to the nursing staff, as well as the patients. He says that the trainee doctor does not respect the nurses, and it causing problems within the team. How important to take into account are the following considerations when deciding how to respond to the situation?

1) The nurse is well placed to observe the trainee. **Very important**

2) Dr. Sellers should not make any decisions without seeing what the trainee doctor thinks – he may disagree, which would suggest a different issue. **Very important**

3) The patients would be able to tell Dr. Sellers if they are happy with the standard of care they are receiving from the trainee. **Very important**

4) This would inform the decision of Dr. Sellers on what to do, assuming the trainee was in fact causing problems. However it is more important to establish the facts first. **Of minor importance**

5) The university should be informed, but as they are not involved directly with his training on the ward, their view should not matter.**Not important at all**

8. A patient is being treated in A&E for a stab wound to his leg. The patient insists to the nurse that the stab was accidental, but the nurse does not believe him as there have been similar incidents reported recently. He informs the doctor, and suggests that the doctor contact the police due to the suspicious nature of the incidence. How important to take into account are the following considerations when deciding how to respond to the situation?

1) The safety of the public is extremely important, and may trump the patient's confidentiality **Very important**

2) The safety and health of the patient should be at the forefront of the doctor's mind **Very important**

3) The patient should be involved with any decision made as it is him who will face the consequences **Very important**

4) The patient should not lose trust in the healthcare system. However the safety of the public may trump this.**Important**

5) This could help the doctor decide the likelihood that the stab wound is accidental.**Of minor importance**

9. A patient comes in to see her doctor about a developing complaint. The doctor reviews her condition and suggests prescribing her a specific medication that is relatively new on the market. The patient is unsure, and asks the doctor what he would do in her position. How important to take into account are the following considerations when deciding how to respond to the situation?

1) The clinical guidelines have been set up by experts who have weighed up the evidence. They should be followed where possible **Very important**

2) The doctor's personal view is not important as it is the patient who will be taking the medication **Not important at all**

3) The doctor's professional view is important as he will be able to inform the patient about risks/benefits **Important**

4) This could allow the doctor to reassure the patient **Very important**

5) The risk to the patient is very important, the doctor should look to do the least harm **Very important**

10. A patient comes into the clinic for a regular check-up. Her doctor knows she has been subject to domestic abuse in the past, and finds out that her husband attacked her a few days ago. The doctor suggests that she contact the police, but the patient refuses. How important to take into account are the following considerations when deciding how to respond to the situation?

1) The patient's health and safety should be at the forefront of the doctor's mind at all times **Very important**

2) The patient should be able to trust her doctor. However her safety may be of a higher importance. **Important**

3) This is the patient's life, so her opinion is the most important. **Very important**

4) The level of abuse may indicate whether the patient needs to stay in a refuge, and whether she requires protection etc.**Of minor importance**

5) The fact that the husband has attacked her is enough to warrant police involvement. However if the patient refuses, this is a factor to take into account**Of minor importance**

11. An elderly patient has been hospitalised with a serious complaint. The only treatment option available is surgery, which carries high risk. The doctors believe that it may not be in his interests to undergo surgery, and that they should discuss palliative care. The patient is unable to make the decision for himself, and his son and daughter disagree with how to proceed. How important to take into account are the following considerations when deciding how to respond to the situation?

1) As the patient's family cannot agree, any previous indications may give an insight into his wishes. **Important**

2) Whoever has power of attorney is able to make the decision **Very important**

3) The patient's primary carer may have a greater insight into the wishes of the patient, however all family members should have an equal say **Of minor importance**

4) This would inform the family and medical team whether surgery would be useful **Important**

5) The medical team would be able to give their professional views, however ultimately it is the family's decision **Of minor importance**

12. A junior doctor has come to see her senior consultant about some basic failings of care on the ward. He has noticed other people making several mistakes recently. Although there are no specific staff members at fault, the junior doctor is concerned that eventually one of these mistakes could lead to a severe incident. How important to take into account are the following considerations when deciding how to respond to the situation?

1) This could provide an indication of if there is a specific reason for the mistakes **Important**

2) The fact that there are mistakes is most important. The type could help the consultant decide what action needs to be taken – training, or simply awareness.**Of minor importance**

3) This would help the consultant decide what action to take – people may need further training. **Very important**

4) There is no reason to suggest the junior doctor is not telling the truth. However a second opinion may help the consultant isolate the incidents**Of minor importance**

5) This is not important as he has noticed other people making mistakes. **Not important at all**

13. A GP is in a consultation with a patient who has had a recent fall. The doctor is worried about the patient's ability to cope at home, as she has no support from friends or family. However the patient does not want to involve the social services as she wants to maintain her independence. How important to take into account are the following considerations when deciding how to respond to the situation?

1) The patient's health and safety should be at the forefront of the doctor's mind at all times **Very important**

2) As this is the patient's life, any involvement of social services should be her decision **Very important**

3) The patient should not be inconvenienced where possible. However her safety is also very important **Important**

4) This would help the doctor decide whether help is necessary. **Important**

5) This would help the doctor decide whether help is necessary **Important**

14. Dr. Mellor has recently been diagnosed by epilepsy. Although there is treatment for the condition, he has admitted to having a brief seizure in the operating room that was missed by the rest of the staff. The doctor who is treating Dr. Mellor has to decide whether to inform the hospital of Dr. Mellors condition. How important to take into account are the following considerations when deciding how to respond to the situation?

1) Dr. Mellor's confidentiality should be respected, however in this case the safety of the patient's where he works is more important **Of minor importance**

2) This is of utmost importance, especially due to where he works – his condition should not harm others **Very important**

3) The fact that he has had a seizure in the operating room means it could happen again **Of minor importance**

4) This should be mentioned to his employers, however the fact that he has had a seizure at work means it could happen again **Of minor importance**

5) This is very important as he is involved with lots of patients, each of whom could be in danger **Very important**

15. A patient with a terminal illness is admitted to hospital after attempted suicide. The attempt has left her severely brain damaged, and she is on a ventilator. The medical team have to decide whether to keep her on the ventilator. How important to take into account are the following considerations when deciding how to respond to the situation?

1) If she is not able to make a decision, her family should be informed (or whoever has power of attorney). **Very important**

2) The doctor's should not do anything illegal when deciding how to act. **Important**

3) If she is not able to make a decision, her decision should be passed on to next of kin. **Very important**

4) This is important as if she is going to have a severely reduced quality of life, then it may be better to take her off the ventilator. **Very important**

5) The medical team should give their professional advice to the family, but ultimately the decision rests with the family. **Of minor importance**

16. Two patients require an organ transplant. One is aged 33, the other aged 60. The medical team have to decide who to give the organ to. How important to take into account are the following considerations when deciding how to respond to the situation?

1) The age does not matter as the organ should go the person who needs it most. **Not important at all**

2) The organ should go to the person who needs it most. **Not important at all**

3) The clinical need is what should determine who receives the organ **Very important**

4) The hospital ethics board would be able to decide impartially who needs the organ the most **Very important**

5) The organ should go to the person who needs it most. So in this case, the patients family's would not have a say. **Not important at all**

Concluding remarks

- We strongly advise that you get a good night's sleep the day before your test. Being rested will ensure that you deliver your best on the day. Ensure that you leave in good time to account for any delays in travel, or any unforeseen incidents. This will enable you to arrive early at the test centre and just relax.

- If during the test, you get anxious or your mind goes blank, don't panic! Take a few seconds to breathe and get your thoughts together. Remind yourself that this is a perseverance test as well and now is not the time to give up.

- Old format questions are good; they use the same skills you need for the new format of questions. They will help you develop a good sense of understanding.

- Use real life as you your best resource.

- Work on your weaknesses, improve yourself.

We hope you make the most of this resource combined with others around you and wish you all the best with your UKCAT!

If you enjoyed the book please do leave us positive feedback on amazon.

If you have any questions or queries with regards to this book, please feel free to email us at:

info@ukcathelp.com

By purchasing this book you also receive access to

over 2,000 questions online; simply enter the code VBIT1loml at the checkout at ukcathelp.com.

www.ingramcontent.com/pod-product-compliance
Lightning Source LLC
Chambersburg PA
CBHW081424090426
42740CB00017B/3174